To Jaime —
I hope this
book will help
you with history —
you're great —

Love,
Mom & Dad

Manuel Alvarez, 1794–1856

Manuel Alvarez
1794–1856

A Southwestern Biography

Thomas E. Chávez

University Press of Colorado

The University Press of Colorado is a cooperative publishing enterprise
supported, in part, by Adams State College, Colorado State University, Fort Lewis
College, Mesa State College, Metropolitan State College, University of Colorado,
University of Northern Colorado, University of Southern Colorado, and
Western State College.

The paper used in this publication meets the minimum requirements of the Ameri-
can National Standard for Information Sciences—Permanence of Paper for
Printed Library Materials.
ANSI Z39.48–1984

Library of Congress Cataloging-in-Publications Data

Chávez, Thomas E.
    Manuel Alvarez, 1794–1856: a southwestern biography /
Thomas E. Chávez. — 1st ed.
        p. cm.
    Includes bibliographical references.
    ISBN 0-87081-211-4
    1. Alvarez, Manuel, 1794–1856.   2. Mexicans — New Mexico —
Biography.   3. New Mexico — History — To 1848.   I. Title.
F800.A77C48 1990
978.9'02'092 — dc20
[B]   90-12365
                                                                              CIP

Contents

Acknowledgments

Biography seems an easy medium in which to write history; then begins the research and biography becomes more difficult because a human being is complex. Making sense of cause and effect — the motives for the subject's actions — requires more than the mere listing of dates of birth, of death, and the milestones in between. If done well, biography can be a conduit: A life's story becomes the history of both life and times. The subject's life illustrates a period of history, and, conversely, history is the story of human beings, like ourselves, who laughed and cried, loved and hated. What could be more natural than writing a biography?

This story of Manuel Alvarez evolved from a couple of graduate seminars at the University of New Mexico. After years of effort, the process of research and writing has, I hope, culminated in a book of some worth. Such an endeavor is not limited to one individual, especially when research is involved. Historical sources such as manuscripts, documents, and books must be collected, stored, preserved, and arranged before they can be used. Hundreds of people are involved before the researcher begins work, and many more assist the historian in the search. All these unsung people deserve credit for every history book written. Unfortunately, time and a faltering memory invariably overlook some of those who contributed along the way. With apologies to those omitted, I thank the following people.

The initial incentive came from professors Donald Cutter of St. Mary's University and the University of New Mexico, Richard Ellis of the Center for Southwest Studies at Fort Lewis College, and Frank Szasz at the University of New

Mexico. These scholars taught me the techniques of history: how to research, organize notes, and compile the accumulated information. They also proofed and corrected the initial drafts; in short, without their guidance nothing could have been done.

Other historians contributed through suggestions, questions, shared information, and encouragement. Marc Simmons and Mary Jean Cook — private historians in Santa Fe — Janet Lecompte of Colorado Springs, David Weber of Southern Methodist University, and Robert W. Larson of the University of Northern Colorado not only suggested source materials but, more importantly, published books on related topics. Their works helped provide some clarity. Donna Pierce of Santa Fe provided encouragement and support, and David Lavender's monumental *Bent's Fort* has been a solid basis for much of my work. Daniel Tyler of Colorado State University published a book listing source materials for the Mexican Period that has been a tremendous asset not only to me but to all in the field. Manuel Servín, formerly of the University of New Mexico, always had time to help with transcriptions and translations of documents written in Spanish. In Santa Fe, the late Bruce T. Ellis's very life was an inspiration. His love and enthusiasm for southwestern history had no bounds. The honor of being his friend was encouragement enough to keep working.

A lifetime's experience of reading books written by a family member or listening to others talk of his work no doubt had an influence. Fray Angélico Chávez, my uncle, has been an inspiration since I was old enough to read. Others, such as Myra Ellen Jenkins, retired state historian of New Mexico, provided incentive merely out of a desire not to disappoint them.

Part of the experience of publishing a book is the opportunity of working with all the people who finally put together the finished product. Editors, designers, copy editors, typesetters, and those responsible for marketing must work with the author to produce the book that ends up in the public's hands. Under the dynamic leadership of Luther Wilson, the staff at the University Press of Colorado has provided this author with a true education in the world of producing a book. Jody Berman, the staff editor, has been very friendly, clear, and patient in taking me through all the necessary steps of getting this book to press. Because of her professionalism, I have never felt lost in the process. In fact, the contrary is true. Copy editor Pam Ferdinand took a subject that could have been a mystery to most readers and turned it into something that will be understandable to anyone. Her insightful questions and comments have saved this author from many embarrassments. The design speaks for itself. Obviously, bookmaking is an art form, even for "boring" history books, and Carol Humphrey, who doubled as the typesetter, deserves the credit for this book's handsome appearance. Also, I want to thank Peter Hammond, the marketing director, whose good sense is reflected in his product, and office manager Judy Wilson, whose demeanor and knowledge of the operation reflect the joint effort it takes in the publishing profession.

No list of colleagues would be complete without naming my co-workers at the Palace of the Governors. Richard Rudisill, Arthur Olivas, Pamela Smith, Charles Bennett, Diana DeSantis, Orlando Romero, Karen Gordon, Sarah Laughlin, and Art Taylor are true friends as well as fellow professionals. Karen Gordon and Diana DeSantis typed, worked on the computer, and corrected copy, while maintaining my sanity. Charles Bennett, a good friend, deserves special accolades for his editorial help. Regina Johnson of Santa Fe contributed a great deal of time doing the final two edits before submission.

No inspiration, no encouragement, no amount of patience, available records, or formal education is as important as a family's love and support. Printed words cannot express the appreciation I have for my daughters Nicolasa Marie and Christel Angélica and their mother Jennifer Townsend White.

Nor can I describe the debt I owe to my parents. This biography was attempted to make them proud. With the hope that the goal has been achieved, this first book written by their eldest son is dedicated to them:

Judge Antonio E. Chávez
and
Marilyn S. Chávez

Manuel Alvarez, 1794–1856

Introduction

The Man and His Times

From 1598, when Juan de Oñate led the first settlers up the Río Grande and founded the "kingdom of New Mexico," the central government, based in Mexico City, paid more or less minimal attention to the new settlement. High expenses and recurring, if minuscule, problems contributed to officialdom's lack of enthusiasm. Historically, Mexico's concern mounted only when foreign encroachment threatened, just as the fear of French influence dominated Spain's interest in its own northern frontier for most of the eighteenth century.

With the culmination of the French and Indian War, called the Seven Years War in Europe, French influence in North America was replaced by British plans for the continent. Those plans were disrupted when thirteen British colonies successfully revolted and, after the 1783 Treaty of Paris, were formally recognized as the United States of America. Spain feared the enthusiasm of the new country, and the new Republic of Mexico inherited Spain's suspicion. So it was that New Mexico suffered under the different policies of, and growing rivalry between, the United States and an economically struggling, politically chaotic Mexico.

As both the oldest seat of European civilization in the Southwest, and the home of most of the Pueblo Indians, the Río Grande valley in New Mexico offers a good sample of cultural adjustment, a convergence of cultures particularly evident in the years surrounding the Mexican War. The Mexican years of the Southwest are characterized by a cosmopolitan frontier population, among them Spaniards, traders from the United States, French trappers, Indians, and Mexicans. The major groupings were subdivided and frequently at odds with one another — rich and poor, local and federal authorities, Anglo and non-Anglo, and American and Mexican. However, certain occupations, such as that of merchant, cut through all cultural and ethnic barriers.

During the twenty-six years of the Mexican Period (1821–1846), many changes and developments necessarily resulted from the effects of Mexico's recently won independence: the expulsion of Franciscan priests from Mexico as a result of their supposed loyalty to Spain; a major revolt in 1837 against Santa Anna's central authority, which fed New Mexicans' desire for home rule; the Texan–Santa Fe expedition; and an increase in the number of Indian attacks, to name just a few.

New Mexican–born secular priests trained in Mexico played an important role in developing national patriotism for the new Republic of Mexico. Texan border claims to the Río Grande only heightened New Mexican anxiety for defense and illustrated Mexico's inability or lack of desire to help. The central government's lack of interest reinforced the department's defensive posture, for New Mexicans now faced another threat besides nomadic Indians: the United States.

Expansion and exploration of the western frontier, a part of the doctrine of Manifest Destiny, increasingly imposed the United States' culture on that of northern Mexico. To be sure, the new country's frontier had not lingered long on the eastern seaboard or Appalachian mountain range. Before 1800, pioneers had moved into that part of Spanish Louisiana later known as Missouri. These forerunners were quickly followed by others, when, in 1803, President Thomas Jefferson took advantage of problems in Europe to purchase the vast, undefined Louisiana Territory. Population quickly increased as new settlements were founded in the lower Missouri and Mississippi river valleys, where rich soil, combined with lead and salt deposits discovered during the French and Spanish regimes, promised opportunity. The rivers provided natural highways that stimulated trade. The Ohio River, flowing from the east, and the Missouri River, from the northern plains and the Rocky Mountains, converge on the Mississippi, the main commercial artery of the West. The potentially lucrative natural resources along these waterways made Missouri the center of Anglo-American immigration.

Land speculation was a natural result of the population influx but drove prices up so that farmers found they could not meet payments on their property with the returns on their produce. As produce prices spiraled down, farmers had an increasingly difficult time selling their goods and getting or extending credit. During the national panic of 1819, the frontier suffered economically, especially from a lack of hard specie. The bullion waiting in north central Mexico beckoned as the perfect cure for the West's economic woes. Missouri became the base of operations for western exploration and, eventually, commodities, such as bullion and mules from Mexico and fur pelts from the mountains. The Santa Fe Trail, one of the main routes across the Great Plains or the "great American desert" thus developed as a route that would focus on, and take advantage of, a distant province in northern Mexico. New Mexicans were easily susceptible to American influence, for distance and a rugged topography had by this time severed close, loyal ties to Mexico.

Beginning in the 1830s, some of New Mexico's native sons attended Missouri's St. Louis University, a Catholic school. In time, over half the trade between Missouri and New Mexico was run by native New Mexicans.[1] Santa Fe and Taos benefited from the rise of the trapping industry, and, to a great extent, these two communities became trapping's commercial center in the southern Rockies, playing roles similar to that of St. Louis for the central and northern Rockies. As a result of the fur trade and the Santa Fe Trail, a new mercantile connection developed with California. By the middle 1830s, the Old Spanish Trail between New Mexico and southern California had opened, and flocks of New Mexican sheep were sent west in exchange for money that could be invested in trade bound for Missouri. The discovery of gold in California increased the sheep trade, and eventually the more direct Whipple route was established via present-day Flagstaff, Arizona.

Nonetheless, problems accompanied the financial advantages being realized. Geographically, New Mexico was perfectly situated to become involved in the annexation issue, for, with independence in 1836, the new Republic of Texas claimed the Río Grande as its western border; half of New Mexico, including its capital and commercial center, Santa Fe, fell within that claim. New Mexico was equally well placed between the United States and the Californian ports of San Diego and San Francisco. Possession of those ports on the Pacific Ocean would give the United States a distinct advantage over other nations in competition for the Oriental trade. President Andrew Jackson had tried to get Texas to extend its western border claim to include California, and, during the Mexican War, California was the prize when the US Army of the West marched through New Mexico on its way to the West Coast.

In secluded New Mexico, poverty was the rule and people had developed an independent attitude toward central government.[2] New Mexicans played no part in the revolution that resulted in Mexico's independence in 1821; most were not aware of the war until months afterward and probably would not have participated had they known. They had become so accustomed to local rule and seclusion and felt so little kinship with the central authority that they increasingly resisted any belated attempts at dominion from the south. This, in turn, left the province subject to foreign influences, and so it was that a society traditionally belligerent toward Mexico City was subdued, almost without a fight, by an alien society and government. In 1846, Brigadier General Stephen Watts Kearny marched his army into Santa Fe, militarily accomplishing an American occupation that had, in fact, begun some time previously.

The year 1846 thus marked one of the more significant events in North American history. From thirteen states clustered on the Atlantic seaboard, the United States had expanded over a vast territory to become a transcontinental nation. The Spanish, too, had been busily expanding their settlements northward out of central Mexico, culminating in what historian Herbert E. Bolton called the Spanish Borderlands. Hispanic settlement in the North American Southwest was an accomplished fact long before the Pilgrims landed in New England. The two cultures met in the Spanish Borderlands. Although Texas and California each played a role, the pivotal geographical position belonged to New Mexico, which had a larger and older Hispanic population than either Texas or California had. To Mexican minds, the Department of New Mexico had a more established importance relative to the other frontier communities.

These two factors — an established population with a historical sense of independence, and geographical location — did nothing but cause problems for the territory after it came under the United States' rule. Trying to achieve statehood when the United States hovered on the brink of civil war proved no easy task: New Mexico became an integral part of the 1850 Missouri Compromise. It suffered the consequences of many biased opinions about Mexicans and Roman Catholics and became deeply involved in Texas's border claims. The United States seemed to have an almost complete lack of concern for the people, and from the beginning New Mexicans protested. The net result delayed New Mexico's acceptance into the Union as a state until 1912.

Manuel Alvarez was a man able to adjust to the varied conditions of this crucial time and place. He seemed to embody everything that would cause his downfall, but he was able to use his intelligence and winning personality to become an integral member of the complex New Mexican society. A peninsula-born Spaniard, a purported Mexican citizen, and US consul to Santa Fe, he was fluent in English, Spanish, and French, and at various times was a traveler, trapper, merchant, stock-raiser, ex officio judge, politico, and elected official. Although he was formally educated, his intelligence was apparently of the sort well able to use practical experiences, for he quickly adapted to life on the frontier of two countries.

There are many historical "giants" of the Mexican Period, but Manuel Alvarez has not yet been considered among them, even though his presence influenced the historical process. Because of his low profile, historians have overlooked his contributions despite the volumes of papers he left in various archives. Apparently, Alvarez was one of those figures who worked best behind the scenes, thus escaping public attention, and the historian is faced with the problem of establishing both his role in, and his impact on, New Mexican and western affairs.

As a fur trapper, Alvarez became a captain charged with a party of over forty men; he spent five years in the central Rocky Mountains and was one of the discoverers of the wonders in present-day Yellowstone National Park. He used this experience and his friendship with Charles Bent to become a prominent merchant in the Santa Fe trade. As US consul in New Mexico, Alvarez served the same function as did his counterpart in California, Thomas O. Larkin. Larkin has been given credit for preparing the way for the US takeover of Mexican California, but expansion into California was contingent on successful occupation of New Mexico. History seems to indicate that Alvarez succeeded in readying New Mexico for conquest. Did he play as important a role in US expansion as Larkin did?

As consul, Alvarez had the duty of overseeing the rights of American citizens who came into Mexico's northern settlements. These people were usually merchants or trappers who, more times than not, complained of Mexico's techniques in imposing taxes. At times, American citizens became embroiled in events that would cause Alvarez virtually to risk his life. After occupation, however, Alvarez sided with the occupied peoples, probably to make the transition as painless as possible. In 1847, when a revolt broke out in Taos, casualties included Governor Charles Bent among other Americans and their supporters. The US Army quelled the violence when they stormed the church at Taos Pueblo and captured the remnant of the insurgents who had sought sanctuary there. Accused rebels were tried and prosecuted by many relatives of the deceased. Because the insurgents were charged with treason, Alvarez was asked to inquire into the legality of the trial. Were they traitors or were they Mexican citizens and patriots resisting an invading foreign army? It proved to be a difficult question to answer.

At the war's conclusion, Alvarez again took up the cause of the New Mexicans, this time as leader of the statehood party, which came into direct conflict with the ruling territorial-military party. As elected lieutenant governor and acting governor, Alvarez and his cohort Richard Weightman made their voices heard in the highest councils of the United States. It was a battle Alvarez and his side would at once win and lose, and his last great endeavor before he passed away.

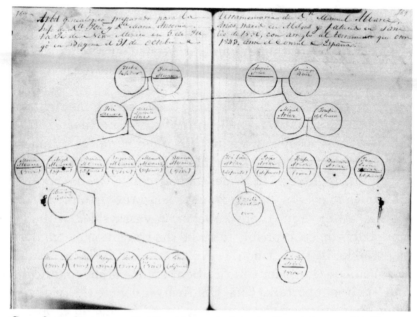

Geneological tree compiled by Alvarez before the Spanish consul in France on October 31, 1843, and recorded in the Santa Fe County book of Inventories and Reports of Wills and Testaments, 1846–1862, pages 168–69, after his death. *Original in, and courtesy of, New Mexico State Records Center and Archives, Santa Fe.*

1

The Traveling Spaniard

Manuel Alvarez was born in 1794 and spent his early years with two brothers, Angel and Bernardo, and three sisters, María, Basilía, and Engracía, in his native mountain village of Abelgas, located on the southern slope of the Cantabrian Mountains in the Region of Leon in northern Spain. Under the watchful eyes of his parents, Don José Alvarez and Doña María Antonia Arias,[1] Alvarez became proficient in both French and his native Spanish and harbored a youthful ambition to become a writer. This eventually led him to draft memorials and official documents and even to publish a few articles for a Madrid magazine. He read avidly and became thoroughly familiar with the writings of Thomas Carlyle, Sir Walter Raleigh, and Benjamin Franklin, as well as many Spanish writers. His interest in history is reflected in his private notebooks in which he wrote on the American Revolution and Hernán Cortés's conquest of Mexico, and compared the works of the famous Mexican Jesuit Francisco Clavijero, who wrote *La Historia Antiqua de México,* and the Prussian nobleman Alexander von Humboldt, author of *Political Essay on the Kingdom of New Spain.*[2]

Perhaps the word *curious* appropriately describes Al-

The village of Abelgas, Region of Leon, Spain, in August 1987, where Manuel Alvarez was born. Many Alvarezes and Ariases — Manuel's mother's maiden name — still live in the village. *Photographs by the author.*

varez: He was interested in people and new lands, and his curiosity is evident in his notebooks, in which he faithfully recorded his impressions, thoughts, and ideas. He expressed a sincere concern for his adopted country: "Mexico must not flatter herself that the world is humbly on its knees seeking admittance at her ports. No[t] so. The country needs an influx of foreigners, artisans and laborers. But before such people will be attracted," he continued, Mexico "must prove herself worthy . . . by the peaceful and prosperous future she provides to secure them." Many, if not all, of his conclusions came from his knowledge of history, a subject he defined in a quotation from Thomas Carlyle: "History . . . is Philosophy teaching by example. Before philosophy can be taught, the philosophy has to be in readings; the experience must be gathered and intelligibly recorded."[3]

The highest praise he recorded for another man was bestowed upon Hernán Cortés, the Spaniard who had defeated the Aztecs and had founded Mexico City in 1522. Alvarez wrote that Cortés had been, at best, "but a great pirate around whom a troop of needy adventurers and brave soldiers had gathered with all the appetite for conquest and the temper of freebooters. [Nonetheless,] it is undeniable that he [had been] a man of extraordinary capacity — brave, sagacious, cool, enduring, intrepid; a statesman, orator, historian, soldier, poet. He united in himself every manly attribute and accomplishment, indomitable resolution . . ."[4] Alvarez was obviously interested in Cortés the individual. A quotation attributed to Robert Walsh a few pages further into Alvarez's ledger divulges another aspect of Alvarez's interest in the accomplished man: "Endeavor, without intermission, and with what good and soever to think justly, act uprightly, and live usefully. For the accomplishment of these great ends of natural being constitute, in fact, the main securities of worldly happiness."[5] Alvarez understood historical context and studied the possibilities of how an individual contributed within that context. He understood that he, like Cortés, had some negative aspects and that the achievement of positive attributes depended on the resolve to strive toward worthy goals.

In 1818, at the age of twenty-four, Alvarez became restless and left for Mexico, in search of adventure. There he witnessed the chaos leading to Mexico's independence from Spain in 1821. In 1823, he left the new republic for Cuba, which was still part of the crumbling Spanish Empire. In Havana he received a US passport from Spanish authorities and, wasting no time, first sailed to New York, then traveled to Missouri within the year. There, he probably made the acquaintance of Eugenio Alvarez, a carpenter and merchant who was one of the original Spanish settlers in St. Louis. Although it is not known if Eugenio Alvarez was related to Manuel, his acquaintance probably proved beneficial to the new arrival, given Manuel's ambitions in business. Eugenio could have introduced him to many an influential person and would have been a fountain of information.[6]

Nonetheless, once in the border state, Alvarez must have been anxious to return to Mexico. As well as meeting remnants of the Hispanic population, he could not avoid meeting the many trappers and traders who congregated in St. Louis. He learned from them about the recently opened Santa Fe Trail and the many opportunities awaiting in Mexico's northern department, New Mexico. He began preparations for a return trip by petitioning Missouri's Governor Alexander McNair for a passport. Eleven companions were to accompany Alvarez, including Louis and Esadore Robidoux and Antoine Lamanche. All were American traders and most had French or Spanish surnames. Alvarez and his companions received their traveling papers on September 3, 1824. In these documents, written both in Spanish and English, McNair praised the men, commenting that the "traders to Mexico are citizens of the United States to me well known." His passport described Alvarez as five feet, two inches tall and clean-shaven, with black hair and brows. He had an aquiline nose and a light complexion, which would eventually darken from his years of exposure to the Southwest's fierce sun.[7]

On September 30, 1824, the already well-traveled Spaniard set out on the journey across the plains for New Mexico. One had to travel 1,500 miles over forbidding terrain inhabited by hostile Indians to reach Santa Fe from Mexico City; Alvarez trekked over 800 miles, still a perilous route but not quite as harsh or hostile. Trade between northern Mexico and the western United States had become lucrative. Whether by design or accident, Alvarez had found a place and a time singularly suited to a young, adventurous man with aspirations to succeed as a merchant.

The trip proved to be a beneficial experience for Alvarez. Aside from immediate dividends, the introduction to adventure and camaraderie was to remain useful throughout his life because the Robidoux family, which included nine brothers, played an influential role in the fur trade of the Southwest and continued to have dealings with Alvarez for many years. After the party's arrival in Taos in late November 1824, Alvarez was employed by Francisco Robidoux, brother of Louis and Esadore, and the next year became involved in a Mexican embargo of his employer's merchandise. Robidoux and Alvarez solved the matter by paying the responsible Mexican official a sum of money, ostensibly due from a previous debt.[8]

The Spanish national immediately applied for Mexican citizenship, but it was denied because of the passport papers Governor McNair had written, which referred to Alvarez as a US citizen. While waiting to sort out this matter, Alvarez began exploring the area surrounding his new, adopted home. Something about Santa Fe, a frontier village, struck his fancy; perhaps the topography and climate reminded him of his native Leon. Santa Fe lies at 7,000 feet above sea level, at the base of the Santa Fe, or Sangre de Cristo, Mountains, which tower to an elevation of over 12,000 feet. The Santa Fe River, really a stream, as well as some local springs, provided ample water. The stream contained tasty trout, a fish with which Alvarez was probably familiar from a stream of the same size in his home village of Abelgas. Thick aspen and alpine forests gradually gave way to shorter piñon trees that grew in the town before they were used up for firewood. Oak and cottonwood trees also grew around the stream.

Despite distances, arid climate, and hostile Indians, Alvarez determined to stay in New Mexico, making his home among a people who were Hispanic like himself, and whose ancestors had first braved this frontier over three centuries before. At the time of his arrival, most New Mexicans lived in settlements strung up and down the Río Grande valley from El Paso to Taos. None of the settlements, besides Santa Fe and Santa Cruz, were large. They were small communities, each having a population of under 1,000 people who lived in flat-roofed adobe houses seemingly scattered about at random.[9] Approximately 5,000 people lived in Santa Fe — hardly a metropolis compared to some of the cities through which Alvarez already had traveled, even though it had been New Mexico's capital since 1610. The most apt characterization of the community in the early nineteenth century came from Lieutenant Zebulon Montgomery Pike, an American soldier taken prisoner in the Spanish territory in 1806: like a "fleet of the flatbottomed boats which are seen in the spring and fall seasons descending the Ohio River."[10]

Well-worn dirt paths passed for streets, and Santa Fe could not boast of anything but dirt floors in its houses until the 1830s. The plaza was faced on the east by the Parroquia, the parish church, named after San Francisco. Private residences, business establishments, and a military chapel faced the south side of the plaza, and on the west side were more residences and businesses. A long, one-story, flat-roofed building facing the plaza to the north housed the governor, his staff, and the regular soldiers who made up the military garrison that had, under Spanish rule, amounted to as many as 110 men. The building was originally constructed as a presidio, or fort, with the founding of Santa Fe and was called the Casas Reales or El Presidio Real — the royal houses or fort — for most of its history. Apparently because of the recently ended revolution, the citizens of the new, independent republic called the building the Palacio del Gobierno (Government Palace).[11] Although other foreigners often criticized the mud-brick houses in which the Mexicans lived, Alvarez appreciated their worth in that environment. Adobe was familiar to him, for his native province utilized some of the same building techniques.

Alvarez was quick to take advantage of his new home's potential for profit. While the prerevolutionary Spanish government had maintained a mercantile system forbidding foreign commerce, the postrevolutionary Mexican authorities did not hesitate to throw open their borders to international trade. New Mexicans, long starved for utilitarian goods, had eagerly welcomed the opportunity. In November 1821 Governor Facundo Melgares had warmly received William Becknell and his small group of merchants, the first legal trade mission from the United States. Within four months after Governor Melgares had sworn allegiance to Mexico, three trading parties had entered Santa Fe. The future looked good to New Mexicans.

Americans were equally interested in new markets. Many Missourians, mostly farmers, were forced to trade in the Indian country to support themselves, but mines in north central Mexico produced hard specie — silver and gold. In 1822, when Becknell returned with glowing reports about the Santa Fe trade, the Missourians' eagerness to sell was matched only by the Mexicans' desire to buy.[12] Santa Fe was a transfer point for Missouri's goods and Mexico's specie: The

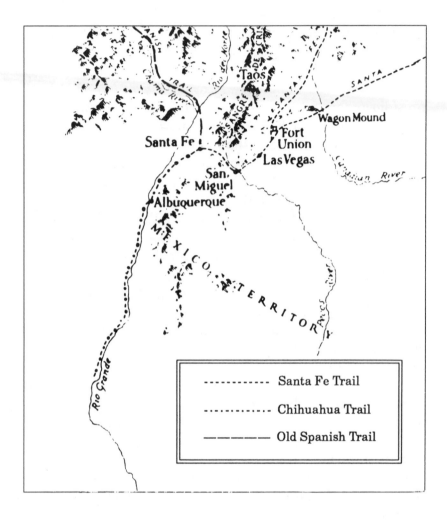

Santa Fe Trail terminated in the departmental capital and the Chihuahua Trail continued on from there, farther into Mexico. Thus, within a year after Missouri's entry into the Union, geographical and economic circumstances had formed a commercial partnership between the new state and the new country, a partnership that meant a new source of wealth for the traditionally neglected frontier town of Santa Fe. By the time Alvarez arrived in New Mexico, caravans to and from Missouri had been making huge profits for three years.[13]

Alvarez's profession partially fulfilled Mexican stereotypes of *peninsulares* — those born in Spain — as businessmen who garnered wealth at the expense of the criollos, the Mexican-born Spaniards. Indeed, the criollos' jealousy of peninsular Spaniards was one reason for the Mexican Revolution. The fact that Alvarez had left central Mexico only to reenter the country at the remote northern frontier, first as an American citizen, then as a claimant of Mexican citizenship, and had finally established himself as a prosperous merchant at a new port of entry, made his activities even more suspect, for he seemed to incorporate all the traits criollos considered threatening.

With money he may have earned in Mexico, Alvarez immediately opened a store in the old capital city — a store he personally operated until 1829 and controlled for the rest of his life. His business enabled him to remain in contact with the many traders from Missouri and with the trappers from the vast, uncharted lands beyond Santa Fe, and he sought to learn at first hand about the increasing fur trade in northern New Mexico.

While William H. Ashley was developing a new system of fur trapping and trading for St. Louis, northern New Mexico made the same transformation, but more quickly. Ashley deserves credit for drawing the industry in general away from its dependence on river travel and for developing the rendezvous system in which men stayed in the mountains and the company picked up their harvest, but the men who worked out of New Mexico had never relied on waterways. There simply were no major, navigable rivers leading to their markets. With furs coming into the conveniently located northern New Mexican towns of Taos and Santa Fe, Alvarez and others managed to turn a profit using the Santa Fe Trail to St. Louis.[14]

In connection with his new business, Alvarez made two more trips to Missouri. His first trip — with Louis Robidoux, Vicente Guiron, Thomas Boggs, Paul Padilla, and ten others — proved very profitable when they arrived at Franklin, Missouri, in 1827 with about $30,000 in specie and several hundred mules.[15] Immediately after their return to Taos in November, Padilla and Alvarez began bidding for more pelts. Alvarez went to Abiquiú to place his bids, purchasing at least twelve furs from Bernardino Váldez.[16] Under the prevailing conditions, buying pelts was more economical than was trapping without a license, and most trappers avoided falling foul of the law by purchasing furs from Mexican citizens who, in turn, had acquired them from Indians, usually Ute. There remained the risk of rousing the suspicions of Mexican authorities, who seemed to assume that any American trapper in possession of a pelt had come by it illegally. Alvarez became involved in such a case when Guiron's furs were confiscated by the *commandante* of Santa Fe on February 21, 1828. Guiron used Alvarez as a translator at the hearing before the first alcalde of Santa Fe, Juan Estevan Pino.[17]

On March 20, 1829, the central Mexican government issued a proclamation that all Spanish citizens had to leave the country. Spaniards in New Mexico had one month to leave the frontier and three months to leave Mexico, and those who lacked resources would receive money to get them to the United States. Alvarez's name appeared on a list of *españoles* in New Mexico and so, along with nine others, he had to leave. It was an opportune moment to head for the mountains and the life of a fur trapper.[18]

The fur trapping and trading industry was in full stride when the thirty-four-year-old Alvarez entered the field. Competition was keen between various fur companies as well as between countries; many expeditions and trappers had used the Santa Fe and Taos area as an operational base after Mexican independence. Alvarez and his partner, fellow Santa

Fe merchant J. Halcrow, operated as free trappers in association with P. D. Papin and Company, a group that had earlier established business ties with Alvarez's store, and perhaps one of Alvarez's motives for going into the mountains was to increase his store's business with fur companies.

Much of the territory north into Colorado and Utah had long been familiar to New Mexicans. Trade with the Utes had been established under Spanish rule and continued until 1847, when the Mormons settled in Utah. In the not too distant past, Taos had been host to the famous trade fairs where Spaniards met with Pueblo and Plains Indians to barter. Fur trappers discovered Taos to be a virtual paradise where they could rest in comfort. With Halcrow, however, Alvarez went beyond those neighboring regions; the two traders serve as an illustration of the role men from Mexico's northern frontier played throughout the North American West. On his first expedition, Alvarez operated out of Fort Teton and trapped on the Teton, Little Missouri, and Yellowstone rivers.[19]

In 1831, Papin and Company came under control of the American Fur Company, and Alvarez and his partner trapped under its auspices for Andrew Drips in the northwest portion of what is now Yellowstone Park. Alvarez spent the winter of 1832–1833 with Drips and a brigade of the American Fur Company at the forks of the Snake River. February proved mild and the ice broke in March, so Drips put about forty trappers under Alvarez, who departed up Henry's Fork intending to hunt on the Yellowstone River. Drips led the rest of the men elsewhere and eventually met Alvarez on the Green River at the end of the spring hunt. The early thaw did not bring continued mild weather, however, and Alvarez was soon stalled on Henry's Fork by snow two feet deep. As soon as conditions allowed, Alvarez led his party into the Yellowstone River area, making history when he encountered the boiling pots and great geyser basin. Until this time, such things as geysers had been myth and rumor. Although other Euro-Americans may have seen them, only Daniel T. Potts is known to have visited the area in 1825.[20] While looking for fur and avoiding the Blackfeet, Potts had seen some of the geysers and at least had heard the explosions of Old Faithful in 1826. Although he apparently did not think the geysers were a great discovery, he did describe what he saw in a letter to his brother: a number of "hot and boiling hot springs, some of water and others of most beautiful clay" that throw "particles to the height of from twenty to thirty feet." Potts added that in other places pure sulfur "is sent forth in abundance," accompanied, in one case, with "tremendious [sic] trembling" and an "explosion . . . resembling that of thunder."[21]

Alvarez shared his discovery at the 1833 rendezvous, piquing others' curiosity and leading to others' visits, the most notable by Warren A. Ferris and Osborne Russell, who traveled to the geysers the next year after meeting with Alvarez and his men at the rendezvous.[22] Ferris noted that water shot 150 feet into the air even though "the party of Alvarez who discovered it [the largest fountain], insists it could not be less than four times as large." From their experience, Ferris and Russell wrote the accounts that popularized the area.[23] Myth and legend had turned into hard fact.

Alvarez proved no less successful in outdoor adventures than he had been with his store: He advanced to "captain" or brigade leader for the fur company, and, at the Green River rendezvous in the summer of 1833, he received a note from Lucien Fontenelle, acting agent of the American Fur Company, for $1,325.98.[24] Once again he had demonstrated his capabilities by performing above the norm and being paid accordingly. His ability to excel at whatever he attempted, and to make loyal friends in the process, became a significant trait.

Apparently, the passage of five years relaxed Mexico's desire to expel all Spaniards, for in 1834 Alvarez was back in

Santa Fe operating his store with a new partner, Damaso López, another peninsular Spaniard who had business experience and had come to New Mexico as early as 1820.[25] In 1833, López had become involved with the José Francisco Ortiz mining claim twenty miles southwest of Santa Fe. In his official capacity, he inspected the mine site and approved the claim for Ortiz and his partner, Ignacio Cano. Since neither of the partners had any mining expertise, they took in López as a third partner but, once the mine began to produce, invoked a law of the Mexican Republic forbidding foreigners to mine; López, being Spanish, was eliminated. Revenge could have been a hidden motive for the whole affair: López, on behalf of a Chihuahuan merchant named Lorenzo, had brought an earlier suit against Ortiz and Fernando Delgado in Santa Fe on June 19, 1820.[26] Whatever the reasons for his separation from the Ortiz-Cano mining venture, López shortly thereafter joined up with Alvarez.[27]

With many acquaintances, the new knowledge he had acquired as a trapper, and the addition of López, Alvarez was better equipped to handle the trading end of the fur industry, even though his fur sales in St. Louis would never amount to a significant portion of his overall trade.[28] As early as 1830, there had been indications that the trapping industry was in demise,[29] although even in 1835 otter pelts, less cherished than beaver, could still get as much as $3 per pound in New Mexico.[30] The British had trapped out the Oregon Territory and the central Rockies were being depleted at an alarming rate. Competition among companies, and with and among independent trappers, and the growing popularity of the silk over the beaver hat, meant an end to beaver trapping as a profitable occupation. Indeed, the American Fur Company, for which Alvarez had worked, had changed owners; the previous management, including one of the most famous and influential of mountain men, Jedediah Smith, knew when to get out. Smith and his partners were typical of many experienced trappers who left the fur trade,[31] but others either risked their lives by trapping farther north, in the territory of the hostile Blackfeet, or moved into the southern Rockies. This, in turn, gave northern New Mexico an opportunity to garner some of the fur trade that traditionally had gone directly to St. Louis.

Meanwhile, the eyes of Mexico City were finally turned northward toward the distant Department of New Mexico, and Alvarez was caught up in the sometimes violent changes that followed. As early as 1835, the Mexican president, Antonio López de Santa Anna, had sought to centralize his government by gaining more control over Mexico's distant departments. He appointed Lieutenant Colonel Albino Pérez, one of his followers, governor of New Mexico. Living in virtual seclusion from Mexico City's politics, New Mexicans had become accustomed to having a local *jefe,* or "chief," govern them — and to life without taxes. Local theory held that the risk of living beyond the frontier, in a land surrounded by hostile Indians and in which the central government left defense chiefly up to the local inhabitants, was taxing enough. So, along with the new, and married, governor's involvement with a local woman, his implementation of new taxes ripened the population for revolt. On August 1, 1837, resistance broke out over the arrest of the alcalde of Santa Cruz de la Cañada. The alcalde, Juan José Esquibel, had flouted the governor's authority by releasing a relative from jail, and had then refused the governor's direct order to rejail the man and pay a fine. This episode was the most obvious of Esquibel's affronts and finally forced the governor to order the alcalde's arrest. He was immediately freed by a mob, and the violence that ensued resulted in several deaths, among them that of Santa Anna's governor and of Pérez's major opponent, José González.[32]

With the outbreak of hostilities, the loyalist forces led by Governor Pérez had been forced to rely on foreign merchants, including Americans, for supplies and money. The merchants had acquiesced, for it "would not have been very safe to have refused them advances."[33] Besides, they had gladly done business with these people before, and the salaries of government officials had usually been sufficient collateral. If the salaries did not suffice, the local customs house would stand behind the debts by offering the proceeds of the next caravan as collateral.[34] American traders did not expect that the government forces would be defeated in the initial battle, after which the revolutionaries divided the spoils; they showed no intention of assuming the debts of the vanquished.[35]

Manuel Armijo, a *rico,* or wealthy New Mexican, from the Bernalillo area southwest of Santa Fe, emerged as the new governor. The revolt initiated his legendary reputation for military savvy, not to mention his ruthlessness when he ordered González executed. Alvarez, Spanish by birth, Mexican by expediency, and trader by inclination, sympathized with the New Mexican case for local rule. After all, Santa Anna's conservative policies could only hinder his business interests, and Armijo operated under the sanction of the central government. There were no funds forthcoming to repay the loans made by American merchants, and the future of the non-Mexican merchant class loomed darkly. Armijo apparently sanctioned the bill, by a central assembly convened on August 27, 1837, in which the insurgents had formally approved "the division of the property of the deceased persons [Governor Pérez, González, and associates] among the principals of the party now in power, thus leaving the creditors of the deceased without any hope of collecting their debts."[36] Because Armijo was an official of the same government to which the merchants had been forced to lend financial support, they were surprised by this move. The governor did, however, thank the Americans for their financial aid. Alvarez and others felt that one way toward a future repayment for their initial aid was to demonstrate their support for, and good

Manuel Armijo, ca. 1845. Alvarez's main adversary in New Mexico during the Mexican Period, Armijo served as Mexican governor of the northern department for three terms (1827–1829, 1837–1844, and 1845–1846). *Courtesy of the Museum of New Mexico, Santa Fe. MNM 50809.*

faith in, the new administration with a contribution of 410 pesos for the "reestablishment of order in New Mexico."[37]

Left with no recourse, the Americans wrote a memorial to the US minister to Mexico, Powhatan Ellis. They felt that justice could be done only through the Mexican national government; the local general assembly having decreed they would not be paid, the problem was seen as a deliberate act of the New Mexican people. Only the Mexican national government could remedy the situation. Among the signers of the memorial were Alvarez, Josiah Gregg, P. W. Thompson, L. L. Waldo, and Esadore Robidoux, all prominent traders. The document appears to have been written in part by Alvarez.[38] It does not seem that Ellis took much interest in the affair,[39] and the Mexican national government paid no more heed than had the local government. Neither the Mexicans nor the merchants were ignorant of the fact that Texas had revolted in 1836, for much the same reasons that would motivate the insurgent New Mexicans a year later. It would not have taken much imagination for Mexican officials to assume that foreigners had led the revolt in New Mexico, as they had in Texas.

Nevertheless, Alvarez persisted, even though the local government refused to budge. In August 1838, he received an answer to one of his inquiries when the secretary of state relayed another denial from Armijo. The communiqué ended with the statement that the government needed time to conclude *"otro negocio"* (other business)[40] — in other words, Armijo's administration did not want to bother with the petition.

Two years after the initial petition, Alvarez put his signature at the top of a list attached to another memorial, a second attempt to receive payment for the claims stemming from the 1837 disturbances. Among the cosigners was Alvarez's friend and fellow merchant Charles Bent,[41] one of four brothers who had moved west from Missouri. Along with his brother William and Ceran St. Vrain, he had formed the Bent–St. Vrain Company and built Bent's Fort on the upper Arkansas River in the early 1830s. He had married a New Mexican and resided in Taos where he operated a store. Despite the fact that this second petition, like the first, proved unsuccessful, Alvarez's efforts prompted the American traders to write a letter of gratitude to the Spaniard in 1840. They praised him for "the very prompt," unyielding stand he took "under every grade of circumstance . . . vindicating our rights."[42] Alvarez best summed up the whole affair in a passage he copied from the "libro de Brantz Mayen" on December 10, 1843; in part, it spoke of the 1836 Texas revolt: "I hold this revolt to have greatly affected the mutual interests and feelings of Mexico and our Union."[43] Alvarez might well have copied those words with a whimsical smile on his face.

Despite these distractions, Alvarez did not allow his feelings to interfere with his intention to petition the new governor for a land grant of four square leagues (approximately 9,300 acres) along the Ocaté River near Mora, northeast of Santa Fe. Alvarez had become intrigued with the idea of transporting sheep along the Old Spanish Trail to California. Damaso López, who had the expertise, apparently wished to join him and supervise the operation. Alvarez was interested in increasing wool output and toyed with producing better wool by integrating merino sheep into his stock. In contrast to his reaction to the Americans' petition for retribution, Armijo approved the petition for land on October 16, 1837.[44] Although López eventually did take some sheep to California, the enterprise was, for the time being, held in abeyance because of more pressing matters.

2

Citizenship and Diplomacy

Exequatur — The authority formally vested in a foreign consul by the country to which he is sent and by virtue of which he is able to exercise his official functions within its territorial limits.

James A. Ballantine
Law Dictionary with Pronunciations, 2d ed.

After Mexico's independence, the close proximity of New Mexico to the United States became crucial because Mexico officially sanctioned foreign trade. This new policy opened the gate for Anglo-American influence in Mexico's northern department. By the 1840s the area had become an important element in the United States' plan for expansion to the Pacific Ocean,[1] and Mexico had become somewhat apprehensive about its frontier outposts. New Mexico also had to contend with the young Republic of Texas and, caught in the middle, was soon to feel the squeeze: First came Texan boundary claims, then invasion.

Because of its geopolitical location, New Mexico, and especially Santa Fe and Taos, became cosmopolitan. As frontier outposts to both Mexican and Anglo-American society, these

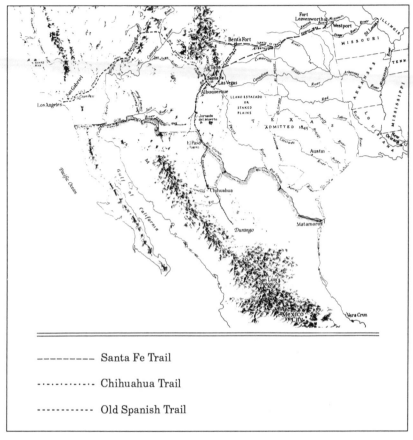

Mexico and the United States, showing the trade routes converging on Santa Fe.

towns of northern New Mexico became commercial centers, representing important political entities, and were vital to American expansion at a time when Manifest Destiny came into vogue. In the midst of such historical developments, citizenship became exceedingly important, but citizenship of one country or another could be either an advantage or a liability depending on the circumstances. Anglo-American merchants tried to meet this problem in many ways: Some became naturalized Mexican citizens or attempted to maintain dual citizenship; others married Mexican women in hopes of establishing rapport with Mexican officials. Some of the more famous examples of this latter solution are Charles Bent and Christopher "Kit" Carson, who married sisters. During his engagement, Carson converted and was baptized a Roman Catholic by the local curate, Padre Antonio José Martínez.[2] Finally, there were those who pretended they were naturalized citizens: They allowed Mexican officials to believe them legal residents, while at the same time they remained citizens of the United States.

Many traders operated under the "protection" of US citizenship, although on occasion the Mexican government chose to ignore such protection, as when Governor Armijo refused to lend assistance to the Americans captured in the Texan expedition that invaded New Mexico in 1841. The governor was at least consistent: He did no more for Thomas Falconer, who was an Englishman. Even those Anglo-American residents of the area who had been naturalized in Mexico received no favors from the governor's policies. In January 1841, Armijo sent out a circular lambasting foreigners who "pass back and forth" under protection of American laws while paying no attention to local laws.[3] About a week later, a letter was delivered to Alvarez notifying him of an official order to deport all foreigners who did not have official papers.[4] The effect of this new policy became evident when, three days later, Alvarez received a letter from an American, Simeon Turley, in Taos. Turley had been officially asked about his citizenship and harassed, so he claimed, by the local authorities. He requested Alvarez, who in 1839 had been appointed the US consul, "to procure . . . a letter or something that will secure me."[5]

If playing citizenship games was a method of survival for non-Mexican residents, Manuel Alvarez was the master. He demonstrated a capacity to play off the rights of citizenship of one country against those of another many times. Yet, this game could create problems and had the potential to backfire. Until 1842, the question of Alvarez's legal status was one of the major mysteries surrounding his life. He applied for Mexican citizenship on three different occasions between 1825 and 1826. Unfortunately, trouble arose over his passport papers, which Governor McNair of Missouri had written, because Alvarez was included among those referred to as US citizens. This seemed suspicious indeed to the Mexican officials; no doubt, too, a few eyebrows were raised when Alvarez's name appeared on the list of Spanish citizens to be deported in 1829.

There is some doubt that Alvarez was ever granted Mexican citizenship, although he consistently claimed he was entitled to it. Many documents refer to him as a "Spanish native and Mexican citizen," he held Mexican passports,[6] and Governor Armijo corroborated Alvarez's argument when he employed it as justification for arbitrarily using the Spaniard's property.[7] The petitions Alvarez submitted are liberally strewn with prose indicative of his determination to be naturalized.[8] Perhaps one reason for his doggedness was his stated zeal for the Catholic faith.[9] On another front, Alvarez argued that, under the Mexican Constitution, he had "the rights of citizenship . . . by living in their country at the time of their independence." Although in reality he remained a Spanish citizen, he apparently managed to convince the Mexican authorities and many other people of his naturalized status.[10]

That Alvarez was not beyond creating a façade by allowing others mistakenly to assume his status is patent in documents relating to his US citizenship. Many examples adequately demonstrate his laxity in keeping the record straight. In each case his assumption of American naturalization hinged on an advantage he wished to achieve. In his petition for US citizenship on October 16, 1834, Alvarez established the fact that he was not yet an American citizen, and he did not want to be considered a citizen of Mexico or Spain. He renounced, in his declaration made at the Circuit Court of St. Louis,[11] "all allegiance and fidelity to every Foreign Prince . . . whatsoever, particularly to Isabelle, Queen of Spain, whose subject I then was." Inability to meet the five-year residency requirement led to a refusal of his petition, and he did not become a citizen until April 9, 1842, when he repeated his declaration in the same court.[12]

Alvarez had carelessly assumed the status of American citizenship as early as 1824, when he received his US passport. Possibly, he felt being a Spaniard would not suffice to get him back into Mexico because that country had just completed a successful revolution in which Spain and peninsular Spaniards were the enemy. Be that as it may, his new "cover" was sufficient to accomplish his goal. On March 4, 1839, Alvarez procured another American passport that proclaimed him "a citizen of the United States," issued in Washington and signed by Secretary of State John Forsyth. Alvarez again proved himself adept in the game of multinationality: Perhaps to avoid any unnecessary problems, he never signed the document in the designated area.[13] The wily merchant may have had another motive, for on March 21 he was appointed US consul to Santa Fe by the same Forsyth.[14]

By this time, Alvarez had a prosperous and well-established store, landholdings, and many connections in the Santa Fe trade. The fact that he was a native of Spain boded ill; if he lost his Mexican citizenship, his place of birth would make it easy for the Mexican authorities to destroy him financially. So, upon receiving the appointment, he decided to try persuading the Mexican authorities that he could function in the apparently contradictory roles of Mexican citizen and US consul, a feat of expostulation it would not be easy to accomplish.

Armijo, who occupied the governor's office for all but one of the years Alvarez held his diplomatic post, was a master

politician and might not want this peninsular Spaniard officially defending the rights of all Americans.[15] Furthermore,
Alvarez had to act quickly. Mexico had a law that eliminated
rights of citizenship for any person who held office for a
foreign country. This meant that if he had not lost them
already, he could lose his presumed citizenship rights as soon
as Mexico City became aware of his appointment. Formal
recognition through the granting of exequatur could certainly
mean the end of his naturalized citizenship, at least in the
eyes of Mexican officialdom. Apparently, Alvarez had expressed his desire for naturalization to the governor, for
Armijo wrote to Luis G. Guevas, the Mexican minister of the
interior, in early August 1839 recommending approval.[16] It
would have been inane to ask Forsyth or the US minister to
Mexico, Ellis, to delay the process; after all, Alvarez had the
secretary of state believing he was a citizen of the United
States.

In late August 1839, Alvarez formally informed the New
Mexican government, specifically Armijo, that he wished to
continue to enjoy his rights under the Mexican Constitution.
He expounded on the dilemma created by the recent honor of
his appointment by the "Señor Presidente de los Estados
Unidos" and the fact that the laws of Mexico could take away
the citizenship he enjoyed before coming to the point: Would
the governor help him retain his Mexican citizenship while
fulfilling the office of US consul by petitioning the supreme
congress in Mexico City on his behalf? Armijo accommo-
dated the Spaniard's unusual request by forwarding
Alvarez's letter, with another stating his own recommendations, and reiterated his report in another letter a week
later.[17] Undoubtedly, the ensuing flurry of correspondence
complicated the process of granting Alvarez an exequatur.
Although Ellis officially learned that unstable conditions in
New Mexico were causing the delay,[18] Alvarez's citizenship
controversy must have been part of it.

Neither the Mexican government nor Alvarez appears ever to have informed Washington, DC, that he had sought to retain his rights of Mexican citizenship, but those officials nevertheless hesitated to issue him official recognition. Not until February 12, 1840, was Alvarez's certificate signed. Forsyth had a letter drawn up in which the consul was formally informed of the Senate's confirmation of his nomination, but the letter was never signed because Ellis informed the State Department that the Mexican government had refused to acknowledge Alvarez as consul.[19]

On February 18, 1840, the day after the unsent letter had been drafted, Alvarez received word from the secretary of the Department of New Mexico, Guadalupe Miranda, that the local government had recognized him as consul in order to maintain internal tranquility.[20] Armijo had yet to receive from the central authorities an answer to Alvarez's request to maintain his Mexican citizenship. Although Alvarez was completely unaware of it, his petition had hindered his diplomatic recognition by both the US and Mexican national governments. Alvarez was officially recognized only within the Department of New Mexico. Shortly after, however, Governor Armijo received an official dispatch from Minister Guevas. The president of Mexico, said Guevas, granted permission for Alvarez to "administer and perform the duties" of consul "without prejudice of his rights of citizenship." Guevas then requested that the minister of foreign relations expedite Alvarez's exequatur as soon as the Spaniard's certificate of appointment was presented.[21] Armijo quickly fulfilled Guevas's wish and informed Alvarez that the central government had granted his petition and now waited upon the presentation of his commission. The governor also had a circular sent out announcing Alvarez's official recognition.[22]

Alvarez's appointment to consul was not unusual within the US government's diplomatic branch; it served the logical need to have in office an individual familiar with local circumstances. Also customary was the absence of pay; Alvarez's official certificate of appointment stipulated that he would serve without salary, although he did receive a small expense account.[23] This miserly policy risked developing a self-interested and inactive diplomacy in the borderlands, as had certainly been true in the case of Alvarez's predecessors, Augustus Storrs and Ceran St. Vrain — neither apparently even took up residence in Santa Fe[24] — but inactivity would not be a characteristic of Alvarez's tenure. Alvarez's official standing became a complicated matter, for the US and Mexican governments held contrary views on official recognition. Such a situation could only be perplexing to the man involved, and the confusion was magnified by the historical context. Being at the "flash point" of two countries, New Mexico provided a tough problem for the chief representatives of the involved governments.

Governor Armijo, Alvarez's adversary, also had problems. New Mexico, a traditionally poor outpost, sometimes waited as long as three years between supply trains from the south. Noting that his department abutted rebellious Texas, Armijo constantly tried to get supplies and men from his superiors. Such attempts nearly always proved futile. Although Americans and Texans considered Texas's severance from Mexico complete with the Treaty of Velasco in 1836, the Mexican government continued to view the Texans as subjects in conflict with their legitimate government. The threat of an invasion, fulfilled in 1841, plus Texas's western border claims, based on the Treaty of Velasco, which included not only Santa Fe but half of New Mexico, heightened Armijo's anxiety. Armijo was an efficient and able administrator during difficult times, and he did not rule independently of Mexico City. He understood his people and governed with sensibility and, importantly, according to the custom of his land. The United States was an expanding and aggressive society, and this was no secret to the New Mexican governor, especially since local

Anglo-American merchants kept him supplied with newspapers from the States. He could read of the development, prejudices, and ambitions of "Young America." Armijo was getting no support from the central government, and he found himself, in 1839, constrained to tolerate an energetic consul in the person of the newly appointed Alvarez, who represented the very people Armijo suspected of being, at worst, Texas's agents or, at best, potential troublemakers.[25]

Alvarez received his official consular papers either in, or just before he arrived at, Independence, Missouri, while on his way back to New Mexico. Enclosed with his papers were instructions that he formally execute an enclosed, blank consular bond. Alvarez also needed a certificate from an attorney in the United States to certify his papers of office. He took the bond to L. L. Waldo, a member of a wealthy St. Louis family; Waldo's brother, David, had become an acquaintance of Alvarez in the Santa Fe trade. Unfortunately, Alvarez left Missouri before Waldo was able to perform the proper task; they apparently missed each other during "the bustle of the caravan setting out from Independence."[26] As a result, Waldo did not certify the bond, but by the end of June, Alvarez had arrived in Santa Fe confident that his diplomatic papers were in order. He found out that Ellis would apply for his exequatur from the Mexican government and then forward his formal recognition to Santa Fe.[27] He was further instructed by Secretary Forsyth that he was not "authorized to perform any act as Consul until an exequatur had been granted him or unless properly accepted by authorities in Santa Fe."[28] However, it appears that he actually began exercising his consular authority even before arriving in Santa Fe. Matt Field, a journalist for the *New Orleans Picayune,* had been sent on a western writing venture by his editor, George Wilkins Kendall, and apparently received his passport in Missouri on June 1, 1839, from the newly appointed consul.[29]

Because Waldo had failed to act on the bond, Alvarez

technically had violated his instructions from Secretary Forsyth.[30] The new consul wrote an apology to his superior and a
dispatch to L. L. Waldo requesting that the bond be sent to
the State Department without delay. Additionally, Alvarez
wrote Forsyth that he lacked the paraphernalia of his office,
notably "an American flag, a coat of arms, and a Consular
Seal." He suggested that his predecessor, Ceran St. Vrain,
had never cared enough to get the vitally needed seal —
judiciously not accusing the department of deliberately with-
holding it.[31] The seal was important to the function of his
office because it legitimized all official correspondence; it was
a formal means of recognition. Alvarez could only conclude
that delays in getting official materials to him originated in
the US capital, so he requested a seal from Minister Ellis in
Mexico City, who replied that "the articles in question are not
furnished to the Legations of the United States for distribu-
tion among their Consuls." Not recognizing the significance
of obtaining the seal and coat of arms through official channels to a man of Alvarez's background and temperament,
Ellis sent an impression of the seal used by the consul in
Mexico City, with the suggestion that Alvarez have one
"made to order" in St. Louis. In any case, the government
would foot the bill.[32] Alvarez would not accept this carefree
attitude; he continued to insist that the State Department
should provide the seal.

The difficulties Alvarez had with the US government over
his appointment paled in contrast to the delays in getting
formal acceptance from Mexico City. Alvarez had both intelligence and a tricultural background, but there were other
merchants who had equal familiarity with Mexico's northern
frontier and could also speak fluent Spanish; most had the
added advantage of being US citizens as well, yet here was
Alvarez issuing passports to them. In Mexico City, Ellis went
through the normal process of submitting Alvarez's commission to Manuel Eduardo de Gorostiza, Mexican minister of

foreign affairs. Gorostiza was asked to pass the paper to the president so that exequatur could be granted as usual,[33] but the president of Mexico declined Alvarez's exequatur because of the 1837 rebellion in New Mexico. He felt that a recognized American agent stationed in northern Mexico would be ill-disposed to his government, especially since US citizens had played a demonstrable role in the 1836 Texan rebellion. Until he felt assured that loyal officials could establish "constitutional order,"[34] no recognition would be forthcoming. Judging when that time had come was left up to the governor of New Mexico, Alvarez's adversary Manuel Armijo. Interestingly, not a word was conveyed to Ellis about Alvarez's citizenship status when Gorostiza justified his government's action by claiming that no US consul had been previously stationed at Santa Fe — conveniently forgotten were the terms of Augustus Storrs and Ceran St. Vrain. Official denial of Mexican recognition took one day — very fast indeed![35] A month later, Alvarez was petitioning in Santa Fe to keep his Mexican citizenship rights. More significant is the fact that both governments had left the problem of Alvarez's recognition in Governor Armijo's hands.

Meanwhile, the consul comfortably believed all was well, so he was somewhat surprised when, by December 1840, his exequatur had still not arrived in Santa Fe: "I continued to perform the duties of consul," wrote Alvarez, "not doubting that the exequatur would be sent to me by Honorable P. Ellis."[36] Aware that he was in violation of his instructions not to act until he had received his exequatur, he limited his activities to avoid trouble as much as possible. Impatience, however, finally caused him to inquire of Ellis about his formal recognition: "Being named Consul would give me in Confidential relations in behalf of our fellow citizens [that] which is formally denied."[37] A month later he repeated his inquiry, to no avail, and in the end, he never received his exequatur, for which he blamed Governor Armijo, who,

claimed Alvarez, was granted powers from Mexico City to
withhold national recognition — without which Armijo held
all the diplomatic cards. Given his power and his purely
personal considerations, Armijo did not care to allow Alvarez
to "exercise the duties of Consul independently of his influence."[38] Besides, it would conflict with the governor's plan of
monopoly of the Santa Fe trade.[39] Armijo could informally
recognize Alvarez when he wished and withdraw recognition
whenever it became convenient. Alvarez felt that this was
contrary to Guevas's instruction and that Armijo's flexibility
illustrated Mexico City's weak control over the department,
but he did not consider that the Mexican government's acqui-
escence in granting Armijo such autonomy might have been
due to its suspicions of Alvarez himself.

The Mexican authorities never knew about the troubles
the consul was having with the US Department of State, nor
did they know that Alvarez's instructions prohibited him
from performing his duties without a seal and his exequatur.
Meanwhile, Alvarez confidently acted on the assumption that
the US government was totally behind him. In connection
with an 1839 case involving a US citizen, heard before Felipe
Sena, the first alcalde and judge of Santa Fe, he verified an
official document for the court, inscribing below Sena's signature: "This is to certify that I believe the signature to be that
of Don Felipe Sena first Alcalde of Santa Fe and not being in
possession of a seal of office I hereunto place my private
seal."[40]

As one of his first official acts, in 1839 he wrote a five-and-
one-half-page memorial to the prefect of first district in Santa
Fe, certifying his claim and those of other merchants for
money and goods given to Governor Albino Pérez prior to the
1837 revolt. This petition proved as unsuccessful as the earlier one. Ironically, each page was written on officially
stamped paper of the Mexican government.[41] Within a
month, Miranda advised him to use his own *papel de sello*

(officially stamped paper) for official communications.[42] Alvarez started drawing his "official seal" and then resorted to labeling all his official correspondence "Consulate of the United States of America."

When Secretary of State Daniel Webster received Alvarez's letter asking that he be indemnified for injuries to his property and person suffered during the Texan invasion, Webster, being a little more thorough than were Forsyth and Guevas, replied that he had no information pertaining to Alvarez's citizenship; before the State Department could do anything "it should be informed on that point."[43] Webster would not assume anything; the burden of proof fell on Alvarez, who, disarmed of his one weapon — tactful assumption — used a new rationale that allowed him to withdraw gracefully. Then in Washington himself on an 1841–1842 trip, Alvarez innocently explained that he had accepted the US consulship "under the full impression, that, I was by virtue of that office entitled to protection as an American citizen"; and "under these circumstances I am of the impression that I might be considered as an American citizen, and entitled as such."[44] It is interesting that Alvarez did not cite the 1839 passport Forsyth had issued to him, as it would have lent weight to his argument. Of course, Forsyth had made the appointment, his awareness of Alvarez's proper citizenship is an open question, and producing the passport might also have produced an answer. In his reply, Webster did not even mention Alvarez's claim to citizenship through the consulship, apparently taking the consul's answer for an explanation. Because Alvarez had not fulfilled the requirements for naturalization and was not a legal citizen of the United States, Webster issued him "a special passport, which may be useful to you on your return to New Mexico."[45]

Seemingly contradicting himself, Alvarez had previously asked Governor Armijo to protect the rights of American citizens, including himself, as a result of the same incidents

Daniel Webster, ca. 1850. Alvarez had to deal with Webster during
Webster's two terms as secretary of state. *Courtesy of the Museum of New
Mexico, Santa Fe. MNM 99235.*

for which he had sought reparations. To this the governor had replied through his secretary of state that protection of Americans would be addressed. However, Alvarez's position as US consul would not entitle him to those privileges: He would be treated as any Mexican citizen, for Alvarez had convinced Armijo to petition successfully for retention of his Mexican citizenship.[46] The US and Mexican governments were in agreement on one point: Alvarez was not a citizen of the United States, even though neither government realized he most likely had never given up his Spanish citizenship. As a native of Spain successfully functioning as a merchant, he probably could not have remained in Mexico had he not assumed or received Mexican naturalization or become the consul for the United States, which appeared to give him the protection of that country.

Nothing could be greater evidence of Alvarez's astuteness in the matter of what his status meant than an episode involving one of his mules. Although a relatively insignificant matter, Alvarez thought it important enough to relate to Secretary of State Webster as an example of "their [the Mexicans'] eagerness to seize every opportunity to do injustice to the citizens of the United States."[47] He felt he could say this, even though he was not such a citizen; however, his motivation in telling Webster appears to be an attempt to fool the Mexican authorities. On August 9, 1841, Alvarez was informed by Francisco Robledo, one of his employees who was at San Miguel del Vado, that the *juez de paz* (justice of the peace) had asked for a mule to take on an expedition against the Comanches. Alvarez referred to a treaty of April 5, 1841, between the United States and Mexico that included an agreement that property of American citizens could not be pressed into public service. He implored the governor "to demand of that Mayor" not to "dispose of my property nor of the property of the American citizens."[48] This phrasing must have startled Miranda and Armijo because they had just

Lithograph of San Miguel, New Mexico, 1857. Known as San Miguel del Vado, or Vado, this town is where the Santa Fe Trail crossed the Pecos River. Alvarez kept an agent here. *Courtesy of the Museum of New Mexico, Santa Fe. MNM 71388.*

granted Alvarez permission to serve as US consul while retaining his rights of Mexican citizenship. Armijo immediately had his secretary of state reply that the mule could be pressed into public service by right of Alvarez's Mexican citizenship, which he had been given permission to retain while occupying a foreign office. This answer was written and received the same day on which the complaint was made,[49] and it was the answer that Alvarez should have expected. Alvarez, curiously, regarded the governor's stand as one of choosing "to ignore that Mexican citizenship is forfeited as soon as [one] accepts office from a foreign government."[50] In reality, Alvarez had connived and fought for the retention of that citizenship.[51]

Undaunted, the Spaniard penned an elegant letter using a standard salutation to ask Secretary of State Miranda to have "la bondad de presentar mis respectos al Eximo Señor Governador" (the goodness to present my respects to his excellency the governor) and "completely to resolve that the property of the United States Consul and that of American citizens should in the future be free from government confiscation." With tongue in cheek he concluded the letter: "Con este motivo virtuoso a V.S. mis consideraciones y aprecio" (with this virtuous motive I send you my consideration and appreciation).[52] Here was a bold move on Alvarez's part — a test to see how far he could push the local authorities. The consul, significantly, labeled all his letters as coming from the "Consulado de los E.U. de América," thus implying the full weight of authority of Mexico's neighboring Goliath. Equally significant and, at first appearance, ludicrous was that the crux of the whole matter was one mule to be used for one day on a campaign that would benefit all inhabitants of the area. In reality, Alvarez was wise to press this test case over an unimportant matter; something of such little consequence as a mule would not raise the ire of Governor Armijo. On the other hand, Alvarez, by virtue of his recognized citizenship, took calculated risks. Given his position and his cunning, a distinct possibility exists that he assumed the US government would protect him. Thus, he applied the argument that he later used on Daniel Webster.

It took Armijo a couple of days longer than necessary to answer, but eventually he granted Alvarez's petition. Alvarez and the Americans had won protection for their property, even though the governor considered Alvarez a Mexican citizen.[53] As the merchant said later, the answer was "worded as though he was in a bad humor";[54] and well might Armijo have been angry — his Spanish adversary had taken advantage of him by employing the threat of a third nation. Alvarez had succeeded in his test and assumed that all had worked out well:[55] He had won the same property rights as other US citizens, while by the official correspondence of both governments he still assumed and enjoyed Mexican citizenship. But he was premature, for Armijo enjoyed a good contest.

Nine days later, the alcalde of San Miguel again expropriated a mule from Alvarez's clerk — now it was the Spaniard's turn to be taken aback. He sent an immediate complaint to Miranda, terse and without niceties. The first line rather quickly stated the point of the entire missive: Alvarez informed the secretary that the alcalde's action was a direct contradiction of the last communication in the matter and expressed surprise that the alcalde, who could not possibly be ignorant of this, would so blatantly disregard the law. He also informed Miranda that he expected some sort of reparation.[56] Alvarez included mention of his US citizenship, for he was always cognizant of his position. The point of the whole affair may have been to establish just where the Mexicans stood in relation to American citizens. The governor took the easy way out: Probably both the consul and Armijo knew all along that the ultimate defense was to plead ignorance on the part of the alcalde. In doing so, Armijo absolved himself and the government he represented, and by arguing that Alvarez should be aware that an alcalde cannot be expected to comprehend the confusing laws governing the various peoples,[57] the way was left open for repeated disclaimers based on the ignorance of a lesser official. Thus, Armijo recouped some of the ground he had originally lost to his cantankerous friend. When it came to the failure of minor officials to implement laws, ignorance proved an excuse rather than a reason.

Alvarez was typical of the many merchants, trappers, and *extranjeros* (foreigners) in Mexico's frontier department, with the difference that he played the nationality game all the way to the upper echelons of government. From an original misrepresentation on a passport in 1824 to confrontations with Daniel Webster and Manuel Armijo, Alvarez ran the gauntlet. While in Mexico, he successfully achieved a role of dual citizenship, deceiving the Mexican government into assuming he was a Mexican citizen and then convincing them to allow him to serve as a US consul while retaining his Mexican rights. Then, he took the opposite position: that his diplomatic job endowed him with the rights of an American citizen — and Armijo concurred! Alvarez used citizenship as a basis to bolster his diplomatic and economic position relative to Mexico. Although Webster had refused to be tricked into paying unwarranted reparations, Alvarez's recognized Mexican citizenship precluded any duties on his business imports into Mexico. Citizenship, however, stays with an individual until his death: Alvarez's status came back to haunt him on occasion; so, too, did Daniel Webster.

Notwithstanding his lack of official recognition, Alvarez became increasingly persistent in performing his consular duties. He felt justified in acting, as he explained to Webster, because, now and then, he had been recognized by Armijo. Moreover, the inhabitants of Santa Fe recognized him as consul.[58] But no matter how hard he worked, Alvarez always realized the true nature of his situation. Any effort to deal with the Mexican government always held the possibility that his diplomatic recognition would be terminated because he lacked an exequatur. By the middle of 1843, he had become convinced that the United States needed a duly acknowledged consular agent "who could publically [*sic*] represent" any problems "to the supreme authority of that country."[59]

Alvarez was not the only one aware of his limitations; his good friend, business partner, and informer from Taos, Charles Bent, enumerated the many disadvantages under which Alvarez worked. After implying that the consul had been invested with something less than full powers and citing New Mexico's distance from the US minister in Mexico City, Bent declared his belief that Alvarez could not possibly operate with total effectiveness. Yet Bent could see the positive effect of the consul's exertions, "notwithstanding these great disadvantages."[60]

3

The Duties of a Consul, the Interests of a Merchant

Not lack of recognition, citizenship problems, nor antagonistic relations prevented Alvarez from performing his duties as US consul. He occupied a strategic position and, even against his instructions,[1] refused to continue the desultory tradition of his predecessors. To be sure, Alvarez limited his activities so as not to be conspicuous, especially before the incidents of September 1841.

As early as November 1839, Alvarez participated in a form of frontier jurisprudence commonly practiced by merchants, involving a business suit between two litigants, Powell, Lamont, and Company, traders between Chihuahua and Missouri, and Philip W. Thompson, a Missouri resident and trader whom Alvarez had known at least since 1838 when he had been asked to straighten out some official papers for Thompson. It had been Thompson who had written Alvarez from Chihuahua to inform him that Armijo had been officially appointed governor after the 1837 rebellion.[2] A year later, attorney David Waldo, representing Powell, Lamont, and Company, brought suit against Thompson for the sum of $8,000. The defendant represented himself. After filing com-

plaints and answers before Louis Robidoux, the first alcalde
of Santa Fe, in the court *de primera instancia,* both sides
informally agreed to submit the case to arbitration. David
Waldo petitioned Robidoux that "expressing full confidence in
the qualifications of Louis Lee and Manuel Alvarez, merchants in this city, the parties have mutually agreed to name
said Lee and Alvarez as arbitrators." On November 4, three
days after their nominations, the two men appeared before
Robidoux and accepted the responsibility. The alcalde gave
the arbiters eight days, all the pertinent documents, and
subpoena powers. They decided not to be bound "to the rules
of law," a proposition to which the litigants concurred, and,
after hearing testimony and reviewing fifteen pieces of docu-
mentary evidence, Alvarez and Lee ordered Thompson to pay
Powell's company $6,149.84.

Initially, the judgment seemed to satisfy all the litigants,[3]
but Thompson soon had trouble paying the award. Obviously,
the decision was not totally to his liking, and a prior agreement that a $3,000 fine should be imposed if either litigant
appealed closed that avenue of redress. Thompson hired
Abiel Leonard, an attorney from Fayette, Missouri, to bring
suit against an uninvolved third party.[4] Leonard found it
difficult to obtain evidence from far-off Missouri and decided
to form commissions in Santa Fe and Chihuahua to solicit
information pertinent to the case. At the suggestion of a
colleague, he convened the Santa Fe commission in Alvarez's
store,[5] where he took depositions on July 27, 1840.[6] Such
legal functions were a fairly low-key, safe activity for Alvarez,
and his involvement was indicative of the faith in his "experience and integraty [*sic*]" that others felt.[7]

Eventually, Alvarez attempted to represent foreigners
who came in conflict with native New Mexicans. Charles
Bent was a great aid, for he kept Alvarez constantly informed
of events in the north and along the Santa Fe Trail. Bent,
possibly assuming he could manipulate the consul, occasion-

ally presented Alvarez with some petty problems: Once, he located a horse that had been stolen from him at Bent's Fort by Indians who had then traded it to some New Mexicans. When he asked if he could regain legal possession of his property, Alvarez replied negatively after inquiring into New Mexican laws and suggested that Bent take better care of his livestock.[8] The legal position was illustrative of the New Mexican government's feelings regarding activities for which they held Bent responsible. As proprietor and eponym of the company that operated Bent's Fort, a place considered a source of American evildoing, Charles Bent operated at a distinct disadvantage when dealing with Mexican officials.

Perched on the Arkansas River, the recognized international border, Bent's Fort had always been under suspicion. One of the problems stemmed from the use of alcohol for trade with Indians. Although forbidden by US laws and regulations,[9] frontier companies continued to use the contraband until, as in the case of the Bent–St. Vrain Company, success no longer required its use. Manuel Armijo wrote, early in 1840, to the Mexican minister of war in Mexico City, complaining about the excessive contraband trade being carried on at Bent's Fort.[10] In fact, by 1840, the Bent–St. Vrain Company was campaigning against the use of alcohol, primarily as a ploy to restrict competition — most notably from a renegade fort at Pueblo, Colorado.[11] The post, which had started its trade that year, was supplied by Taos stills run by such adventurous Americans as Simeon Turley. When Alvarez inquired about a suitable location for a US government fort, Bent seized the opportunity to suggest that such a bastion be placed at the mouth of the Fountain Creek, right next to Pueblo.[12]

While the United States had a strong legal tradition opposing the use of alcohol, Mexico's laws were silent on the subject, and the national government did not seem inclined to make any effort to remedy the problem.[13]

Alvarez was passing on information of potentially hostile Indian activity to Armijo, information that usually came by way of Bent's Fort and included advice that the suspicious governor rarely followed. In early 1841, Alvarez received reports that the Plains Indians had become restless because they believed the Mexicans desired to enslave them. Several groups, including the Arapaho, Sioux, and Comanche, had a "big powwow on the Arkansas" River to determine what to do about the problem.[14] Some Arapahos even traveled to Taos to trade one horse for each Arapaho prisoner released, and Charles Bent advised that the offer be accepted to avoid hostilities.[15] A month later, Bent reported his fear that the Arapahos might have united with the Comanches. This worried him, especially when the Indians threatened war if their people were not returned. With a thousand lodges erected on the Arkansas and another alliance, between the Cheyenne and Comanche, giving momentum to the cause, Bent took the threats seriously.[16] Alvarez relayed all this information to Armijo, who questioned the accuracy of Bent's sentiments.[17] The following month, Alvarez received a dispatch from Bent, who was crossing the prairie at the time. He found Arapahos camped on the Las Animas River, replete with Spanish scalps and ten stolen horses. Bent feared an eventual attack on San Miguel.[18]

On October 6, 1842, Andrew Drips, Alvarez's old mountain boss, was appointed Indian agent for the Upper Missouri Agency,[19] with specific duties centered along the South Platte and upper Arkansas rivers. The appointment indicated a renewed government effort to suppress the alcohol trade, for Drips's sole job was to act as an undercover agent against the contraband. He even had a list of suspected violators.[20] Nevertheless, many contemporaries, including Drips himself, felt he was ineffective,[21] but Alvarez held that agents such as Drips were necessary. He wrote Secretary of State James Buchanan that a major cause of distrust between the peoples

Ink drawing, by Lachlan Allan MacLean, of Bent's Fort, 1846. Original in the collections of the Palace of the Governors. *Courtesy of the Museum of New Mexico, Santa Fe. MNM 147645.*

of the neighboring countries was the constant traffic upon the mutual frontiers "in the article of ardent spirits."[22] Such trade led to robbery and murder, not to mention deterioration of relations with Indians. Alvarez believed Drips was succeeding, for he reported "our agents" along the Missouri "entirely prevented our traders from halling [sic] the article."[23] Nonetheless, there was as much liquor being passed as before: The deficiency had been made up "from the Valley of Taos." One of the major funnels, he claimed, was operated in conjunction with some unlicensed American traders at a fort above Bent's post. Alvarez had his own solution to the problem: "Could some understanding be had with the Government of Mexico, so as to prohibit the transportation of Spiritous Drinks across the Mountains to within our territory[?]"[24] Such a treaty would enhance relationships between citizens of the two countries and lead to an eventual amelioration of a hazardous situation among the Indians of the area.

Bent, and now Alvarez, fingered Pueblo as the major culprit. Officials in Washington were slow to act on the suggestions of either man — possibly because preparations for war with Mexico had supplanted concern over a relatively few unlicensed and foreign traders, but also possibly because Alvarez and Bent were close friends and business associates. However things brightened in November when the US government, apparently responding to Alvarez's letter, sent a company of dragoons to Bent's Fort. Their purpose, according to Drips, was to stop the whiskey peddlers coming from the Spanish country. At the same time, Drips's men, with enlisted Indian help, succeeded in curbing the trade on the South Platte and upper Missouri rivers.[25] The inception of the Mexican War and the march of Brigadier General Stephen W. Kearny's Army of the West ended the program. Liquor trade also terminated, but only temporarily, while Kearny's activities erased the international boundary along the Mexican and American frontier.

Alvarez received many official representations expressing concern about Bent's Fort and used the occasions to raise another, more important (to his way of thinking) issue. It seems that, periodically, Alvarez became testy in his role as go-between for Armijo and Bent. If his advice to Bent that he take better care of his livestock seems sarcastic, it was not more so than his answer to one of Guadalupe Miranda's inquiries about what he was doing to solve the Bent's Fort problem. Alvarez caustically pointed out that he could not and would not do a thing "in consequence of having not yet been recognized United States Consul."[26] Nonetheless, it did not take long for Alvarez to become more involved in American affairs.

A growing number of murders, an increasingly biased

taxation of foreign goods, and a jaundiced discontent with Mexican justice all spurred Alvarez to be a feisty consul. The murders started with William Langford's killing of Sermon Nash in 1839. At Bent's request, Alvarez petitioned Governor Armijo to have the murderer brought to trial — asking the local government to try a foreigner was the kind of activity that did not create problems. Langford was a "hardened villian [*sic*] destitute of all feeling of humanity" with "not the least remorse of conscience for the violent outrage he has committed." If freed, "he is a man capable of again committing murder mearly [*sic*] to satisfy his inadinant [*sic*] thirst for blood."[27] The governor would have no trouble bringing such a man to trial.

From the time of Alvarez's appointment up to the ill-fated Texan–Santa Fe expedition, the number of killings mounted with startling regularity. Andrew Daley, Joseph Pulsepher, Joseph Bradaux, the deaf and mute François Lacompte, and — mentioned almost in passing — a Mormon killed near Taos were apparently murdered by Mexican culprits, not Americans.[28] Alvarez, if not prodded into action by his own conscience, was pushed by the insistence of the American residents and merchants. It seemed to the Americans that the responsible parties never received punishment. Writing about a murder near Mora, Bent declared that it was the fourth such occurrence "within the last few years," and no perpetrators had been punished.[29] Alvarez brought up such issues with the government and, in some cases, had to intervene when certain Americans decided to take things into their own hands, as was the case when William Dryden attempted to lead a mob after Daley's murderer.

Daley's violent death in 1839 near the placer mines southwest of Santa Fe probably received the most attention at the time. Although the two men responsible were eventually convicted and imprisoned, Alvarez felt this was a result of the exertions of American citizens who, enraged, presented the accused to the authorities and insisted that the law be allowed to take its course. Despite his expressions of appreciation to Armijo, the consul refused to give the Mexican authorities credit when corresponding to his own superiors (such bravado was also in part a ruse by which to press the US government into the realization that he should receive the full authority of his office).[30] Alvarez was perplexed when, a few months later, one of Santa Fe's alcaldes released both men through, as the consul saw it, an alteration of the law.[31] Sometime before Alvarez made his 1841–1842 trip to Washington, the culprits were returned to jail, only to be released again, along with Pulsepher's murderers. Between August and December, the government incarcerated the men again, but by the middle of December, Alvarez decided to enclose in a dispatch to the US minister in Mexico City a written order by Armijo that, once again, directed the release of Daley's killers.[32]

In 1839 Alvarez was entrusted with collecting goods that had been stolen from two Americans on the Santa Fe Trail near Fort Leavenworth. The crime had been committed a year and a half before, and the merchandise had somehow gravitated into the hands of the *juez de paz* of Mora, the man with whom Alvarez had to deal. Alvarez requested the aid of Armijo, who agreed to help secure the stolen goods. Unfortunately, this case became confused with other problems, and eventually Miranda informed Alvarez that the governor could not help. The property was never retrieved.[33] Alvarez's attitude toward the Mexican government in such matters became jaundiced, yet he continued to correspond heavily with Armijo's officials. Upon hearing that the governor would pursue the matter of an American's death "with all [the] diligence [with which] justice should be ministered," Alvarez commented dryly on the wide gap between Armijo's actions and his words. In his capacity as consul as well as merchant, Alvarez wanted the Mexican government to set an example and thus discourage the growing frequency of robbery and murder of extranjeros. Such barbarous activities, he pointed out, could be to no one's advantage.[34]

There were, of course, also cases of natural deaths of Americans within Alvarez's jurisdiction, and on these occasions, the consul had to collect, appraise, and account for the deceased's effects; if at all possible, he used these assets to pay for funeral services. If the case of David White is a good example, the bill usually came to about $34.25, $11 of which was expended for the coffin. In a similar case, the most expensive item listed was the priest's services.[35] Not all duties involving the effects of the dead were simply executed; in late 1840, Alvarez arranged for a deceased person's property to be transferred from Las Vegas to Santa Fe. The dead person's son, a Doctor Hobbs, and his friends were to travel to Santa Fe, where they would receive a list of the items, compiled by Alvarez, and take possession of the goods. Unhappily, the property disappeared in a bureaucratic shuffle.[36] Alvarez's lack of diplomatic recognition had allowed the local authorities opportunities to enrich themselves while "the legal representatives" received "nothing." In light of the fact that many merchants regularly imported over $100,000 worth of goods, this kind of corruption could be very expensive. Certainly it points up the importance of Alvarez's achieving full diplomatic status.[37]

Nonetheless, Alvarez was not without wiles and guile, which he used to the fullest extent in the case of Doctor John H. Lyman, a New Englander traveling to Chihuahua in search of better health. In Santa Fe, Lyman had loaned $900 to Francis Valentine Tayon of St. Louis. Tayon agreed to repay the loan with a $100 interest fee within a day and at Taos. Lyman, who did not want to make the sixty-mile trip from Santa Fe to Taos, proposed that, instead, Tayon repay the original amount of $900 in the capital city. Tayon repaid his debt with money borrowed from Stephen Lee, and, with his money in hand, Lyman continued on his trip into interior Mexico. Meanwhile, Lee discovered that Tayon could not repay him and complained to Governor Armijo, who had Lyman detained at Algodones, forty miles southwest of Santa Fe.[38] Alvarez became involved when he explained Doctor Lyman's innocence to Governor Armijo, who obligingly ordered the American's release. No one informed the luckless Lyman of the favorable order. Instead, the local *juez de paz,* Antonio de Montoya, his secretary, and Armijo's messenger forged an order transferring Lyman back to the capital city. By this time, the poor prisoner was expecting the worst and decided to procure his release by accommodating Montoya with a solicited bribe. The three Mexican officials accepted $50, then demanded $200 more, which Lyman — apparently allowing righteous indignation to conquer fear — stoutly refused. Soon thereafter a friend told the doctor about Armijo's order and Montoya's forgeries. Angered, Lyman determined to return to Santa Fe and "demand justice."[39]

With Alvarez at his side, Lyman took his complaint to the governor. Armijo returned the doctor's bribe money along with the expenses incurred during his delay. The governor also explained that Montoya's secretary would be held in irons for one month, but in truth none of the implicated officials received punishment.[40] Lyman wrote that he was "satisfied that no Americans" could "ever attain justice in any court . . . under the influence of Governor Armijo" and, as proof, pointed to "the different Americans assassinated . . . within the past two or three years, whose murderers *are not punished.*"[41] The good doctor requested that Alvarez secure him a passport and left New Mexico less than a year later as a member of the Rowland-Workman party. Whatever health problems had originally led him to the Southwest, Lyman proved to be a colorful and elusive character, once, according to one account, refusing to give up a good fishing hole during an Indian ambush, even though arrows showered around him. His relatives in New England, worried about him, sent a letter of inquiry to Alvarez that, if it accomplished nothing else, demonstrates the state of mail service: It was written on October 9, 1842, and Alvarez forwarded it to the US consul at Monterey, California, where it arrived in April 1844.[42]

Frontier violence and frontier eccentrics could not distract Alvarez from the financial issues that rankled and irritated the Americans the consul represented. Fees and taxes continued to be a potent source of conflict with New Mexican officials. In one case, Alvarez exchanged a number of letters concerning the marriage of an American man to a local girl at San Miguel. The local prelate had charged the groom $30 above the normal fee, and the consul immediately confronted the governor and inquired of Vicar Don Juan Felipe Ortiz on the man's behalf, citing international treaties as well as fair play. This acrimonious controversy ended in favor of the groom, who paid the usual fee[43] — no doubt a satisfying outcome even though a marriage fee was a small matter compared to customs taxes.

Levies on trade attracted Alvarez's attention in two ways: As a merchant he had a financial stake; as consul, he had a diplomatic interest. Alvarez applied his most intense diplomatic effort trying to rectify these taxes. As the tax was arbitrarily set by the governor, Americans questioned Armijo's motives. In 1839, for example, Armijo decided to tax each incoming wagon $500 — a law that, with reservations, Alvarez could accept and Americans could and did sidestep simply by packing their loads on as few wagons as possible. However, when Mexican officials required that only extranjeros pay the tax, the consul acted to neutralize the seemingly unfair economic advantage granted to Mexican merchants,[44] initially by complaining to his superiors. Alvarez's motives were twofold: He believed the governor ruled with such a personal hand that any representations directed to him would be ill-advised — he "might consider himself offended"; on the other hand, the consul felt effective pressure could be applied at the ministerial level. Alvarez appealed to Powhatan Ellis and later presented Armijo with a petition signed by the merchants,[45] a step more appropriate for an unrecognized consul than was direct, official action. Technically, Alvarez believed such laws violated the ninth article of the current treaty between the United States and Mexico[46] and, correctly, thought that the governor had determined to use taxation "to draw from the market the competition of the industrious and enterprising" citizens of the United States.[47] He saw Armijo's actions as unprincipled, even though he could understand the governor's trying to give his own people the competitive edge. Armijo was acting to aid the Mexican populace he governed, and, indeed, American traders may have been far better off than they could have been; they were not, after all, paying what the Mexican law required or intended.[48] Nonetheless, Alvarez's actions hinted of the American merchants' bitterness about this double standard. They refused to compete at a disadvantage because it hurt business.[49] Months later, the governor relented and taxed all merchants alike, even though individual occurrences of unequal tax levies on Americans continued.[50] Perhaps underlying more immediate discontents, the claims for debts accrued during the 1837 revolt still remained unpaid, although contrary rumors constantly surfaced and Alvarez continued to press for reparations.

And what became of Alvarez's business during his years as US consul? Luckily, business could never be separated from consular duties; each occupation easily lent itself to the needs of the other, although at times, circumstances would dictate that one job take on at least the appearance of precedence. Despite the many tussles and problems of his consular duties, Alvarez never held his commercial enterprises in abeyance. With Damaso López still his partner, Alvarez's business seems to have progressively increased. Although both diplomatic affairs and the purchase of merchandise required trips, he customarily remained in Santa Fe and bought through some trusted friend at the other end of the trail. By 1839, L. L. Waldo's had become the major firm through which Alvarez dealt. On November 20 of that year, he settled his account with Waldo for the sum of $2,247.59;[51] in a different ledger, dated two months later, Alvarez recorded business with the same individual to the sum of $15,176.21.[52] Obviously, business promised better returns and a safer occupation than a diplomatic career could offer. Personal debts were more likely to be paid off than were reparations claimed from the US government.

Some interesting facets of his trade emerge from Alvarez's records. As late as October 1839, the merchant still dealt in furs, even though by the time of his 1833 retirement from active trapping the pelt industry had started its decline. In an apparent contradiction to popular belief, he managed to make money, for L. L. Waldo sold approximately 270 furs for him, which on the Independence market, grossed $1,313.25. Less transportation and Waldo's 5 percent commission, the net proceeds amounted to $1,231.75. Broken down, 253 beaver skins grossed $1,244.75 or approximately $4.92 each; four otter skins sold for $20 and a damaged bearskin brought $5 — prices that compare somewhat favorably with prices during the height of the trade. The buyers were Pierre Chouteau and Alexander MacKenzie of the St. Louis branch of the American Fur Company.[53]

Although Alvarez's business was based in Santa Fe, its influence was felt over the length of the Santa Fe Trail to Missouri. The other side of this shiny coin was the accumulation of debts owed to Alvarez; during his absences from Santa Fe, the merchant paid commissions to designated individuals to collect these monies. This was especially so after 1840, when his longtime partner López apparently ceased to be a part of the business. Alvarez designated Charles Blumner as his agent when the events of 1841 required that he travel to Washington, DC. Perhaps because of Alvarez's near assassination and the delay in getting his passage papers to the States, he waited to choose a collector until the very day of his departure. Besides collecting debts, Blumner essentially handled all of Alvarez's business affairs. A reflection of his employer, he was unfailingly prompt, arranging for repayment of one debt only two days after his boss's departure.[54] On the other hand, Alvarez never strayed far from maintaining his business: Just two days before his hurried departure, he had collected a debt for the Giddings and Gentry Company, which, in itself, speaks to the consul's punctuality. The circumstances of the collection and payment are of interest, because the two notes, totaling $60, were owed by Guadalupe Miranda, the second highest official in New Mexico and the same person who had come to Alvarez's rescue two months previously.[55]

In two legal documents, Alvarez wrote in Spanish that all the people listed owed him the sums indicated and that they should pay his proxy as they would pay him. During Alvarez's absence, Blumner crossed off names as debts were collected and noted in English and Spanish at the bottom of the lists how much those people who had paid in part still owed.[56] With one exception, the list of debtors left with Blumner consists solely of Hispanic names; if Alvarez compiled another list of non-Hispanic names, it has not survived. By habit, perhaps reflecting his Hispanic tradition, Alvarez did not differentiate between male and female customers. Indeed, he corresponded freely with New Mexican women, and they, in turn, apparently felt comfortable placing their respective orders and occasionally asking for credit. None of the letters allude to anything but the business at hand and the confidence of his customers in his sense of fair play. All of his New Mexican ledgers in which names are listed include Hispanic women.[57]

List of debtors to Alvarez, October 25, 1841. Alvarez charged Charles Blumner with the authority to collect payment while Alvarez was away on a trip to the United States. The list includes women: Señora Linda del Sargento Sánchez; Doña Margarita Labadia; Doña Luisita Lopes (de Chama); and María Josefa Esquivela. Alvarez left New Mexico primarily to present his complaints on behalf of US citizens to Daniel Webster, but he had the presence of mind to tend to business matters as well. *Original in Alvarez Papers, Business Papers. Courtesy of New Mexico State Records Center and Archives, Santa Fe.*

In some cases it appears that Alvarez was not beyond giving extra service to his female customers. On one occasion he helped an elderly, crippled lady without even making her acquaintance. For his service of keeping another woman endowed with basic supplies while extending credit, he received her infinite gratitude.[58] Compassion was not his only reason for enlightened business practices. Women such as María Rosalía Baca, Luisita Baca, and one listed as Señora Linda del Sargento Sánchez provided steady business. They also, by virtue of Alvarez's records, give testimony to the social status of their sex in Mexico's northern province. Not only were women allowed to negotiate their own business and receive credit, some of them were literate enough to record their own dealings[59] — and this was at a time when frontier women were supposedly subservient and illiterate!

The consul did not limit his business to the boundaries of Santa Fe. In 1841 he continued the pattern of his initial dealings in such places as Abiquiú. Other markets included San Miguel del Vado, Chama, Peña Blanca, Pojoaque, Pecos, La Joya, Mora, and locales he merely grouped under Río Abajo and Río Arriba. Naturally, he did business in Taos with Charles Bent and with Simeon Turley, who, despite Alvarez's disapproval of his liquor trade, freely corresponded with the consul. Once, Turley supplied the consul with an ox, not the one ordered because that animal had died, Turley related, in someone else's care. On another occasion, Turley asked Alvarez to collect a debt from P. W. Thompson and one of the Robidoux brothers, thus indicating that Alvarez collected for him.[60]

To be sure, a merchant who dealt in trade to the extent Alvarez did would incur expenses at places outside New Mexico and Missouri, but up until his forced 1841 trip, he preferred to do business through Missouri-based merchants. They, in turn, would fill orders through suppliers all over the eastern United States. All extra costs, such as storage, insurance, and shipping, were paid in full by the merchants for whom they ordered. As Alvarez began to make more frequent trips, he cut out the middleman as buyer, although because of the quantity of goods he bought, he continued to rely on eastern agents to oversee passage and storage. If he so desired, he could wait at St. Louis or Independence and then escort his goods down the trail to Santa Fe. Alvarez concentrated on the Santa Fe end, leaving all the eastern business with such dealers as L. L. Waldo, Giddings and Gentry, and David Waldo. In May 1840, he was billed $970.34 for a shipment of goods from Pittsburgh to Independence; the cargo had been purchased by L. L. Waldo, who charged a 5 percent commission on the $5,600 cost. Insurance en route cost $155; freight "to Pittsburgh" from points east cost $201.14; freight from Pittsburgh totaled $103; and "hawling [*sic*] from River" was a $15 expense. Arrangements for transferring freight were intricate, and every incidental had its separate bill.[61] In a different ledger for the same company, Alvarez was billed for the salary of one teamster: At a scale of $25 per month, John Smith, the wagon driver, received $32.70 for his employment from March 20 to May 9, 1840, and his assistant received $15.66 for his aid in getting the wagon back from Taos to Independence.[62]

By 1840, another interesting item began to appear in Alvarez's business dealings. One of the major reasons for the instant success of the Santa Fe trade was the availability of hard specie or silver in Mexico. The other end of the trail had a distinct lack of hard specie and was in an economic crisis. Because of this, trade did not terminate in Santa Fe but carried on to the silver deposits around Chihuahua City; silver was thus not a rare commodity on the Santa Fe Trail. Gold, however, was scarce until at least 1838, if Alvarez's records are any indication. In October of that year, he sold a little more than 255 ounces of "Bullion Gold" at a rate of $19.30 per ounce, grossing $4,934.52 in that single transaction.[63] The originating point of the bullion is unknown, but Alvarez did some business with Chihuahuan merchants. Indeed, many of the men with whom he dealt traveled to that city, and it is possible that they took Alvarez's goods along or sold their own, returning with the precious specie to pay debts owed to Alvarez. There is, however, no evidence of any other business as extensive as his dealings in Santa Fe and the United States.

One other possibility, somewhat infeasible, is hinted at in an astounding letter written to Alvarez by Juan (John) Rowland. Sometime in late April or early May 1840, a Portuguese man arrived in Taos from the upper Arkansas (Napeste) River, where he claimed to have discovered gold and silver on different tributaries. To prove his point, he introduced two samples. Rowland, cautious about the reputed discovery some twenty-five miles upriver from Bent's Fort, expressed a desire that his and Alvarez's friend and experienced miner "Don Damaso" have a chance to verify the story.[64] Damaso's appraisal indicated the samples were of poor quality, and the Portuguese's discovery went unheeded until the great Colorado gold and silver rushes. No matter, after 1838 Alvarez seemed never to lack hard specie in the form of gold. Merely five days after Rowland had written his letter about the potential discovery, Alvarez is credited in L. L. Waldo's account for delivering almost twelve ounces of dust. On May 8, 1840 — the same day L. L. Waldo's account notes the delivery of twelve ounces — Alvarez delivered $2,000 worth of "silver in bag" to L. L.'s brother David. In the same ledger, next citation, David received $2,028.37 in gold dust. Even more startling is that the two men dealt a whopping 532 ounces of "gold dust" at a relatively low price of $19 per ounce, for a total of $10,108.[65]

A few months later, David Waldo exchanged some gold bullion at the US mint in New Orleans. The specie proved to be of very fine quality with a fineness rating of 935 per thousand. Just under 500 ounces netted $9,485.99.[66] Alvarez received a copy of the treasury memorandum because the agreements of exchange on the frontier were contingent upon the findings at the mint: If the bullion should bring a higher price in later transactions, Alvarez would receive the difference; if, on the other hand, the gold proved to be of low grade, then Alvarez would be obligated to make up the difference.[67] Five months after David Waldo had exchanged this bullion, he reported to Alvarez that he had sold, among other things, some of Alvarez's mules in New Orleans. Some of the gold dust he had brought with him apparently belonged to Alvarez, for Waldo was ashamed to admit that he had made a bad loan to a person who was "broke to hell, not being able to pay more than fifty cents on the dollar." Waldo promised, however, to get the full value back.[68]

Such minor setbacks were to be expected, and Alvarez, by now very much experienced, continued his business dealings. Waldo's misadventures in New Orleans did not preclude the Santa Fean from obtaining more gold dust or, for that matter, from using it as he did to pay other business houses such as the Giddings and Gentry firm.[69] By 1841, Alvarez seemed to have easy access to the valuable metal. Such an abundance of specie gave the merchant freedom to take full business advantage of his trips to the United States, although the 1839 and 1841 trips were also important journeys for his diplomatic career. By 1842, Alvarez had become something more than a local store owner; he had become a prominent merchant — indeed, a precursor of the larger mercantile capitalist who would follow.[70] Gold aside, he collected as much as $5,000 in outstanding debts in 1841 and at the same time entrusted David Waldo with a herd of mules to sell at Independence.[71] Obviously, Alvarez had diversified.

Returning as a naturalized US citizen in 1842, he found the climate in New Mexico unchanged. Some accused murderers of Americans had been released, and, in October, an enraged Armijo, accompanied by his secretary of state, paid a visit to Alvarez's home. The governor had lost some goods, worth $18,000 to $20,000, in the Missouri River[72] when the steamboat *Lebanon,* in transit from St. Louis to Independence, had sunk. Armijo accused Alvarez of involvement in a conspiracy resulting in the loss, then threatened his life.[73] He added his belief that 6,000 Texans were marching toward Santa Fe. The consul was not given a chance to defend himself against the governor's charge because, meanwhile, a mob of locals had formed outside Alvarez's door. At that perilous moment, his life depended solely on a furious Armijo. Alvarez most likely saw visions of a similar scene almost a year earlier, but Armijo fortunately controlled his anger enough to prevent a complete reenactment. A relieved and somewhat forgiving Alvarez reported to Waddy Thompson, the US minister to Mexico City, that "we are to be made responsible for his [Armijo's] accidental lapses."[74]

Alvarez's friend in Taos did not escape the wrath of the locals, either. Bent, who had been sued for $800, went to court unsuccessfully and was not allowed an appeal. He found himself incarcerated when he refused to pay, but the populace's ugly mood convinced him to change his mind, and he obtained his release when one of his employees arrived with more than enough money for the suit. Immediately after being freed, Bent fled to his company's fort on the Arkansas. Alvarez, who had intervened on Bent's behalf, later wrote that while he could not prevent what happened, his pleas did avoid a more unpleasant situation.[75] These incidents, plus the recurring rumors of a new Texan invasion, helped entice the consul to leave on another trip.[76] Besides, he needed to attend to some unfinished business, for he had been requested to check into the efforts to secure reparations from 1837 and 1841. Charles Bent had spread word that the US government would pay all claims and then collect from Mexico.[77] Alvarez, who knew nothing of this solution, was anxious to find out officially what, if anything, had been resolved.[78] Also by this time the profit margin had fallen in northern Mexican commerce. Such a condition directly influenced Alvarez, and as consul he was in a position to do something to mitigate its effects. His trip east would have a threefold mission: He could make official representations; purchase merchandise; and get away from the volatile Armijo.

A new administration in Washington and an act of Congress opened the way for a solution to the consul's ambiguous position. One provision of the law, popularly called the Drawback Bill, passed by the second session of the Twenty-eighth Congress, created the position of consul or commercial agent to Santa Fe. James K. Polk's administration realized that the US government could avoid, even ignore, Mexico's unwillingness to grant exequatur by creating a commercial agency rather than a consular post: The functions of a commercial agent would not require official recognition.[79] Alvarez was the natural nominee for the newly created position. With this in mind, his old friend David Waldo set out to make sure that the Polk administration knew of the Spaniard. Waldo wrote a recommendation to the secretary of the treasury, Robert J. Walker, asking that the esteemed merchant be appointed: "No gentleman stands higher in this Section of our State than Mr. Alvarez, and from his acquaintance with the Spanish and French tongues would much facilitate the transaction of business, among foreigners in Mexico."[80] Waldo's recommendation included a petition in support of Alvarez signed by 142 merchants in the Santa Fe trade.[81] The letter and petition were forwarded to the Department of State, with no result. Over a year later, Waldo tried again. Noting that the government had not officially appointed Alvarez as commercial agent, he pointed out that Alvarez had suffered much as consul at Santa Fe and that recommendations with hundreds of signatures had been forwarded to the secretary of state the previous summer. His appointment was very much desired, continued Waldo, because "Mr. Alvarez is a worthy, honest man as well as the most qualified person to execute consular duties under the Drawback." Waldo's persistent efforts seem to have had no effect, for the bureaucracy refused to be prodded, even if the matter was "all important to traders."[82]

The perceptive Alvarez may have been the person who suggested to Buchanan the advantage of bypassing the necessity of exequatur when he wrote in reference to the petition his friends sent. He asserted that though the Mexican government would likely make no objection to granting the exequatur because Armijo was now out of office,[83] there was always the possibility that the resilient ex-governor would return to power. In that event, Alvarez wrote to Buchanan, "should the Department deem it advisable to forward the Seal corresponding to the commercial Consulate," with the proper papers, he would accept the appointment "with pleasure."[84] In other words, the government should create a commercial agency and thus avoid any further problems. About eight months later, Buchanan finally sent Alvarez's appointment as commercial agent to Santa Fe, having taken his consul's advice and withheld the appointment until Armijo had, indeed, returned to office. On March 19, 1846, the secretary of state sent a letter enclosing Alvarez's appointment, general instructions, and the long-awaited seal of office. Buchanan later explained to Alvarez that the president was unwilling to appoint a full US consul instead of a commercial agent because Armijo had returned to office. The secretary also expected the Spaniard to report semiannually.[85]

Alvarez had used the delay to take a business trip through the northeastern United States and England, Spain, and France and returned from his trip unaware of Buchanan's action just nine days before. Arriving ahead of the mails containing the appointment, he quickly jotted off his recurring request to the secretary of state: "This Consulate is without an official seal and to remark that such a seal is

The Consular Seal for the agency in Santa Fe. This seal, made of brass, was sent to Alvarez too late to be used. *Collections of the Palace of the Governors. Courtesy of the Museum of New Mexico, Santa Fe. MNM 146019.*

particularly necessary now . . ."[86] His last known official correspondence to the secretary of state was to acknowledge receipt of the appointment and the coveted seal of office, which had been delayed by the outbreak of the Mexican War. Although grateful, he wrote to Buchanan: "It was detained, as General Kearny ordered the commercial caravan to march in his rear . . . and [it was] only delivered a few days since. Owing to the change of Government I think it unnecessary to have the bond filled up, I am also in receipt of the Seal of Office and the accompanying documents, I will under the above impression defer giving the bond, unless otherwise directed."[87] Brigadier General Stephen W. Kearny was leading the Army of the West to New Mexico and on to California, Santa Fe was an occupied town, and Alvarez resignedly felt the agency had been rendered moot.[88]

Thus ended a tragicomic diplomatic career in which Alvarez was never fully recognized by Mexico or by the United States, even though he spent the whole of the time seeking recognition. He had to perform his duties clandestinely in a very difficult situation. Despite problems with his citizenship, the elusive exequatur, and local politics, he fulfilled the functions of his unofficial position as well as did any recognized consul, and he struggled through an invasion that, in part, foretold the occupation of New Mexico by Kearny's Army of the West — the Texan incursion of 1841.

4

The Trouble with Texans

There was nothing that could have prepared Alvarez for the reality of the Texan–Santa Fe expedition in 1841. It embodied the worst fears of local Mexican authorities, involved a third country, and seemed to implicate the Anglo-American citizens of New Mexico in a conspiracy to undermine the Mexican government. The pending arrival — the expedition was no secret — of over 300 armed Texans did not sit well with New Mexicans or their national government. Agents for General Mariano Arista, commanding general of the Mexican Army of the North, reported to him in Chihuahua as soon as the Texans left Austin, and Governor Armijo knew soon thereafter. The invasion created real problems for Alvarez, who, as a representative for American citizens, was somewhat alienated from the Mexican population. Although Texas had claimed independence, the Mexican government did not recognize it. Coupled as it had been with a threat of French invasion, Mexico had reacted adversely to Texas's insubordination, and this new activity was seen as a national insult.[1] Mexico still considered itself as trying to suppress a rebellious department that had violated national integrity "the day they [the revolutionaries] usurped the territory of Texas."[2] Native New Mexicans saw the Texans' approach as an attempt to extend the trouble.

Some historians have argued that the expedition was merely a commercial venture. Whether the president of Texas, Mirabeau Lamar, or his commander, Major General Hugh McLeod, intended forcibly to prove their claims to further territory is moot, for the Mexicans in the northern department were already up in arms and believed that Americans were in sympathy with the Texan cause. This was true in some cases, but not true of the majority of extranjeros, although one motive for the expedition undoubtedly came from the innocent activities of American merchants trading with New Mexico. Especially important was a successful 1839 caravan that Josiah Gregg had taken to Santa Fe from Van Buren, Arkansas, which had attracted Lamar's attention. The second president of Texas reasoned that his new government would benefit considerably from Santa Fe trade via a southern route and, to that end, appointed William Dryden commissioner to New Mexico in 1840.[3] However, Dryden soon ran afoul of New Mexico's Governor Armijo. Angered over the government's apparent lack of interest in finding the murderer of Andrew Daley, Dryden led a protest. Although the ensuing confrontation with the Mexican militia[4] was nonviolent — faced with armed soldiers, Dryden and company dispersed — the result was that Dryden had very little, if any, respect for Mexican people and the local government probably cared even less for him. Dryden eventually fled New Mexico when local authorities claimed to have found a damning letter, addressed to him, on one of the prisoners from the Texan expedition.[5]

As early as January 1841, the Texans' plans were public knowledge, and the potential effects of their proposed visit had New Mexicans worried — not without cause.[6] American merchants and New Mexican residents, such as Thomas Rowland, William Workman, and Charles Bent, were accused of being Texas's agents.[7] Tom Rowland denied the accusa-

DON FERNANDO DE TAOS.

Lithograph, from W.W.H. Davis, *El Gringo,* of San Fernando de Taos, 1857. Taos was home to many foreign merchants and trappers in northern New Mexico. *Courtesy of the Museum of New Mexico, Santa Fe. MNM 9777.*

tions, and his house in San Miguel was ransacked, resulting in $1,000 in damages for which he subsequently sought restitution through Alvarez.[8] Bent and Workman responded more aggressively when accused of complicity with Texas by Juan B. Vigil, a Taos lawyer. Influenced by the recent February decrees to deport *extranjeros,* the two *taoseños* had little faith in Mexican justice, and, uncharacteristically, they resorted to frontier-style justice: They immediately found their accuser and demanded he prove his charges. Apparently Vigil's answer was not sufficient, for Workman started beating him, first with a whip and then with his fists, until Bent called him off.[9] As Bent explained, such violence was necessary because Vigil expected it, adding he "would rather wipe [*sic*] a man . . . then [*sic*] have him punished by the law."[10] Bent advised Alvarez of the incident and, when he was later arrested, asked the consul to solicit the governor's aid: "You will recollect the promises [of gunpowder] I told you that had been made to one in Santa Fe. Now they will be tested." Alvarez was to tell the governor he would get the promised powder.[11] The local judge, wishing to confer with Armijo, suspended the case and confined Bent to his house. The next day, Bent sent to Armijo, through Alvarez, one keg of powder and ten kegs of coffee. The consul received a set of seven volumes of history for his efforts,[12] and Bent was duly released. Vigil, undeterred by Bent's methods, continued to accuse other Anglo-Americans, even threatening the local judge. In March 1841, Bent and four other men planned to give Vigil a more severe drubbing, but barking dogs allowed the intended victim to beat a hasty retreat. Vigil took refuge in Córdova, where he asked for an armed escort out of the valley. A few more scares, thought Bent, and the problem would be solved.[13]

Meanwhile, those people who felt insecure under the Mexican government's protection met secretly at Abiquiú to leave for southern California. Any connection, no matter how remote, with Texans aroused suspicions, and, fearing for their families' lives, Workman and some friends decided that they would be better off elsewhere. The situation worsened for the extranjeros when Armijo received definite word on September 11, 1841, from some Comanches who reported that the Texans were getting close; they had progressed as far as El Capulín. The governor gave assurances that Americans would be protected.[14] Four days later, two deserters from the Texan expedition, an Italian named Brignoli and a New Mexican from Taos whose name was Carlos, arrived in Santa Fe. Both had been employed as guides for the Texans. Alvarez got wind of a rumor that the deserters had named some prominent Americans in New Mexico as spies for the expedition.[15] Such rumors upset the public, and confirmed Alvarez's worst fears, months of Armijo's warnings, and the local clergy's chauvinistic sermons. The lives and property of many Anglo traders were in danger, and, at one point, the local militia had to disperse a mob in the Santa Fe plaza. As US consul, Alvarez was the only official to whom the Americans could turn, and he could only hope that his previous exchanges with Armijo would serve him in good stead. Alvarez had used a mule, along with other incidents, to set a precedent and gain experience; the situation now amounted to an international incident and Alvarez had to draw on his experience to protect lives.

As the Texans approached, Armijo became more impatient,[16] and Alvarez kept abreast of events, partially by keeping a running tabulation of the musters of the Mexican militia. He reported 150 men from Río Arriba on September 15, ninety men under Don José Chávez from Río Abajo on the seventeenth, and eighty men under Don Cristóbal Chaves and 400 under a Captain Muñoz on the nineteenth.[17] Matters came to a head in late September.

Immediately after the Comanche reports, Alvarez had a personal conference with Armijo to express his concern for the Americans' safety. The consul officially petitioned that all alcaldes and *jueces de paz* of towns in which foreigners resided respect their persons and property. This the governor verbally promised, reiterating his assurances in a letter written a day after the conversation. Alvarez was satisfied that the necessary precautions would be taken and pleased that the governor would openly inform him of the Texans' approach.[18] He felt that "this proposition appeared to me just and to inform me of it [was] kind, for which I am infinitely gratified."[19] Miranda replied on behalf of the governor that Alvarez could be assured about Armijo's word: He "*dará toda protección conforme a los tratados*"[20] (will give all protection in conformity with the treaties) between the neighboring countries. However, Armijo offered protection only on the condition that the foreigners give no aid to the Texans. The next day, when Carlos and Brignoli arrived, Alvarez received information that some Americans had been insulted by local

Mexicans.[21] This knowledge, plus mounting excitement over the arrival of the deserters, caused him to repeat his previous requests,[22] although he did not blame the governor for the incidents — for he realized Armijo could not be responsible for everything. Alvarez received a conciliatory reply from Armijo. Such incidents were bound to recur in the height of excitement: In a drunken stupor after celebrating the capture of 200 Texans, some Mexicans broke into the house of John Scolly, another extranjero merchant.[23]

Good feelings notwithstanding, some worried American citizens drafted a letter to Daniel Webster expressing fears of robbery and murder,[24] fears that were realized within a few minutes after Armijo and his army had moved out of Santa Fe. Intent on getting a look at some recently captured Texans, the governor's nephew, Ensign Don Thomás Martín, his friend Sergeant Pablo Domínguez, Bartolo Montoya, and about seventy others galloped into the plaza. They took a Texan prisoner out of jail and, with a crowd of locals, entered Alvarez's office in an apparent attempt to harass the consul. Alvarez was convinced that their goal was assassination. Martín got to Alvarez first and, as the victim relates it, just as "I was about to master him" Domínguez came to Martín's aid.[25] The mob followed, shouting, *"Ságuenlo* [sic] *afuera! mátenlo!* [sic]" (Drag him out! kill him!)[26] Alvarez was wounded by a knife thrust in the face, and had not Armijo's secretary, Guadalupe Miranda, ridden up and dispersed the mob, Martín could easily have killed him.[27] Although there is no evidence that Governor Armijo had prior knowledge of the incident, it evidently did not upset him. Martín and Domínguez soon received military promotions, while the subsequent treatment accorded Alvarez was, at best, unpleasant. The episode created for the consul a martyr's reputation, and virtually anyone who has mentioned him in writing has made some reference to it. It was an event that brought everlasting fame to the merchant.[28]

During the next few days, the consul and the Mexican government bombarded each other with correspondence, in which Alvarez correctly expressed concern about the intentions of the Texans and the safety of American citizens. In his official capacity, he had to deal with the Texans — their country had been recognized by the United States. To this end, he sought permission to meet with the expedition's leaders, a request that made the governor suspicious:[29] Could the US consul be seeking to inform the Texans of something? Another of the myriad requests for assurance that Americans be protected led to a disgruntled reply on September 22, 1841. When Alvarez explained that he felt it his duty to see the approaching Texans, Armijo withdrew his official recognition of the consul,[30] thus, from the governor's viewpoint, eliminating any need for Alvarez to leave town. Alvarez therefore refused the governor's offer that he join the Mexican camp.[31] The idea of keeping Alvarez and others under control and preventing them from providing any information to the Texans resulted in a circular that prohibited all travel in the direction from which the Texans were coming.[32]

In December 1841, the John Rowland–William Workman party of twenty-three Anglos and three Mexicans reached their San Gabriel, California, destination.[33] All were acquaintances of Alvarez, and one — the irrepressible Doctor Lyman — even had asked him to bribe an official, Don Agustín Durán, for a passport.[34] Many people continued to correspond with Alvarez, thus establishing one of the earliest New Mexican–Californian connections, which later developed into profitable business operations, especially in sheep. Alvarez eventually would receive reports from ex–New Mexicans on the progress of the Mexican War in California. As his friend who had needed a passport wrote, "And now farwell [*sic*] to you my very much respected friend. I shall often think of you and your very great exertions on my behalf both as a friend and in your official capacity as American consul."[35]

These were the sentiments of most American travelers in New Mexico, and it was a respect well earned.

The California-bound party had been able to slip away unnoticed because all attention was centered on the San Miguel area, southeast of Santa Fe, where the first of the hated Texans struggled into view. Most of the anxiety New Mexicans had felt proved wasted: The Texans had undertaken an ill-planned, ill-equipped, and ill-directed journey through the plains, where the Indians had provided a much better defense of New Mexico than the ragamuffin militia that met them could do. A little trickery, such as unkept promises of good treatment, was enough to make the invaders give up their arms. The prisoners were kept under guard at San Miguel until Armijo, dressed in his finest uniform, could address them before they were forced on a treacherous march to El Paso, where eventually they received better treatment. Another victory was thus added to the legend of Armijo's military prowess since his rise to power in 1837, as he claimed to have saved Mexico's northern department twice within four years. Because of the distance between Santa Fe and Mexico City, appearance mattered every bit as much as reality.

As the news of the captive Texans came in, the harried Alvarez scarcely had time to tend to his wounds, much less to complain about American rights. The most astonishing captive, surely, was a native Mexican — Antonio Navarro, an ex-senator in the Mexican government[36] — but several Americans and one English citizen, Thomas Falconer, were also among the prisoners.[37] One of the Americans was George Wilkens Kendall, editor of the *New Orleans Picayune,* who had sent Matt Field out west in 1839. Two years later, Kendall had set off for Santa Fe strictly as a journalist, but, unfortunately, he had used the Texan–Santa Fe expedition as a means to get there. Even though he and Falconer had proper passports, Governor Armijo refused to act, insisting that they remain prisoners with the rest. Undaunted by his close scrape with death, Alvarez sought Kendall's release. Observing the governor's belligerence, the consul protested that to incarcerate American citizens among the Texans was to disgrace the US government.[38] Alvarez met with Charles Bent and James Magoffin, a longtime trader on the trail, to discuss extralegal means of securing Kendall's release. Together they raised $3,000 and offered it to Armijo for the release of the American editor and the Mexican, Navarro, "to shew [sic] that we were not altogether partial to the Americans."[39] Armijo rejected the offer, and Kendall, Navarro, and Falconer perforce marched on with the rest of the prisoners to Mexico City.

Governor Armijo, fearing that other Texans, possibly a second force, might be heading toward Santa Fe, extended his order forbidding travel toward the southeast.[40] This prohibition caused a critical delay, nearly a month, in granting Alvarez a passport for the United States, where he was no doubt anxious to be received because he had a list of complaints for which the US government could justifiably demand reparations; foremost among them was the US consul's having been physically abused and robbed, an act far more blatantly hostile than any incident of the 1837 revolt. The wait for his passport only served to prove his point, especially since winter was fast approaching.[41] On September 28, the governor reaffirmed his decree on travel and refused Alvarez's petition to rescind the order.[42] A few days later, Alvarez received an unwelcome answer to another of his petitions: Neither he nor any other foreigner would be allowed to leave New Mexico[43] — in any direction. Although Alvarez had urgently wanted to leave from as soon as a week after the Texans' arrival, it was not until October 25, 1841, that he and fifteen Americans received their passports.[44] Presumably, Armijo had by then become convinced that no new Texan threat was developing.

Fearing that the governor might change his mind or that the weather become nasty, the Alvarez party left Santa Fe the next day,[45] bypassing Bent's Fort on the upper Arkansas River and taking the hazardous Cimarron cutoff. The party then divided, five members detouring down the Arkansas River and four others going ahead of the main group. Alvarez took a risk crossing the plains in late October, and it was a gamble he almost lost. The winter snows caught up with his small band of travelers near Council Grove at Cottonwood Creek, where they were stopped in three feet of snow and found themselves unable to keep a fire going. By then, the main body had caught up with three of the four men who had gone ahead. John Richmire, one of the four, froze to death four miles from the camp,[46] and two others were so badly frozen and sick that Alvarez decided to leave them with one healthy person while the rest struck out to seek aid from Missouri settlements. They made it to Independence on December 15 and by the seventeenth, help had worked its way back to Council Grove. Unfortunately, a second man had died before the rescuers arrived.[47] Not one of the original Alvarez party escaped frostbite, and some of the survivors had suffered severely. Only Alvarez's insistence that everyone keep moving had saved the remainder.

Alvarez's friend and an experienced frontiersman, Antoine Robidoux, was leading a party of men behind Alvarez's group. They, too, got caught in the same blizzard, losing one man and over a hundred mules and horses.[48] The consul later tallied his absorbed losses at a total that proves him to have been something more than a poor man — $8,210. Taking a trip, during an inclement season, for the primary purpose of presenting a formal complaint to the US government did not necessitate a lot of baggage, yet Alvarez lost two riding horses, one buffalo horse, "two Jacks of superior size and breed," thirty-six mules, one gun, and other utensils, as well as personal items.[49] No wonder some of the party tried to make better time!

By February 1842, Alvarez was in Washington, asking Secretary Webster what the State Department planned to do about the injuries suffered by American citizens in New Mexico.[50] He had been careful to bring all his official correspondence with him, and, after his safe arrival in Missouri, he had dashed off a letter telling Webster both where he was and that he planned to "proceed to the seat of government." Although Alvarez had included a memorial "nearly agreeing with the facts" for the department's inspection, Webster had no way to predict what his intelligent, if wordy, consul had in store for him: The memorial was a thirty-two-page narrative meticulously footnoted, with the original documents attached; those letters written in Spanish were accompanied by English translations (upon his request, the State Department returned the original letters in exchange for Alvarez's own handwritten copies).[51] In all, Alvarez had included over sixty letters substantiating the text of the memorial.[52]

An amazing historical document of the time, the memorial formed but one part of Alvarez's evidence — a statement signed by American residents of New Mexico would be presented at a personal interview, which the consul asked to delay until "after some repose which is necessary to recruit my health impaired by a troublesome journey."[53] Alvarez also wanted to remonstrate to Congress, so he collected letters of introduction, hoping to meet the speaker of the House, John White, and even to persuade someone to use his "aid and influence with Mr. Clay and other friends."[54] To all this activity, the State Department replied that Waddy Thompson, recently appointed minister to Mexico, would be personally instructed "to make proper representations to that government."[55]

A couple of weeks later, Alvarez entered a second petition on his own behalf. He reiterated the attempt on his life, emphasizing that outrage by claiming that even though the

Mexican government had initially recognized him as the US
consul, the local Mexican authorities had done nothing by
way of reparations or apologies; for this he asked for an
indemnity of $2,500. For the deaths of two men on the trail,
caused by the "arbitrary detention" that prevented them
from leaving Santa Fe until late fall, he asked $12,000 more;
indeed, Alvarez felt the detention, or arrest, as he claimed,
from September 16 to October 25 was itself worth $5,000.
Finally, he wanted $8,200 for the property losses he had
calculated he had incurred on the trail.[56] This amazing petition did not faze Webster. In a succinct and brisk letter
demonstrating the stern New England mettle for which he
was famous, Webster told Alvarez that his lack of US citizenship prevented the United States from seeking reparations
from the Mexican government for him. Because he was never
granted an exequatur, Webster concluded, "there cannot, for
the present at least, be anything done in your behalf."[57]

Governor Armijo had always hesitated to answer Alvarez's requests for personal protection because he thought
the consul was a Mexican citizen;[58] now, Webster was reasoning that the United States could do nothing because Alvarez
was not an American citizen.[59] It was as a result of Webster's
attitude that Alvarez decided to reapply for US citizenship,
and on April 9, 1842, in the St. Louis Court of Common Pleas,
he became a naturalized citizen. Alvarez had two witnesses:
Theodore Papin, a relative of Alvarez's old boss, P. D. Papin,
and Pascal L. Cerrí, one of the charter members of the Papin
company. Both had to bend the facts until they broke to gain
the coveted citizenship for him, certifying that Alvarez had
resided in the United States for "at least five years, and in
the State of Missouri at least one year, immediately preced-
ing this application."[60] Almost a month passed before Alvarez
worded a two-sentence letter to inform Webster of his naturalization and let him know that "I leave [for Santa Fe]
tomorrow."[61] It is clear he was bitter at the lack of apprecia-

tion he had received for his consular efforts. The people for whom Alvarez had so bravely labored were equally disgusted with Webster. George Kendall and Josiah Gregg drew clear portraits of Alvarez's heroism in their respective works *Narrative of the Texan–Santa Fe Expedition* and *Commerce of the Prairies,* in which they wrote that, although Alvarez had risked his life for his countrymen and only narrowly escaped, the US government did nothing to assist him.[62]

Alvarez returned to New Mexico to find that his trouble with Texans, now seeking to disrupt the Santa Fe trade, was not over — on a subsequent trip he confronted it head-on when he met Colonel Jacob Snively and 180 men at the Arkansas crossing. Snively and his band had camped there waiting for a westbound caravan under the protection of Captain Philip St. George Cooke of the US Army. As soon as the caravan crossed the Arkansas River into Mexican territory, it would no longer have the benefit of Cooke's protection, or so the Texans felt, and Snively patiently lay in ambush. Alvarez felt that such brigandage hurt trade and opined that something should be done.[63] Not surprisingly, he and Charles Bent got actively involved.

Alvarez and Bent had dinner with Captain Cooke in his camp at the fork of Walnut Creek and the Arkansas River on June 16, 1843. The itinerary of the caravan escorted by Cooke was known to be dangerous, and a Texan ambush would surely alienate all Santa Fe Trail merchants. Bent volunteered intelligence of Governor Armijo's plan to lead a force of 600 men to the Arkansas River for the purpose of taking over the caravan at that point. Captain Nathan Boone added an unconfirmed rumor that a force of Texans — "those land pirates" — may have defeated the Mexican governor.[64] His statement probably raised some eyebrows, but, although they could not know it, Boone's rumor was true. The Texans had successfully ambushed Armijo's advance guard, led by Captain Ventura Lobato. It was a blow (which, as will be seen,

Charles Bent, 1844. Alvarez's friend and business partner and first US governor of New Mexico. Copied from a painting that hung in the Taos home of Bent's daughter, Teresina Scheurich. *Courtesy of the Museum of New Mexico, Santa Fe. MNM 7004.*

was partially caused by Alvarez) that would lead to further bloodshed four years down the road.

Alvarez also had valuable information for Cooke. Perhaps remembering the forces called up during the Texan–Santa Fe expedition, he estimated that Armijo, if pressed, could raise as many as 1,500 militia and Indians in about a week and march to Bent's Fort in ten days. From Cooke's point of view, the situation was grave: Events along the Arkansas could grow from a few Texan ambushes to an international incident. The crux of the problem had to be Snively and his Texan volunteers, but how could he legally get to them if they were south of the Arkansas River? Alvarez, and perhaps others, offered a solution when he suggested that Texas's northern boundary did not continue to the headwaters of the Arkansas; Alvarez thought that Texas's western boundary struck the river at or above Chouteau's Island far below Bent's Fort. Cooke, utilizing that assumption, concluded that if he could not enter Texas's territory to arrest Texans, the Mexican authorities would ignore him if he crossed the upper Arkansas into Mexican territory, under the pretension that it was the United States' land, for the same purpose. After all, Texans, so far, had committed depredations solely on Mexicans.

Cooke and his command eventually encountered Jacob Snively and his force of something over a hundred men, "a ruffian crew" of "outcast citizens of the United States." Cooke, after consulting with his officers, repeated Alvarez's border claims and announced that no country, including Texas, had a right to carry on its warfare in a neutral's — that is, the United States' — territory. If they did so, the neutral had a "rightful power and duty" to disarm the intruders, which Cooke proceeded to do. He also announced that Texas was determined to disrupt a peaceful trade between the United States and "a friendly power," a trade the Union wished to protect. Cooke's act caused some international squabbling between the United States and Texas, but it effectively ended Texan marauding along the trail while winning Mexican favor for American merchants and pointing out a difference between them and Texans. The only party to complain was Texas.[65]

5

A New Era Opens

Taxes proved a more lasting trouble than even Texans were. Merchants in the Santa Fe trade had to pay two duties for goods imported from a third country to the United States and subsequently shipped over the trail to Mexico. Even though the goods were never removed from the original packages, import duties were required at the entry ports of both the United States and Mexico. Santa Fe traders felt they were being unjustly treated because sea trade had to pay but one duty at a Mexican port; shipment by boat did not include a US import duty. The solution was to eliminate the added tariff for the Santa Fe trade, and this was attempted on three different occasions in the form of the Drawback Bill.[1] Despite the acute interest of Alvarez and others on each occasion, the bill continued to meet defeat in the House of Representatives, following passage in the Senate, once because the House combined "it with some Canadian measure."[2] Although enactment seemed remote for almost the full tenure of Alvarez's consular duties, he continued to marshal arguments in favor of it, pointedly relating the bill to the "big picture." Aside from the benefits of personal profits, such a bill would increase trade "to about two millions of dollars annually, giving employment to from eight hundred to one thousand wagons,"[3] translating into more jobs in the Mississippi valley. Diplomatically, the increased trade would draw northern Mexico further under the United States' influence and thus balance Britain's influence, exerted from that country's base in British Honduras, in southern Mexico. If nothing else, such numerous and huge caravans required as many as 1,500 men, which, in itself, would discourage hostilities from the Indians.

Perhaps Mexico also felt that increased trade would mean increased influence. In August 1843, President Antonio López de Santa Anna closed all northern ports of entry into Mexico; foreigners, such as Alvarez was by birth and on paper, were now prohibited from engaging in retail commerce in New Mexico. Alvarez, caught outside the borders, used the opportunity to start back east. Traveling by way of Chicago and Philadelphia, where he stayed six days, he arrived in New York around September 1.[4] While in Philadelphia, on August 25, Alvarez had traded a little over 791 ounces of gold dust for $15,158.90 at the US mint. It seems he used his gold to fund a trip to Spain, where he visited his family for the first time in a quarter of a century,[5] and to England and France. It was before the Spanish consul in Bayonne, France, Don Francisco de Hormaeche, that Alvarez made his last will and testament. Josiah Gregg and others kept him abreast of events at home while the Spaniard combined business with pleasure by purchasing valued European items for his store.

Even though this was his first trip back to Europe, it was not his first personal venture with European merchandise. The previous year, while presenting memorials, confronting Daniel Webster, and receiving US citizenship, he had managed to outfit a caravan of sixty-two wagons that carried goods from the eastern markets and from England for an estimated total value of between $150,000 and $160,000.[6] This in itself might have been an incentive to go to Europe the next year. He took with him at least two letters of intro-

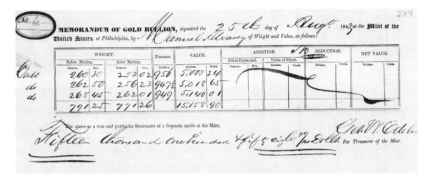

Memorandum of Gold Bullion, August 25, 1843. On his way to Europe, Alvarez went to the US mint in Philadelphia and received $15,158.90 for 771.26 ounces of gold, after melting. *Original in the Alvarez Papers. Courtesy of the New Mexico State Records Center and Archives, Santa Fe.*

duction for England and one for France, all written by some New York business associates — Peter Harmony, Nephews and Company. By all appearances he attended solely to business in London, intending to purchase an "assortment of goods" from such merchants as Lamar, Campbell and Company, and Aguirre, Solante, and Murrieta.[7] Apparently, Aguirre was also part of a Parisian firm that Alvarez wished to visit, and he did most of his business through Aguirre's London-based partnership, which acted as his agent. The consul seems to have left over $3,000 on deposit in a London bank, collecting interest for use as payments. The firm, in turn, was honored to have as a client a man who served as a "Ynoke" (Yankee) consul, reference to which was made on four occasions in one letter.[8]

There is some doubt about Alvarez's itinerary in Europe. He apparently visited the British Isles last, possibly because he planned to do most of his buying there. In Spain he undoubtedly wanted to visit Abelgas and Leon, and he procured special letters from an administrator of the Academia de Nobles Artes de San Fernando for a visit to that institution. It appears that Alvarez desired to visit the academy for purely intellectual reasons, for one of the letters mentioned his interest in "la historia natural."[9] Alvarez's arrival in France coincided with the eve of a major revolution, for in 1848 the liberal views of the eighteenth century would once again encourage reaction against Europe's conservative monarchies. Unlike the situation in England, a visitor needed paperwork to go anywhere in France. Nonetheless, Alvarez received royal treatment: In November he visited the Palais de l'Elysée, possibly attended a royal reception while in the Chapelle Royale de Notre Dame, and had special permission to tour the Palais de Fontainebleau, including the gardens. Obviously, Alvarez's contact, Monsieur de Barcaizteguy, had some influence, for the Spaniard visited places the inside of which many Frenchmen never saw.[10] By the middle of January, Alvarez had arrived in London to tend to business, drafting two letters in which he commented on the Parisian press and its anti-American stand regarding Mexico and Texas.

Despite all his buying and shipping, the trip allowed Alvarez to become reacquainted with his family. Judging from Alvarez's will, which provided that any wealth he left be divided among his surviving brothers and sisters and especially his cousins Luis Arias and Josefina, and from his correspondence while in Europe, Luis apparently had endeared himself to the traveling Spaniard and may even have been privy to some of his cousin's business ventures. Writing to Luis in Spain, Alvarez commented on the trouble merchants had had and on his position as consul, adding that though such events were having an effect on his business, he would be better off concluding his work in Europe, for it appeared his dealings with Aguirre and company would prove successful. Even more important, however, was his mention of his mother: He had sent her a gift and, in turn, was gratified by her happiness on receiving it.[11]

At home in New Mexico, Santa Anna's border closure was creating some problems, but no one doubted that trade with

Tower Hill, London, England, 1860–1861, much as Alvarez would have seen it. *Photograph by the London Stereoscopic Company. Courtesy of the Museum of New Mexico, Santa Fe. MNM 113966.*

Mexico would be reopened. Certainly, Alvarez expected to return to his Santa Fe business; otherwise he would not have bothered to stockpile European and American goods in expectation of that moment, confidently putting his money behind his ability to read Mexican-US frontier diplomacy and, in thorough, businesslike manner, keeping himself informed of the situation. The real uncertainty was not when, but the

Rue de Rivoli, Paris, France, ca. 1860. *Courtesy of the Museum of New Mexico, Santa Fe. MNM 114101.*

political conditions under which, the border would be reopened. On one occasion, Josiah Gregg wrote to Alvarez in Paris, expressing the possibility of revolution in Mexico and further mentioning a loss of hope for the Drawback Bill.[12] Nevertheless, Alvarez prepared and planned with high expectations.

Despite the reopening of Mexico's ports of entry in April 1844, Alvarez did not return hurriedly. By May 1, he had arrived in New York after his prolonged stay in Europe. What

had already become a major business trip was further ac-
cented by Alvarez's stateside activities. It appears that Alvarez spent a couple of weeks in New York, and within two
days after his arrival (assuming that day to be May 1), he had
spent over $2,000 on merchandise. Within the next dozen
days he spent over $4,000. The types of goods procured for the
New Mexican market hinted of the commodities long denied
a secluded frontier area. Predominant in Alvarez's selection
were textiles and related items such as sewing utensils, lace,
and buttons; also included were such common, everyday
utensils as combs, shovels, knives, and belts.[13] Except for his
personal goods, Alvarez wisely limited his purchases to
sturdy goods that would pack and travel well. All things
considered, he invested in merchandise that would bring the
best return. Visiting such firms as Hugh Auchincloss and
Sons; Lockhart, Gibson and Company; Walcott and Slade;
Robert Hyslop and Son; William C. Langley; and Alfred Ed-
wards and Company, among others, Alvarez paid cash, thus
usually receiving a 5 percent discount. That a man from the
frontier would have such cash on hand after an extended
European tour speaks eloquently of Alvarez's wealth and of
the growing prosperity of the frontier.[14]

Alvarez did not stop buying in New York but continued to
purchase items at the same pace for the remainder of his trip.
He went to Philadelphia for a few days and, by May 20, had
traveled to Pittsburgh on his way to Missouri, where he
arrived sometime around June 1. Independence, Westport,
and St. Louis were familiar ground, and the merchant remained in the area for the next two and one-half months
arranging for the shipment of his goods to Santa Fe.[15] Although the record is somewhat sketchy, enough evidence
exists to surmise the extent of his business. One expense that
had not changed much from 1842 was shipping. Alvarez,
however, did not have to solicit shipping companies, for his
reputation seems to have made some firms eager to deal with

him. Even before he left for Europe, one sales representative,
not finding Alvarez in his room at the Groton Hotel in New
York,[16] had left the merchant a note requesting him to "call
on us before making a contract" with another firm. Some of
the major selling points of such companies included low
rates, short transit time, daily service, and the boast that
"none but *temperate men* are employed."[17] Whether or not
that agent was successful is unknown. Alvarez did have to
ship his goods from New York to Pittsburgh, where another
company, simply using its proprietor's name, Anthony
Beelen, contracted to ship the goods down the Ohio River
from Pittsburgh to St. Louis at a rate of thirty cents per
hundred pounds.[18] Beelen charged Alvarez $103.39 for the
job, which translates to a Santa Fe–bound shipment weighing in excess of 34,000 pounds. Needless to say, not everything went according to plan, and Alvarez suffered one small
inconvenience when his shipment from Pittsburgh was delayed under the care of Thomas H. Larkin of St. Louis, "owing
to a Break in the Canal."[19]

After a long journey that had truly spread Santa Fe commerce to Europe, Alvarez procured a passport issued in the
name of Secretary of State John C. Calhoun.[20] In all of his
traveling he had never managed to visit Washington, DC;
this really was a journey of business and pleasure, free of
diplomatic headaches, and marked by renewed ties with his
family in Spain. His favorite cousin Luis had become a
"Chancellor to the Spanish Consulate at Bayonne," and Alvarez used the opportunity of business correspondence with
him to express a desire to return within the next "few years."
He also repeatedly referred to his mother and Josefina. In the
meantime, business between the two cousins would be conducted through the New York firm of Peter Harmony, Nephews and Company.[21]

Alvarez personally arranged the last leg of his goods'
journey with Charles Bent, contracting with the Bent–St.

Vrain Company to ship from Independence to Santa Fe at a rate of nine cents per pound. He had ready for shipment thirty-four bales, six trunks, nine boxes, five "small" boxes, an iron safe, coffee, six dozen spades and shovels, brandy, and a keg of powder — it all added up to 10,485 pounds. The rest would travel with other caravans. The "master" for the voyage was Frank Delisle, who had taken his wagons to Independence on August 26, a day before Alvarez contracted with Bent's company.[22] Even before the formal signing of the contract, Bent had already shipped some of the goods on the steamboat *Omega* from St. Louis to Independence. Bent had planned to leave much earlier than the eventual departure date, but he in fact accompanied Alvarez and his wagons across the plains[23] in late September and October. Alvarez and a portion of his goods arrived in Santa Fe in late October or early November.[24] He assigned Francisco Paula de Robledo, in San Miguel del Vado, to intercept and report on any subsequent caravans carrying his merchandise. On November 3, 1844, Robledo relayed information on the arrival of a caravan in San Miguel.[25] Among its cargo were Alvarez's goods from London and New York — mostly textiles.

Alvarez was kept busy: Along with the usual, varied requests he traditionally received,[26] he had to inventory, store, and stock all his purchases from the previous year. He had been in Santa Fe a month before he wrote to Washington, informing the State Department that he had returned home and still needed to be officially acknowledged. He also exhibited his enthusiasm for the Santa Fe trade: "Within the last two years," he reported, "commercial intercourse" between the United States and Mexico "has increased with an almost unprecedented rapidity." To the merchant-consul, the future seemed even more promising.[27]

A year later, almost to the day, Alvarez made another trip, and, on arriving in Missouri, learned of the recent passage of the Drawback Bill. Joyfully, he informed James Buchanan of his approval. Alvarez decided to appoint Joab "Jeremiah" Houghton, a resident of Taos, temporary consul, justifying the move "by virtue of my appointment" in 1839 and adding that "under the provisions of the late law, many merchants have purchased goods and are on their way to New Mexico." A temporary consul would avert any fear that Alvarez's "absence from Santa Fe might prejudice [American] interests," and besides, Alvarez planned to be away only a couple of months.[28] In a letter to Treasury Secretary Robert Walker, he reiterated his belief that the new Drawback Bill would "greatly augment" prairie commerce and "increase in proportion" the flow of precious metals into the United States.[29]

Between trips east, Alvarez and Charles Bent demonstrated where their loyalties lay as they continued to use their many contacts at Bent's Fort and along the Santa Fe Trail to keep Governor Armijo informed of Indian and Texan raiding parties. Texas seemed to be extremely bitter over the treatment the survivors of the Texan–Santa Fe expedition had received from the Mexican authorities, a feeling exacerbated by the biased publicity surrounding the event. Texans continued to raid outlying New Mexican settlements, and, as Alvarez reported, attacks on trail caravans were avoided only when the Cheyenne runners of William Bent, Charles Bent's half-brother, kept Bent's Fort informed of Lone Star activity along the Arkansas River. Ceran St. Vrain relayed the information from the fort to Charles Bent in Taos, who, in turn, passed the intelligence to Alvarez in Santa Fe. From Alvarez, then, the Mexican traders had a good idea of what was happening along the Santa Fe Trail. One such warning from Charles Bent read that "thare [sic] are people of the single star on the lookout for game on the plains." This particular warning resulted in many Mexican traders not risking the trail at that time.[30] The native traders simply let American traders transport their goods, for the Texans were less inclined to torment Americans. Thus, the Bents' Santa Fe network of communication contributed to the preservation of the trade.

Preparation and good intentions did not completely eliminate the ambushes. One of the more celebrated episodes occurred when Don Antonio José Chávez, a prominent New Mexican, refused to take necessary precautions in light of recurring rumors of Texan forces planning to attack traders. Leaving in February 1843, the wrong time of the year, he took with him some servants, a couple of wagons, some mules, furs, and some gold and silver. He encountered bad weather and suffered its consequences, but the worst of his trip was when he met up with fifteen men commanded by John McDaniel, who had recruited his troops in Missouri for the purpose of joining Colonel Charles A. Warfield of the Texas army. Obviously within US territory, Chávez was made captive at the Cow Creek crossing, robbed, and later murdered. Several of McDaniel's party were arrested and tried in Missouri, and McDaniel and his brother David were executed. Texas disavowed McDaniel's acts and claimed no responsibility because Warfield had commissioned him without consulting the government of Texas.[31] Mexican officials in Santa Fe and Taos kept abreast of the recurring Texan threats and the role of the US Army. Indeed, the *Revista Oficial* in Chihuahua issued favorable reports of the New Mexican army's activities while denouncing the scandalous *tejanos,* but the article made no mention of the Americans' integral role.[32]

By 1846, fifty-two-year-old Manuel Alvarez could have easily reminisced over an eventful life, and the future held even bigger ventures. War was coming between the United States and Mexico. As early as January 7, 1843, Charles Bent had sent a note, along with a sheaf of newspapers, to Alvarez in which he said, "You will see that there is a prospect of war." Governor Armijo also shared in this information since Bent had asked Alvarez to let "the big man" see the papers "as it may please him to see" what is written about him.[33] On

January 24, 1845, sixteen months before the outbreak of war,
Alvarez had received another letter from Bent in which he
conveyed his sorrow over the election of James K. Polk. He
was "fearful that this election will cause difficulty between
this and our country."[34] On July 16, 1845, a letter from a
merchant friend, Sam Wethered, Jr., had arrived in Santa Fe,
telling Alvarez that 70,000 pounds of Wethered's freight on
thirteen or fourteen wagons had been delayed at Independence until September. The reason, said Wethered, was "to
learn all the particulars as respects Mexico and the United
States."[35] The storm was brewing and its winds were beginning to be felt.

In November, Alvarez received information about another
problem that was contributing to a growing anxiety over
American designs on New Mexico. Joab Houghton, Alvarez's
recent choice as temporary consul, and a couple of his American friends seemed to be making a political power play, attempting to place the country and courts under their control.
Houghton and his partners had some clout, as evidenced by
the fact that they were able to remove the Taos prefect from
office in favor of one of their own choice. They had achieved
the same in Río Arriba and were gaining influence over more
of the American community. Theodore Wheaton, a veteran of
the Santa Fe Trail, urgently warned Alvarez that Houghton's
people were on their way to Santa Fe. Alvarez was asked to
inform the governor and William Dryden, an ally in opposition to the Houghton group, because "it may be some time
before Congress legislates for this country and during this
time we shall suffer severely both as to our public and private
interests if we cannot stop this pernicious influence."[36] Wheaton felt the only method to halt this Anglo-American movement in the north was to do it legally through an alliance
between the top Americans and Mexicans "who are disposed
to see the country prosper"; if nothing was done, he felt,

Houghton would impose "worse oppression than that under Armijo."[37] In light of such brash politics, it is no wonder that Padre Antonio José Martínez of Taos delivered Sunday sermons denouncing annexation, or that Charles Bent petitioned the US consul to assure his protection under the Mexican government.[38]

Houghton's actions hint at divisions within the American community that would continue through the next decade. New Mexico became a myriad of factions just before US occupation, but Alvarez seemed to fit in them all. A wagonload of goods came to Santa Fe after Alvarez had received a request and instructions in the mail from R. G. Woods, on behalf of Woods, Langford and Company: The wagon master had died on the trail, and Woods did not feel confident enough to trust the business acumen of the man left in charge, a younger brother of Woods's partner. Would Alvarez take charge upon the arrival of the wagon "as he [young Langford] cannot have the same knowledge treating the matter [of sale] that you have"?[39] (As it turned out, the young man had also died on the trail.)

Alvarez's old friend Josiah Gregg similarly relied on the consul's tact and acumen. Gregg, a veteran of the plains, had had nothing good to say about Governor Armijo in his book, *Commerce of the Prairies*. Now in failing health, Gregg felt another trip across the plains would be his cure-all, but he wondered how Armijo would treat him in Santa Fe: Would his "dear friend" Don Manuel Alvarez "feel the pulse of our *friend* the governor and others perhaps, and see if you can gather from them, how I will be received"?[40]

The fact that Gregg would even inquire about the governor indicates that Armijo could at times look favorably upon *extranjeros*. Indeed, there were Americans who preferred Armijo's rule to that of their fellow countrymen, and the governor was no doubt aware of many services from these enterprising Americans, not the least of which was his supply of coffee. Gregg's letter was penned less than a week before Polk's declaration of war. By the time he wrote again, he had received a hurried appointment to General Zachary Taylor's army as an interpreter.[41]

In the face of somewhat harsh realities, Mexico's northern department had not previously split along racial lines. When news of General Mariano Paredes's rise to power in Mexico City reached New Mexico, Charles Bent opined to Alvarez that war would break out "since Parrades [sic] has come to power," and that "we should be prepared because if [Padre] Martínez is in favor in Mexico Armijo must fall, as he is no friend of the latter."[42] The threat of another Texan invasion — a possibility that had everyone on tenterhooks — made matters worse. Suspicion of Texas had been acting as a unifying factor in the New Mexican populace, but apprehension over another invasion now developed into a suspicion of Anglo-Americans in general. Rumors once again worked many locals into a frenzied state. Such fears were largely after the fact: American influence on the Santa Fe Trail had already made its effect on Mexico's sovereignty in the north, and by the late 1840s, citizens of New Mexico, many of whom had been educated in the United States, owned approximately half of the Santa Fe trade.[43] Once again, Americans feared for their lives and property. Two events justified their anxiety. The first was the murder of an American named Crombeck in a Jicarilla Apache ambush. The incident was pressed on Alvarez by Charles Bent because the northern authorities seemed to take no interest in the death of one foreigner, especially under the prevailing circumstances. Six of the Indians had been brought into Taos with the corpse, which was described as "terribly mangled" with the skull smashed and "the face one third broader" than natural.[44] Bent had wanted five of the Indians held secure and the sixth sent out to bring in the two "murderers" who had not been caught. Instead, the authorities had released four and kept two hostage for the two still at large. Bent complained that the final two would be allowed to escape and pleaded with Alvarez to get an order to have the accused transferred to Santa Fe for trial. Nothing ever came of Bent's protestations, even though Alvarez received an official reply from Juan Bautista Vigil y Alarid, secretary of government, that Armijo had taken steps to punish the Jicarillas involved in the killing of Crombeck.[45]

Then, on May 3, 1846, Alvarez received the startling news from Taos that George Bent, brother of Charles, and Francis (Frank) Blair had been attacked by a mob of *taoseños* the previous day. Ensuing reports indicated that Blair had been left for dead with gashes on the head. Witnesses to the incident were two of Padre Martínez's brothers, one a newly elected justice. None of the attackers had been arrested, and the American community demanded action from Armijo. Alvarez, now much experienced in such matters, presented their wishes to the governor. Charles Bent had sent a message to Alvarez to "tell the governor as his own supreme authority is at stake here," but the consul merely expressed his distrust of the Taos officials and suggested that the offenders be tried in Santa Fe.[46] Charles Bent arranged for guards in front of George's house, where his brother and Blair were being attended. On May 5 Alvarez received assurances from Vigil y Alarid that the *"disagradables seriosos acaecidos* [sic] *en Taos"* — the serious, disagreeable events in Taos — were being investigated.[47] The offenders were indeed incarcerated, only to escape a few days later on June 1.

After news of the pending US invasion reached Santa Fe from traders on June 26, a mob formed in the plaza to listen to inflammatory speeches. As heads got hotter, Alvarez may have recalled the mob that had attacked him during the 1841 Texan invasion. Once again, the local government stopped the uproar, this time by order of Governor Armijo.[48]

The whirlwind of activities in which Alvarez participated seemed to increase in magnitude, if not velocity, perhaps reflecting events occurring on an international scale that would soon involve New Mexico. Meanwhile, Alvarez found time to raise a hundred head of cattle on the Ocaté grant, which, on December 5, 1845, Governor Armijo had reaffirmed — demonstrating that "the big man" was something more than many biased American writers were prone to depict.[49] Two of Alvarez's friends, David Waldo and John Rowland, shared the opinion that Alvarez's interests in his rancho were due to the expectation that New Mexico would soon be under the US government.[50] If selling beef to American soldiers was indeed his plan, the venture would be partially successful, but only after constant haggling with the US Army's quartermasters.

Recently elected president, Polk had campaigned on the promise that his administration would make the United States a transcontinental nation with valuable West Coast ports at San Francisco and San Diego, and he immediately embarked on a strategy of buying the northern part of Mexico, which included New Mexico, Arizona, and California. Mexico's refusal to deal and Texas's annexation into the United States exacerbated the already poor relations between the two countries. On April 25, 1846, Mexican troops crossed the Río Grande at Matamoros and killed or wounded sixteen American soldiers under General Zachary Taylor at the battle of Rescala de la Palma. President Polk used the incident as an excuse to go to war with Mexico. His war message was delivered to Congress on May 11, 1846, and two days later, the legislators formally voted a declaration of war. Soon thereafter, US Consul Alvarez received a "Confidential Circular" from the secretary of state, James Buchanan, which in part stated: "It is our interest . . . that Mexico should

be an independent and powerful Republic, and that our relations with her should be of the most friendly character. . . . We
feel deeply interested that she should establish a stable government. We go to war with Mexico solely for the purpose of
conquering an honorable and permanent peace."[51] New Mexico's long history was embarking on a new era, in which
Manuel Alvarez would be cast in an important role.

6

"Its Brilliant Light Shall Grow"

N ews of war traveled across the plains faster than had Buchanan's message. When Stephen Watts Kearny, commander of the Army of the West and soon to be brigadier general, received his orders to take New Mexico and California, he promptly sent "spies" to confer "with Don Manuel Alvarez."[1] Alvarez was not unprepared for war. In February 1846, he had reported that New Mexico's militia consisted of soldiers demoralized because their government had no money to pay them. They could easily become a mob, and the threat of a *saqueo* (attack) on the extranjero merchants, against a backdrop of talk about annexation to, or war with, the United States, only served to intensify the normal kinds of consular problems with which Alvarez had to contend.[2] He no doubt would have liked to rid himself of the sordid affairs relating to the continuing deaths of American citizens: The distasteful task of trying to account for the deceased's possessions in the face of a governmental policy that tended to auction such goods did nothing positive for the consul's relations with Mexican authorities.[3] Despite his anxieties, Alvarez was careful to point out that there was some strong opposition to annexation and without some kind of military presence nothing would be achieved. He had asked Buchanan

Stephen Watts Kearny, commander of the Army of the West that invaded New Mexico during the Mexican War. *Courtesy of the Museum of New Mexico, Santa Fe. MNM 7605.*

to "appreciate the importance of providing for" protection of American citizens in New Mexico "in view of the anticipated dangers arising from expected events" and suggested that the secretary of state should consider reparations to American merchants "in the proposed treaty with Mexico."[4] Based on his own experiences, Alvarez had reason to be concerned for life and property,[5] and, when all is said and done, he was pleased about having the responsibility of protecting the safety of so many people and succeeding.[6]

Meanwhile, George Thomas Howard had been appointed to transmit the news of war to the various caravans and Americans along the trail and in Santa Fe, where the information arrived on June 17.[7] Alvarez, "on his own initiative, had an immediate interview with Armijo" to try to convince him it would be wise to capitulate. Alvarez argued that it would be far better to be an "inconsiderable portion of a powerful republic, than a considerable one of" an unstable nation. He stressed the historical negligence Mexico had demonstrated toward its northern department and the resulting poverty. Alvarez admittedly had little success with the governor but he found other officials, especially Armijo's advisors, easier prey: "They, not holding such high places, nor so responsible commissions and yet exposed to the same dangers were rather easily won over."[8] Although Alvarez's arguments probably played a considerable role in the initial "peaceful submission of the territory,"[9] how much actual influence the consul had on Armijo is subject to conjecture. He was not the only American to talk with the military commandant, and Armijo seems to have had a lukewarm attitude toward fighting. Although the threat of invasion hung oppressively over New Mexico, he had recently hosted a dinner party in the *Palacio* in honor of American traders at which he had declared that the people of New Mexico would not fight. Armijo's return to office in 1845 had relieved many of the traders, for he installed order and security. On top of this,

Chihuahua did not seem prepared to send equipment and troops to aid in New Mexico's cause. Finally, Armijo's proclamation calling people to arms was less than enthusiastic.[10]

On August 12, Kearny's two emissaries, James Magoffin and Captain Philip St. George Cooke, along with twelve dragoons, rode into Santa Fe under a flag of truce attached to a saber, to parley with Armijo. After an afternoon meeting at which the governor received a conciliatory letter from Kearny, a secret meeting including Cooke, Alvarez, Henry Connelly, Magoffin, and Armijo took place at night. Cooke found Armijo "in painful doubt and irresolution,"[11] indisposed to resist Kearny's army and actually appearing to welcome the council of American representatives. Perhaps the governor was reflecting the effect Alvarez had had on him. Speculation has been that the American emissaries bribed the governor to vacate Santa Fe to Kearny's approaching Army of the West, yet Armijo had any number of reasons for abandoning his defensive position at Apache Pass south of the city. The American army outnumbered his militia, his troops were poorly trained, armed, and positioned, and aid from Chihuahua could not arrive in time to help. Given the circumstances, it would have been surprising if he had insisted on fighting; Magoffin's detailed report to Congress for remuneration does not mention any bribe money.[12]

Kearny's army peacefully marched into Santa Fe on August 18, 1846. Alvarez's efforts to help make the transition as peaceful as possible[13] were rewarded by his appointment as consular agent, a federal post no longer needed and that, as previously mentioned, he declined. He did not, however, receive an appointment to a position in the new territorial government set up by Kearny. Joab Houghton was appointed chief justice of the superior court, fulfilling his earlier ambitions, while twenty-five-year-old Frank Blair had recovered enough from his beating by the Taos mob to become the new attorney general. Alvarez's old friend, Charles Bent, became the new governor, probably on the basis of his long acquaintance with Kearny. Bent attempted to find Alvarez a position in which he could both actively participate in making New Mexico economically self-sufficient with the development of mining and help verify various land grants.[14] Accordingly, when Bent submitted his plans to the federal government, Alvarez was one of the three proposed land commissioners[15] suggested to Missouri Senator Thomas Hart Benton, but since Washington did not follow up on the plans, Alvarez never held that office or any other under Bent's administration.

Alvarez probably preferred to stay at his store; business had never been better. His trip to Europe had set up a couple of subsequent trips to the States, the most recent being during the previous year when he, again, went to New York and Philadelphia, where he exchanged more silver and gold for spending cash.[16] Naturally enough, his enterprise spread beyond agents in St. Louis, for they were in no more advantageous a position to oversee his affairs in Europe than he himself was. Alvarez had kept money on deposit in London and thus received periodic reports from Murrieta and his colleagues. Meanwhile, Peter Harmony, Nephews and Company operated as his New York agent, through which he did business with his cousin Luis in Spain as well as Murrieta in London.[17] Coupled with new advantages under the Drawback Bill and greater profit margins to Santa Fe merchants dealing in European commodities, he managed to set himself up quite well. Not only had he had the foresight to prepare for the reopening of the borders in 1844, but it seems he also had a productive network in operation for the pending, indeed inevitable, change in national government New Mexico underwent. Alvarez's last trip east before US occupation is evidence of his intentions: While corresponding with firms in Europe, he bought in New York. The result was a shipment of goods arriving in Independence on October 10, 1845 — forty-nine bales of two trunks each weighing a total of 10,796 pounds. Once again, the Bent–St. Vrain Company received the shipping contract.[18]

By the winter of 1845–1846, Alvarez had returned to New Mexico, where he spent the final months before American occupation in a relative lull. Robledo continued to report and, on occasion, advise the merchant,[19] and regular notices of accounts with his New York and London contacts indicate that he continued investing, through New York, in Europe.[20] No doubt the reality of the occupation and the subsequent adjustment of the local populace momentarily distracted Alvarez from his business interests, but he was prepared after the army arrived, when business increased and there were soldiers everywhere. Santa Fe had as many as 3,500 armed Americans wandering its streets,[21] for the most part undisciplined Missouri volunteers, and they were eager customers. Since the trail was now free from danger, the soldiers had a wealth of merchandise to choose from, but, unfortunately, they had not been paid. Business was done on credit, making spending easier and risks higher.

Despite the new business, Alvarez did manage to keep up with the events of the continuing war. On October 20, he received a note from somewhere "180 miles below Santa Fe," asking him to collect a debt and adding that "we have no news from Chihuahua nor have we heard from the states."[22] A month later, the same man, Solomon Houck, wrote from Valverde that "[Brigadier General John E.] Wool was not heard of and no chance to get there yet — Taylor took Montirrey [*sic*] and lost 1,000 men in taking it." Houck also reported a rumor that Mexico had sent 700 men from Chihuahua to take New Mexico — part of a stratagem that relied on New Mexicans rising in revolt and joining them.[23] On November 27, Isaac Lightner wrote that it looked as if the Mexicans had only begun to fight, and "it is impossible to say when peace will be made."[24] New Mexico's brief honeymoon

*JnoW.H. Patton immediately after his first fire
at the Brazito on the 25 Dec 1846.*

"John W.H. Patton," Missouri Volunteer. Pencil and ink drawing by Lachlan Allan MacLean, December 25, 1846. The Missouri Volunteers traveled down the Santa Fe Trail as a part of Brigadier General Stephen W. Kearny's army during the Mexican War. *Original in the collections of the Palace of the Governors. Courtesy of the Museum of New Mexico, Santa Fe. MNM 147638.*

ended by December when the peaceful transition to US rule suddenly collapsed.

Many Mexicans had refused serenely to accept the new regime, and some prominent citizens still considered themselves at war with the occupying force. A revolt had been planned for December but was aborted when word leaked out. Two of the leaders, Diego Archuleta and Tomás Ortiz, fled south toward Mexico City, but their absence did not affect the spirit of those remaining. New conspiracies bore fruit when, on January 19, 1847, Governor Charles Bent was assassinated in his home at Taos, before the eyes of his family. Five other people also suffered violent deaths in the Taos area, and simultaneous revolts broke out at Arroyo Hondo and Mora. With news of Bent's death, Colonel Sterling Price, commander of the US forces in New Mexico, took to the snow-covered field. He marched his army to Taos, encountering rebellious forces along the way at La Cañada and Embudo. Having taken refuge in the church at Taos Pueblo, the rebels found themselves quickly surrounded. After a stubborn resistance, they surrendered.

Trials for Bent's murderers were quickly set up. The two judges were Joab Houghton and Carlos Beaubien, whose son Narciso had been killed in the uprising, stabbed and lanced until unrecognizable. George Bent became foreman of the grand jury and the prosecuting attorney was Frank Blair. Not surprisingly, the verdict proved swift and harsh: Fifteen men were sentenced to hang. On April 12, 1847, Padre Martínez complained to Alvarez about a lack of justice and asked him to present a report to Colonel Price on behalf of the condemned.[25] This was a familiar position for Alvarez, the old Hispanic merchant, only now he would represent Mexicans.

The Taos uprising pointedly illustrated the inherent conditions and abuses that drove home to the lay population the nature of their new situation. New Mexicans, whatever their ethnic heritage, had been conspicuously quiet about the finer legal points of occupation: Some had assumed that the territory had become part of the United States; others had felt the land had been occupied by a foreign power. Yet, when those who had thought it their duty to resist were brought to trial in Taos and Santa Fe, no one, including Padre Martínez in his plea to Alvarez, questioned the legality of convicting Mexican citizens for treason against the United States. Not until after fifteen men had been hanged did this question arise during the trial of a seventy-five-year-old man named Antonio María Trujillo.

Trujillo's defense attorney chose to neglect the "who did it" aspect of the trial to assail the indictment on the ground that the defendant was not bound by allegiance to the United States — he was a Mexican citizen. Although the ploy failed and the Santa Fe jury found him guilty, District Attorney Francis Blair referred the question to Washington.[26] Blair seems not to have been the only person to understand the logic of Trujillo's defense, for others, including Acting Civil Governor Donaciano Vigil, wrote to Washington on Trujillo's behalf with many a word about the inconsistencies of a treason charge.[27] Whether or not Alvarez followed through on Martínez's request that the ex-consul intercede for the accused with Colonel Price is unknown, but Blair effectively made the Trujillo case an issue.[28]

Price apparently listened to someone, for he inquired of Secretary of War William L. Marcy on the legalities of prosecuting Mexicans. Marcy passed the problem to the president and wrote an initial answer that left the final decision to Price, assuring him that as military commander he had supreme authority, including the right to appoint a new governor should Vigil resign, but they stressed that they wanted Trujillo's life spared.[29] In a later letter, apparently in answer to continued inquiries, the secretary of war stated that the right of the army to establish a civil government — implying that such a government be subject to the military — was acquired by conquest. Conquest, however, did not make the area part of the United States, nor did it make American citizens of resident Mexicans: It was, then, not "the proper use of legal terms" to try them for treason against the United States because it "would not be correct to say they owed allegiance to the conquerors."[30] Martínez's faith in Alvarez in this matter demonstrates not only the consul's ability to avoid making enemies, but the respect that many held for him: Alvarez had been asked to plead the case of those who had viciously killed his longtime friend.[31]

Most of the killing in the Taos area was done by Indians from the Taos Pueblo, who did not revolt out of any deep sense of loyalty to Mexico but out of a bitter feeling of revenge. Four years before, Taos Indians, impressed into Armijo's militia as auxiliaries, had formed part of an advance guard moving through the Cimarron Canyon to intercept the Santa Fe Trail below the Raton Pass. Such forays were common to protect the trade along the trail, but this had been a special occasion, for Armijo sought to meet a caravan in which he owned fifty-two wagons. The US Army had protected the caravans up to the Mexican territory's border, where the New Mexican militia had taken over. The advance guard, under the command of Captain Ventura Lobato, had marched into an ambush set up by a superior force of Texans. Eighteen New Mexicans had died, all of them Taos Indians, and when Armijo learned of the rout, he withdrew his main force. For Taos Pueblo, the defeat was a bitter loss that became the major factor in their participation in the revolt of 1847.[32] The Taos Indians blamed the deaths of their brethren on the Texans, who were Anglo-Americans, and they apparently accepted the Mexican chauvinists' line: All Americans were in collusion with Texans, and Mexicans and Indians shared a common threat from the United States and Texas. By the time of Bent's assassination, Texas, in fact, had become a part of the United States, and Bent's governorship under the aegis of the new regime did not enhance his stature at Taos Pueblo.

When Bent was murdered, no one realized how close the Indians had come to getting revenge on the actual cause of the Cimarron Canyon tragedy: The viciousness of the revolt was due, in part, to Alvarez himself. Just prior to the ambush, Alvarez and Kit Carson had stopped at Bent's Fort on their way east in the fall of 1843, and there met with Bent. Alvarez had unwittingly told St. Vrain that Armijo planned to intercept the caravan at the border. Before long, everyone knew of Armijo's strategy, and some of the company hunters informed Colonel Snively, commander of the Texan troops. Snively put Colonel Warfield in charge of attacking Armijo while he waited with his main force for the Santa Fe–bound caravan. Warfield proved successful when he destroyed Lobato's advance guard on the Cimarron.[33] It was also one instance when Bent's spy system unintentionally backfired, eventually contributing to his death.

The events in Taos heralded further violence. In December and January as many as twenty-four people were killed in the Taos, Arroyo Hondo, and Red River areas alone. Through the following June an estimated 102 Americans and their sympathizers and 318 Mexican and Indian "patriots" were killed or wounded in fighting that spread from Taos through Mora to Las Vegas. The United States had time, equipment, and manpower on its side, and resistance faded.[34] With its passing, another chapter of Alvarez's life came to a close.

Alvarez had been a prominent man in the many conflicting factions of New Mexico during the Mexican years. Able to get along with Mexican *peones,* he had also worked with the highest officials of the two countries of which he was, at different times, considered a citizen. He was trilingual, highly intelligent, and formally educated, yet he apparently drew his greatest strength from his practical experiences as a traveler, trader, trapper, merchant, stock-raiser, and government official. He had influenced all those who had participated in the Santa Fe trade or traveled into New Mexico. Now many new challenges loomed before him.

The arrival of the American army meant change in every facet of New Mexican life, but none more so than in the political arena where the old order changed: No longer would Americans suffer under real or imagined Mexican injustice or capriciousness; no longer would aristocratic families rule with an independence rooted in a tradition of seclusion; no longer would there be a separate and unequal legal standard. Although socially such divisions continued to exist, positions had reversed as Anglo-Americans moved toward the top.

Kearny, a relatively mild conqueror, was careful not to alienate the local populace and promised them many things. He heard that the clergy had spread rumors of American atrocity: No woman would be safe from the ravaging soldiers, nor would anyone's property remain intact. He realized that the local leaders had stressed that the United States was a Protestant nation that would deny Catholicism to New Mexicans. With this in mind, the victorious brigadier general tried to assure the Mexicans through speeches, strict discipline of his own troops, and by making sure that priests and Catholics were counted among his army's ranks. No shots were fired, there was no pillaging, and many local Mexican officials were retained.

That the occupation, prior to the 1847 revolt, went so smoothly can in large part be attributed to the effect of the Santa Fe Trail, for the previous twenty-five years, on both the economy and the culture of New Mexico. Kearny wanted to take advantage of the situation: His proclamations guaranteed respect for persons and property, and he assured Mexicans that they would enjoy the rights of all American citizens. The problem of marauding Indians would be checked, and a new, more just legal system would replace the antiquated

Mexican code. The job of writing a new code was given to Private Willard Preble Hall and Colonel Alexander Doniphan, both Missouri attorneys, and David Waldo was to translate the document from English to Spanish, although Bent later petitioned that Charles (also called Carlos) Beaubien and Alvarez be paid $125 and $500, respectively, "for services rendered in the translation and preparation of the organic and statute laws of the Territory."[35] The resultant body of law incorporated the Hispanic system into that of American jurisprudence, and, if faithfully carried out, it could have been a just system. Unfortunately, complications arose.

The United States was torn over a war that continued to rage, and sectionalist interests guaranteed that people had different ideas on how to handle the conquered territory: Southerners were wary of incorporating a dark-skinned Mexican population into the mainstream of American constitutional protection because it could set a precedent of admitting Indians and, especially, Negroes to the status of full citizenship; northerners pointed to the danger of providing the South with more slaveholding states, thus destroying the precarious balance between slave and free states in the Senate. Indeed, many people questioned the wisdom of keeping areas such as New Mexico. *New York Tribune* editorials pondered the legal aspects of Kearny's activities, querying whether or not New Mexico was part of the United States and, if so, by what legal method. Quoting from the *St. Louis New Era,* the writer questioned what the status of the "mestizoes, mulattoes, half Indians, and barbarous Mexicans" would be. The conclusion was that Kearny's establishment of a code was illegal and that the addition of New Mexico's degraded population would be "a great national misfortune."[36]

Kearny was in trouble in Washington, too. Members of Congress questioned how an army officer could extract an oath of allegiance from a people still at war: Such an act would make the new "Mexican American" a traitor to Mexico. Even more astounding was Kearny's threat to charge with treason any Mexican who became hostile to the occupying force. Such beneficial features of Kearny's code as separation of powers, elections, and guaranteed rights proved to be lost on national legislators, who had trouble getting past Article 1, which organized New Mexico into a territory of the United States and set the stage for Kearny's "organic law."[37] Parodying the newspapers, Congress debated how New Mexico could become a territory when only Congress had the authority to create such an entity and when the United States was still at war with Mexico. Technically, New Mexico was conquered and occupied territory, and, aside from that, any status relative to the United States had to wait until treaties were drawn up at the war's conclusion.

Congress also suspected President Polk and requested him to turn over all papers and correspondence dealing with New Mexico. Part of the administration's reaction to this congressional petition was to increase its correspondence with Kearny, who, of course, felt he had acted within his instructions: He had conquered a territory and done whatever he could to placate its populace. Part of Kearny's problem was Polk's grand design "to take the earliest possession of Upper California," which necessitated quick action by the Army of the West. He had been instructed by Secretary of War Marcy to establish a temporary civil government, using existing government officials.[38] With mounting congressional pressure, the administration had to save face, although Marcy tried to reprimand his general in a mild manner: He wrote that Kearny's laws "go in some few respects beyond the line designated by the President," and Polk could not approve them. Marcy instructed that the provisions of Kearny's code not be carried out; New Mexico could not be regarded as "permanently annexed" while the war continued.[39] New Mexico's politics were left in turmoil and its people in a quandary, while the administration was approaching that of a military state.

Although ending any immediate chance that New Mexico would enjoy a civilian government, the Taos rebellion and the subsequent trials raised serious questions.[40] At stake were human rights as guaranteed under the US Constitution, and Alvarez and others would directly attack military rule and its minuscule regard for civil rights. Unlike California, where civil government took precedence, New Mexico suffered through resistance and a debate over military rule that resulted in the birth of political parties, as well as other rivalries, and engendered chaos. Generally, those people who had benefited from the military formed a party advocating territorial status, which they felt would continue to benefit them. The opposition represented those who in no way benefited from martial law, and this group won the favor of a majority of the Hispanic population as well as the appellation "statehood party" or "Alvarez faction," both of which are somewhat misleading. Although goals and programs were either disguised or nonexistent, and people switched sides constantly, there were some consistencies: Civil leaders of both parties believed, differences notwithstanding, that civilian government was more palatable than the current condition of effective martial law.

A slight but tangible root for the division of opinion was planted before American occupation: personal ambition. Many Anglo-Americans sensed an opportunity for advancement. Such old hands as Joab Houghton were still seeking to solidify political power, while many newcomers found provincial New Mexico an excellent place to begin a political career. Most of those already in the territory received spoils from Kearny's government, and contrary to his instructions, Hispanic names were noticeably lacking. People such as Alvarez, who had labored hard for the US government, received nothing. In reality, there were no state or territorial factions, but groups of individuals who wanted office, power, and influence. Although the primary motive was to replace the military regime, the question of who would replace it was no small concern. Alvarez's statehood stand was secondary to his opposition to territorial government because he saw his opponents as merely advocating the status quo minus the military. Most of the territorialists held influential positions in the military government and had condemned Alvarez and his like as revolutionary and treasonable.[41] The situation soon deteriorated to the point where one observer wrote: "Everybody and everything in this . . . country appears at cross purposes."[42]

Legal and constitutional problems, cultural conflicts, and military rule made New Mexico a place with a troublesome potential. Although military expenditures meant added wealth, improved buildings, and better roads, and the army provided protection, local citizens saw the soldier on an individual level. That meant an image of debauchery[43] that reflected on all Americans. The clash of cultures, despite many evidences of cooperation, continued to simmer, and contemporaries sensed the problem: One person felt himself sitting on top of a volcano boiling with the "savage Indians, the treacherous Mexicans and the outlawed Americans";[44] another recent arrival described the soldiery as having degenerated into a military mob[45] and echoed the charge that appointed officials were corrupt.[46]

Alvarez was familiar with all of this from previous experiences and had demonstrated his success at surviving many-sided feuds. When and where necessary, he had proved adept at taking a stand; now, he would make perhaps his strongest effort and in the process create his legacy. His involvement started quietly enough as a natural outgrowth of his reputation for fair play. Alvarez had always seemed to side with the underdog, and now the disadvantaged came to him: A petition signed by five Spanish-surnamed individuals, asking if he would consider himself a candidate for delegate to the US Congress,[47] cited his demeanor, ability in languages, and compassion. Even ex-governor and old adversary Manuel Armijo confided in Alvarez, first complaining about treatment he was receiving, then seeking advice, and finally asking, almost wistfully, if he would be treated well in the United States.[48] Alvarez enhanced his sense of justice with a sterling intellect. He had read and absorbed as much as any man in New Mexico, and such enlightened concepts as the natural rights of man, the social contract, and republicanism were not foreign to his mind. Included among his notes are quotations from Rousseau, Carlyle, and Alexander Hamilton,[49] and he had found time to write a treatise on the American Revolution, demonstrating his willingness to understand the history and philosophy behind the institutions of his adopted country. He did this even though no one but himself apparently ever saw his letter books.[50]

Alvarez was eminently qualified to lead a fight for the minority party in an occupied territory, and it seems that he was one of the few Spanish-surnamed individuals who had access to the various factions. Made privy to the sufferings and aspirations of the Mexican community, he also, as a longtime successful merchant in the area, was much sought after in business affairs. James L. Collins, a member of the American army and a man who eventually would politically oppose Alvarez, became the Santa Fe merchant's major source of news when, in July 1847, he and the army went south. Collins kept up a running correspondence concerning a debt he owed to Alvarez. When Alvarez graciously allowed Collins to go beyond his due date, the soldier replied that he "shall ever feel grateful"; the next day, Alvarez received another letter from Collins requesting him to handle some business.[51]

Alvarez seems to have been keeping a low political profile,

but the petition for him to become a congressional delegate, two months after Martínez's complaint about Taos justice and immediately after the trials and the Antonio Trujillo affair, must have encouraged him. In September, he and a friend, apparently on request, rode up the Santa Fe River canyon to the lake at its headwaters. They were on their way into the wilderness but also managed to write a report on the availability of water for the city; although their observations agreed with an earlier report compiled by two American engineers, Alvarez and his friend offered some new suggestions, such as a sluice to control water levels in the lake and river. A mild report, with no expressed hostility, it was published in the Spanish section of the *Santa Fe Republican*.[52] However, the act of publication demonstrated some frustration with the new order, perhaps a demonstration that the Spanish-surnamed were equally capable and interested enough to have an active role in shaping the area's future.

Alvarez's gesture was not the first public hint that not all was right. Nine days before, two days after the report was written, the same newspaper had published an editorial that stated in part: "The people of New Mexico should have a Government of some kind which they can see and feel and understand, either military or civil."[53] Obviously, the conglomerate civil-military structure had begun to cause displeasure among Anglo-Americans as well as in the Hispanic community. The newspaper continued to reflect a rising concern over the strengthening hold of the military. Its publisher, Alvarez's correspondent James Collins, was pro–civil government and very much alarmed when it appeared that Colonel Price did not adhere to the Kearny Code.[54] By late October 1847, people had become disturbed enough to hold a rally in the plaza in front of the Palace of the Governors. Consisting mostly of Americans, the gathering underscored even more pointedly the growing dissatisfaction with the military as they listened to pro–civil and anti–military government speeches. Whether Alvarez attended this rally is unknown, but he did attend subsequent meetings.[55]

A week later, the *Republican* published a Santa Fe grand jury report that proved to be a damning criticism of Colonel Price for usurping many of the privileges that were supposed to belong to civil authorities. The jury charged Price with "arrogating" authority in the civil courts; he had become a self-constituted judge and jury in a case that involved "his own private interest." With Joseph Nangle, a newcomer who later became an ally of Alvarez, as foreman, the jury recommended that all collusion between civil and military authorities be avoided.[56] With few exceptions, those who had begun to complain loudest were relative newcomers to New Mexico, mostly those who, like Collins, Nangle, and, later, Richard H. Weightman, had come with the army in 1846. As factions eventually solidified, a "haves-versus–have nots" feud began to develop: Most of the prominent old-timers such as Joab Houghton and Ceran St. Vrain had received jobs under the military regime. Of course, Alvarez qualified as an old-timer, but so far as the army was concerned, he became a "have not." As a sort of unofficial spokesman for a portion of the Mexican population, his stand on the pending problems became important, and, as one reporter later said, he was a man who did not hesitate to let his views be known: He "never allowed his position to be misunderstood, either politically or socially."[57]

Historian Howard Lamar describes the eventual party lines as the conservative, anti-American, predominantly Spanish faction versus the American territorial party, although he blurs the harshness of this division with qualifications: Racism, although in existence, was not the only nor necessarily the main issue, and the conservative party included many Missouri merchants and Benton Democrats who saw home rule as an advantage to their established involvement in the Missouri trade.[58] This rationale stands in direct contrast to the proposition, made earlier, that old-time merchants who had been appointed to territorial offices opposed any threats to their position. Many men, Alvarez among them, with a big stake in the Santa Fe Trail, found themselves, after occupation, with little or no voice in decisions that affected their mercantile interests, and they had been accustomed to more. At the very least, motives for choosing sides varied, with many examples of people switching positions according to individual advantage. Significantly, almost everyone had a growing distaste for military government.

In accordance with the Kearny Code, which stated in part that a general election should be held in August 1847, and that the legislative body "shall convene at the city of Santa Fe on the first Monday in December,"[59] the general assembly met on December 6, 1847. Alvarez sat in the lower house as one of three representatives from Santa Fe County.[60] Probably the major event of the session was Governor Donaciano Vigil's message, given the first day, in which he advised the assembly to devise a code of laws modeled on those of the other states.[61] Further business resulted in the passage of ten resolutions, one of which called for another meeting the following February. The assembly's activities, for the most part, were totally disregarded, partially because of its ethnic makeup: The council, or upper house, consisted solely of Spanish-surnamed individuals while the house, or lower assembly, counted but four and had twenty-one non-Hispanic members. The council consistently rejected laws passed by the house.[62] The public's expectations of results were most likely typified by the American who casually wrote to his father: "Whether their actions will be approved by the General Government is a matter of doubt."[63] In other words, the general assembly, although allowed to meet as a necessary evil, had no authority. The military could and did choose to ignore it, even though Price voiced his approval of its acts.[64] Nevertheless, Alvarez established himself as one of the leaders, playing a prominent role and serving on two committees;

as chairman of the judiciary committee, he reported on bills concerning enclosures, town incorporations, replevin, mortgages, ejectments, and the election of a delegate to Congress.[65] A *Santa Fe Republican* editorial praised him, Houghton, and Missouri lawyer William Z. Angney, who had come to New Mexico as a captain in Kearny's army, as honest and talented men exerting themselves for the future success of the territory while refusing remuneration.[66]

On February 5, 1848, Price abolished a number of government positions, including those of district attorney and territorial secretary. His action no doubt riled the civilian populace, for it spoke of a complete disregard for civil law.[67] The *Santa Fe Republican* had exhaustively discussed New Mexico's annexation,[68] and Price's activities heightened expectations for the convention that was to meet five days later to consider the question. Nevertheless, hopes abated when the meeting adjourned without taking action: The United States, as all now realized, clearly had determined to keep the area as a territory. With or without Colonel Price's actions, the people really had no choice in the matter, and so things remained until ratification of the Treaty of Guadalupe Hidalgo.[69] Although ratified in Mexico on March 10 and in the United States on May 26, it was not until July 19 that people in New Mexico received word of the treaty and the war's official termination. The news added fuel to the fire, for now the New Mexicans had a new justification for opposing Colonel Price: They had become US citizens in American territory. No longer could they be considered wards of an occupied area — this was the constitutional point on which they would base all future moves.

American merchants of New Mexico had complained of excessive taxes for a long time, and, from the efforts to avoid the heavy burden of Mexican customs to the intensive and successful fight to get the Drawback Bill passed, Alvarez had loudly voiced his stand among the businessmen. Just after

the Drawback Bill had given them relief from American duties on goods shipped to Mexico via Santa Fe, the area had
been occupied and the fight resumed. On March 2, 1848,
Colonel Price issued General Order No. 10, which reimposed
import duties, ad valorem, on all goods entering New Mexico.[70] The new military government saw the tax as an excellent form of revenue, but merchants must have seen the
imposition of what they felt were unfair taxes as an injustice.
So long as the war continued, the army ruled and there was
no legal recourse. Less than a month after people learned of
the treaty, a large group of merchants met in the Santa Fe
courthouse. The rift with the military had by this time grown
to irreparable proportions.[71] The men, Alvarez among them,
resolved that the ad valorem duty was unjust "if not in violation of the spirit of the United States Constitution."[72] Two
days later, on Monday, August 8, they met again to finalize
their petition. The meeting was by far the largest formal
protest of the period, and the petition carried eighty-six signatures. William S. Messervy, chairman, nominated a committee of Wethered, Solomon Sublette, Robert T. Brent,
William McKnight, H. Winslow, Asa Estis, and Alvarez to
present a memorial to Colonel Price. In its final state, the
petition claimed that Order No. 10 became illegal on May 26,
1848, when the Guadalupe Hidalgo treaty became effective.
The tax, at 6 percent per annum, they argued, should be null
and void because the "constitution has priority over" general
orders. The merchants said they would resist paying the tax
and would "use all fair, legal and honorable means to resist."
As American citizens residing in a US territory, they were
entitled to protection under the Constitution that "expressly
guarantees free commerce." Would Colonel Price, they inquired, relieve them of Order No. 10?[73]

Unlike the earlier, elected general assembly, which made
pretensions of a mixture of people, the antitax meeting ex-
cluded Mexicans. On the list of merchants who signed the

petition, every name of any importance is included — but only one man had a Spanish name: Alvarez, who by his attendance again demonstrated his ability to straddle the cultural fence as well as his importance as an advocate for the Mexican cause. There were many Hispanic merchants in Santa Fe and the tax had equally disconcerted them when it passed unanimously. By now some emotion could be noticed, for opposing factions had aligned along vague racial lines.

The local populace had been alternately disappointed and encouraged in their stand on the question of legality of military rule. Senator John M. Clayton of Missouri had introduced a bill for territorial governments in Oregon, California, and New Mexico; although it passed the Senate, it failed in the House. Somewhat discouraged, Clayton's colleague from Missouri, Thomas Hart Benton, advised New Mexicans to meet in convention and establish their own government because Congress refused to act for them. Local division became evident when the convention met at the request of Governor Vigil, who sought to implement Benton's ideas.[74] Sitting in Santa Fe on October 10, 1848, the meeting quickly lapsed into disarray with overtones of racial discord. Although it was clear that many people felt the Guadalupe Hidalgo treaty should have ended military government in New Mexico,[75] there were deeper immediate problems, for a group of the meeting's members, described as mostly Mexican, angrily walked out. James Collins, too, who apparently led the conservative faction's fight for home rule, did not stay for the final days, and his name does not appear on the petition sent to Congress.[76] Alvarez is a mystery figure; his name is not on the petition and his presence at the meeting cannot be established.[77]

Feeling ran high, factionalism developed, and partisans clashed. Apparently to demonstrate cohesiveness, the remaining delegates elected Padre Martínez the convention president and a racially mixed committee to report to Congress. The committee worked out a bilingual memorial in which they asked for a territorial government, "purely civil in character." They also noted their acceptance of a slightly revised Kearny Code, asking that the president fill enumerated offices and give them the right to appeal. The memorial protested Texas's attempts at "dismemberment," demanded protection from Congress "against the introduction of slavery," and requested a local legislature and a delegate to the US Congress. Citing the area's population as well as the liberality of their proposals, they signed the memorial and resolved to forward copies to Senators Benton and Clayton. Of the thirteen men who unanimously passed and endorsed the document, eight had Spanish surnames, including Martínez and Donaciano Vigil.[78]

The memorial immediately embroiled New Mexico in national politics when introduced into Congress: The South opposed the proposal because of its antislavery statement; Texas insisted upon its border claims; and Congress, caught up in the sectionalism issue, did not act.[79] New Mexicans had suffered under military rule, been ignored by Congress, and been encouraged to seek home rule by prominent figures. The time seemed ripe for change, and men began to jockey for influential positions. Naturally, Manuel Alvarez found himself in the thick of it all.

7

Politico and Politics

The new military commander in 1849, John Macrae Washington, might have felt the same kind of apprehension that his soldier brethren had felt in the seventeenth century. He was charged with the not so congenial duty of combining the dual authority of military and civil government while winning support from the local populace, a difficult job not made easier by his unfamiliarity with the region and its people. New Mexicans had always handled their own affairs: Had they not disposed of Albino Pérez in 1837; and was not the 1847 Taos Revolt a resistance to foreign rule? Colonel Washington arrived at his new command at the inopportune time when factions were hardening. All sides resented his authority, which was burdened by Price's legacy and hampered by vague instructions: Until Congress provided for a territorial government, the military was to "protect the inhabitants of the Territory of New Mexico in the full enjoyment of life, liberty and property."[1] Did this mean that he was to establish a temporary civil government? Although Colonel Washington did not suffer from open hostility, the climate was explosive.

Fortunately, the opportunity for change remained in the political arena where such men as Alvarez were forming alliances. The old merchant and his friends received a great boost from the new president, Zachary Taylor, who came out strongly for statehood on the premise that New Mexicans could best handle New Mexican problems. Along with the sentiments of Benton and Clayton, the president's sentiment added fuel to the move for home rule,[2] but Taylor went further, appointing Georgian James S. Calhoun US Indian agent on April 3, 1849. Calhoun arrived in Santa Fe on July 22, 1849, shrouded in mystery;[3] as an emissary from the president, he — it was rumored — had orders to encourage a statehood movement. Almost all subsequent accounts agree that the Georgian carried secret instructions, which were apparently divulged only to William Watts Hart Davis, the man who would eventually succeed him as territorial governor.[4] Meanwhile, Calhoun dutifully met with leading citizens and, not surprisingly, found some support.

Sometime in 1849, the conservative, local-rule statehood party became known as the "Alvarez faction." Because of his influence in the Hispanic community, Alvarez had been approached by the American advocates of local rule, and Calhoun quickly became an ally. Their ideas were not incompatible, and perhaps, as one historian asserts, the always astute Alvarez sensed a chance for office.[5] That summer, Major Benjamin Beall, acting for the absent Colonel Washington, issued a proclamation for the people to elect a full convention of delegates to consider the problem of a civil government. The elections and events that followed demonstrate that those advocating local rule made up a distinct minority. The convention's success, from a territorial point of view, suggested, at the very least, that the military authorities, territorial officials, and a few local officials had allied to use their current upper hand in an effort to end any statehood movement.[6] The territorialists hoped to convince the statehood advocates to give up by making them realize they had only a small following.

James S. Calhoun, Indian agent and governor of the Territory of New Mexico (1851–1852), an ally and friend of Alvarez. *Courtesy of the Museum of New Mexico, Santa Fe. MNM 7835.*

The convention met on Monday, September 24, 1849, in
Santa Fe. Nineteen delegates attended, including Alvarez,
who once again represented Santa Fe County. In a demonstration of things to come, no less than seven of the delegates
had held office under Kearny, among them a man who was
fast becoming Alvarez's foe, Joab Houghton.[7] Padre Martínez
was elected president of the convention, and later voting
reflected the trend followed throughout: On the vote for pro-
cedure, the local-rule faction was voted down, Alvarez being
one of six polling for the losers. The second vote more pointedly reiterated the first when Hugh N. Smith, a territorial
advocate, collected fifteen votes to become the convention's
choice for delegate to Congress. Through these first votes, the
Santa Fe delegation of Alvarez, Doctor E. Vandry Derion, and
William Z. Angney voted together. In opposing Smith, they
cast the only votes for second-place finisher Richard Weightman. Weightman had a strong political ambition and would
become a leader in the Alvarez faction.[8] The next vote, on
another procedural matter, once again saw Alvarez and his
colleagues voted down; the opposition demonstrated their
consistency with their customary fifteen votes. However, the
Santa Fe delegation had added the vote of Joseph Nangle,
who then became the minority's spokesman serving on a
constitutional committee that introduced a territorial document. Nangle gave a minority report that argued for the
formation of a state government if the majority proposition
proved infeasible.[9]

During the evening session on the third day, the majority
report, with appended instructions for the delegate to Congress, was moved for adoption, but Nangle moved that it be
considered section by section. Nangle's motion carried, thus
giving the Alvarez faction an opening: Of the subsequent
changes, over half were initiated by Alvarez's ally William
Angney.[10] The whole of the proceedings did not meet with the
approval of Colonel Washington, who returned to Santa Fe a

couple of weeks after the convention, "for he refused to recognize the results."[11] The military commander's rejection, plus the eventual negative treatment that delegate Hugh Smith received in Washington, could only have discouraged the territorialists. Despite the dominance of the forces led by Houghton, the Alvarez faction had laid down the gauntlet and come out with a minor, if yet unnoticed, victory: The convention had allowed the territorialists to sell their program and lose.

It did not take long for the rift to open for public scrutiny. New Mexico's problems deepened, and the local-rule forces, spurred by a new impetus, began to get their message into the press. The *New Mexican* had editorialized on November 24, the convention's first day, that Congress would not act because of the slavery issue; on the other hand, Californians and the Mormons had begun to act on their own, and New Mexicans, too, "must form ourselves into a State Government."[12] A couple of weeks later, Alvarez and his friends, including Weightman, Calhoun, Angney, and Messervy, published an address to the people: Their message started with the "desire to throw off the slavish manacles" forced upon them by the military and concluded that the "illusory" remedy of a territorial government would not serve the purpose. Territorial status would mean a government run by outsiders, picked by outsiders: How, the writers asked, was that different from the current government? The settlement of grants of public lands and the ad valorem tax continued to irritate[13] and could not be disregarded. The choice was between oblivion and degradation or statehood. New Mexico could not sit back and permit Congress to allow others to make claims on its territory for the sake of preserving the Union. Smith had been snubbed, and why? — because he did not represent a sovereign state. Nothing could stop such injustices to New Mexico but statehood, for then New Mexico would have representation in both national houses. Alvarez's name appeared at the top of a list of fifteen other supporting names,[14] and an editorial endorsement of the address immediately followed.

Two days later, however, another address appeared, repudiating the first and designed to demonstrate statehood's minority status. Over sixty men endorsed the territorial view.[15] His faction obviously at a numerical disadvantage, Alvarez reputedly started publishing a paper called the *Santa Fe Gazette,* a wholly political organ that hammered on New Mexico's delegate, Hugh Smith.[16] Smith, however, did not need a newspaper to change his mind: His report to Congress had been defeated out of committee and he had not helped matters by attacking slavery; finally, the House refused him a seat. Realizing the significance of such a caustic reception, Smith gave up territorial advocacy in April 1850. In fact, he took the Benton, or local-rule, point of view, advising New Mexicans that they, "for the present, rely upon" themselves and assert their "rights by the establishment of a state government."[17]

Meanwhile, another incident occurred that vividly illustrated the long-simmering abhorrence of the military. As Indian agent, Calhoun had been very active, even though he seemed to meet resistance from the army at every turn and complained almost daily of its inability to provide protection over much of the sprawling Southwest. His arguments were given credence by the White party massacre at the Point of the Rocks, near present-day Clayton, New Mexico. Pueblo Indians added to the sanguine accounts by reporting that White's wife, daughter, and, possibly, female servant had been taken captive. Either because he had lost all confidence in the army or because the commander refused to help, Calhoun decided to send out a Mexican trader who was "daring, fearless, and withal a discrete man."[18] A cash reward of $1,000 for the rescue of the captives had been raised through the contributions of Calhoun, Alvarez, François Aubry, and

Messervy, but in the end, none were rescued and all died. In a letter to Colonel William Medill, the commissioner of Indian affairs, Calhoun explained his disgust with the new military commander, Colonel John Munroe, who apparently felt he did not have enough information to act. Many people shared Calhoun's sentiments, placing at least part of the blame on the army's sloth.

The political front heated up, too. Richard Weightman publicly accused Joab Houghton, appointed to the bench by Kearny, of unethical conduct and incompetency — charges that have been confirmed — and Weightman was behind a formal request to Houghton asking that he resign, signed by eight attorneys. Copies were distributed to other judges.[19] Citing the petitioners' jaundiced view of the public interest, Houghton accused them of "private and selfish" motives that would effect a "radical change of government and judiciary."[20] He also quickly fingered Weightman as his adversary, and the two men met in a duel. Fortunately, neither was hurt, for when the command to fire was given, the partially deaf Houghton did not hear it but managed to duck Weightman's shot; the seconds prevented Houghton from firing. Weightman, a relative newcomer, seems to have been a caustic personality given to violence; a few years later he killed a friend and partner of Alvarez in a barroom disagreement.[21]

That Weightman's ambitions alienated some local-rule proponents is conjecture, but at this time the faction lost a valuable ally who at one time had been its spokesman: James Collins switched sides, and with him went his newspaper. Later, as editor of the *Santa Fe Weekly Gazette,* Collins vented his wrath on Weightman, who, he wrote, "seems extremely anxious that the world should know he is a very remarkable man" but used the method of ungentlemanly attacks.[22] Collins believed Weightman to be both overly ambitious and a Texas agent, and wrote a pamphlet in which he condemned Weightman for his violent accusations.[23] Such

prolonged personal vendettas reflected on Alvarez by association; between individual adversaries, the personal enmities
continued after the Spaniard's death.

Beyond the desire that the statehood position should have
an unfailing voice, Collins's defection to Houghton's camp
appears to be another reason for Alvarez to start a newspaper. Alvarez had published in the medium and knew something of its technical operation; one paper had earlier
publicly praised him for the interest he manifested in the
"welfare of this territory" and for his efforts on its own behalf:
"Were it not for the assistance of this gentleman," it would
hardly have been able to continue to operate.[24] Alvarez's
tenure as an editor, however, lasted less than a month. It
appears that the press he had been using somehow came into
the possession of the opposing faction, and by July 1850, he
and his colleagues were in the market for a new printing
press, a prized item on the frontier. At the time, the loss of the
newspaper must have seemed a devastating handicap, or so
it was hoped by one observer, who used the situation to
advance the territorial party's ascendancy.[25] Undaunted, Alvarez and his friends immediately started raising money. On
July 16, Alvarez's name appeared on top of a subscription list
"for the purpose of purchasing a printing establishment to be
brought from the U.S."[26] Everyone on the list, including Angney and José Manuel Gallegos, a future delegate to Congress, pledged $100. Apparently they were successful,
because Alvarez authorized Weightman to draw on him for
$1,500 for the purchase.[27] Weightman, who had gone to St.
Louis, found a press for $700, including both job and accentu-
ated type. More good news for Alvarez was that Weightman
did not draw on his account but arranged with Messervy to
get the money from Santa Fe. The only problems were a
six-month shipping delay[28] and the presence of President
Taylor's new emissary to New Mexico.

Like his predecessor Calhoun, Colonel George A. McCall

had special orders to help stimulate the statehood movement. In November 1849, he had received the details of his mission from the secretary of war, who had explained that the military had been left in command because of congressional "omission." The "embarrassment" needed to be remedied and the people of the territory agreed; McCall should not "thwart but advance" the wishes of the people to organize their own government.[29] McCall had arrived in Santa Fe on March 11, 1850, and had gone to work, executing his plan while fulfilling his instructions that he immediately meet with the area's leading citizens. Sensing that the local-rule faction was very much in the minority, and applying pressure on the military to side with him by virtue of his presidential mandate, McCall apparently decided he would be more successful working with the territorial people.

Certain that the president wanted a movement for statehood, McCall tried initially to convince everyone to join together. The local-rule proponents refused to compromise, but he persuaded Houghton and Vigil, who were busy trying to be noncommittal, that they should lead a new movement for statehood, thus stealing the thunder of the weak Alvarez faction. In light of Hugh Smith's treatment and advice, the failure of Congress to act on New Mexico's petition, and Taylor's apparent stand, Houghton acquiesced and transformed the territorial faction into avid statehood proponents.[30] The presence in Santa Fe of a Texan minister trying to organize that ancient city into a seat for a Texas county proved a bit too much for New Mexicans. Texas's audacity in pushing its border claims posed a real threat, and the common foe proved enough to bind the two opposing camps. Texas and McCall applied enough pressure to get everyone working together a mere three weeks after the colonel's arrival.

On April 13, Houghton and some friends called for a meeting, to be held the following week, to endeavor to draft resolutions for statehood. In actuality, the meeting consisted of old territorialists, who asked Colonel John Munroe, the military commander, to arrange a constitutional convention. Simultaneously, McCall cited the president's wishes to the commander. Munroe complied by calling an election to be held on May 6; delegates would assemble on May 15 and draft a state constitution.[31] The whole process, up to the election, was remarkably devoid of the Alvarez faction. McCall apparently chose to ignore Weightman and company, possibly because they appeared to be so much in the minority or because, as a military man, he was simply more inclined to work with the army and its allies. As soon as the territorialists had become convinced of McCall's plan to seize the statehood banner from the local-rule people, their alliance was won.

The Alvarez faction had immediately expressed its concern about the apparent plot to usurp them, and they had surmised correctly, for Houghton and company had sensed their new strength. Territorialists swept the elections and, during a ten-day convention, passed a prewritten constitution that Houghton was widely suspected of authoring, declaring in favor of a free state in an emphatic stand against slavery (a reaction to Texas's proslavery stand) and subordinating the military to a civil government. While the local-rule advocates charged a "fix" between the territorialists and Colonel Munroe, the victors published a *cédula* (document) calling for election of officers for the new state government and, at the same time, a referendum on the proposed constitution. Convinced of his friends' strong position, Munroe agreed that an election should be held on June 20. The legislature could meet July 1 with the understanding that the government was inoperative until New Mexico was admitted as a state.[32]

Even with this reminder, Munroe and his allies, including George McCall, went into the interim twenty-four-day campaign with seemingly unbridled confidence, nominating

Henry Connelly for governor, Ceran St. Vrain for lieutenant governor, and Hugh N. Smith for congressman (Houghton apparently was held in reserve to be appointed to the Senate). The old territorialists so far had been successful in their strategy of taking up the statehood banner, and a natural result, so they thought, would be winning over the Hispanic population. Even McCall allowed himself to become convinced that they would prove victorious. Nevertheless, Alvarez and his friends had a keen judgment about New Mexican politics and were held in deeper respect among the Hispanic population than anyone gave them credit for.

Realizing the importance of the Hispanics' superior numbers, the Alvarez faction took an immediate advantage by running two Spanish-surnamed candidates opposite Connelly and St. Vrain. Tomás Cabeza de Baca ran for governor and Alvarez for the second slot; old local-rule stalwart William Messervy was picked to oppose Smith. The Alvarez faction immediately went on the offensive as a unified voice denouncing the military administration and pointing out the close connection of their opponents to that maligned government. The argument was simple and logical: the people versus corruption, deception, repressive authority, and bad administration. Territorialists were culpable because of their alliances with the military, federal judges, and prefects who received the backing of that group's newspapers. Alvarez and his colleagues went after the Hispanic, Pueblo Indian, and Catholic vote in an intense campaign.[33]

While both sides worked to fulfil their respective ambitions, all was predicated on the passage of the proposed state constitution. The Texan threat still lingered, and though the presence of agents in Santa Fe and troops in El Paso bolstered the promise of the US president that he would meet Texan border-jumping with the army, the status quo held. The two parties felt that they had to present a united front to illustrate their desire to be their own rulers, and passage of a state constitution would be a perfect demonstration of solidarity. Thus backed, the constitutional mandate was overwhelmingly favored. The electorate endorsed the state constitution by an incredible 8,371 to thirty-nine votes. This, along with his commander in chief's wrath, convinced Munroe to persuade Major Robert S. Neighbors and his Texan commissioners to leave the territory.[34] A complementary goal that in the long run was more important to everyone was to get congressional action. Although Congress had ignored or skirted the issue of statehood for good reason — sectionalism and slavery were threatening the Union — New Mexicans saw such avoidance as a transgression of their rights because they were left with a legally questionable military regime. Maybe a new tactic, in which everyone involved showed unbounded enthusiasm, would move Congress; their representative could point out that New Mexicans were "almost unanimous" in their wish for statehood and that this unanimity was demonstrated by the union of the two parties to achieve congressional action.[35]

The real shock on election day, June 20, 1850, was the resounding victory of the statehood party. Of the three major offices, the Alvarez faction lost only the governorship, and that was a hollow territorialist victory because the winner, Connelly, never set foot in New Mexico for the duration of his term. From back East, he summarily fulfilled his duty by reporting to the president on the state of affairs in New Mexico.[36] The task of chief of state thus fell to the newly elected lieutenant governor: As titular head of the statehood proponents, Manuel Alvarez now actively served as their political leader. In the other races, Messervy became the congressional delegate with his victory over Hugh Smith, and on the local scene the Alvarez faction completely reversed the makeup of the last convention in which the Houghton party had prevailed.[37] Calhoun was delirious with pleasure: the irony, that the party to whom Munroe had allied himself submitted to defeat while the party that had originated the statehood movement embraced victory![38]

Taylor's other agent did not enjoy such happiness, for McCall had totally sided with the losers. In fact, his anti-Alvarez stand caused him to meddle in local affairs: When the new legislature met in July, he backed a plan for all the territorialists to walk out in an attempt to disturb the proceedings. When that tactic failed, McCall switched to a more brazen plan and, in doing so, showed a motive for his distaste of the Alvarez faction. Offended by Alvarez's decision to be an active leader and by his appointment of various allies to state positions, McCall claimed the lieutenant governor handed out offices "without regard to capacity" and tried to undermine the respected old trader by attempting to convince a group of Alvarez's supporters to change their allegiance. He discovered the kind of loyalty Alvarez had built up over the years, but McCall was one who could attribute his failure to the bigoted opinion that Alvarez's followers, "like all Mexicans, easily turned around in their opinions and feelings" (that this could better serve as self-description seems to have escaped him). Such people, he continued, are "led by the nose and used as tools by men like Alvarez."[39]

Although McCall and many others of the Houghton group would have liked to disbelieve it, Alvarez and his colleagues were as literate and, perhaps more important, as determined as anyone in New Mexico. Alvarez's decision to function as a true governmental leader should not have surprised anyone; he had always acted when he felt it justified. Recognized by neither Mexico nor the United States, he nevertheless had diligently pursued his diplomatic activities throughout his tumultuous career as consul. Now, as an acting governor, his intellect had even more justification for pursuing the legitimacy of the new state government while openly flouting Colonel Munroe and his military regime. Alvarez left no doubts about his dedication and intent when he made his inaugural

address and listed some of the territory's problems, number-
ing them one through five: hostile Indians; the loss of legiti-
mately owned property to the "acts of evil doers who live
among us and . . . prey upon our rights and property"; a
prevalence of gambling; corruption and lack of professionalism in the judiciary; and "disuse of the vagrant law allowing"
the criminal element to take advantage of the innocent — all
this in direct condemnation of unkept promises. He then
made some recommendations, including reorganizing the ju-
dicial system as well as allowing the Pueblo Indians to decide
for themselves whether or not they wished to partake in the
US government. If the Indians did not choose that course,
they should be allowed to live "secure . . . in all their ancient
rights and privileges and their internal" governmental sys-
tems. Even more important than more stringent laws, he
proclaimed that the "noblest gift of this newly organized state
to her people would be the establishment of a sound and
economical system of common schools."

Alvarez felt that the events that had led to the new
government's formation were positive: "Confirming in the
people the choice of their public officers is to extend the
sphere of democratic liberty to fix in the servant a just ac-
countability and to beget a wholesome spirit of popular zeal
and patriotic emulation."[40] He reiterated his party's justification for a state government: People had had to endure the
evils of a half-civil, half-military government while their petitions were ignored by Congress. The people of New Mexico,
on whose behalf he felt that he spoke, had always had one
policy: consent. They had given this to the military regime
and, thus, could and did take it away. This was especially
applicable at the termination of the Mexican War because
extension of military rule left New Mexicans in the "strange
position" of being independent people, residing within the
United States yet without a free government. The will of such
people is a sovereign guide that, in a peaceful manner and

reasonable way, is the ruling power and the dominant law. He stressed that recent events, such as the constitutional convention and the elections, had formed the current government and thus legitimized it in all its acts. Alvarez then switched to a more personal note in his address and mandated the respective legislators to act with zeal for the "public will" and, with "ardent patriotism," "reform the abuses that have for a long time existed." Judging by his personal acquaintances sitting in the august body, he knew they would act with prudence and wisdom. He closed with his own commitment to "take part eagerly."[41]

Alvarez's stand put Munroe in a difficult position. Up until the state constitution was adopted and the recently elected officials tried to conduct their duties, the commander had cooperated. Now, however — with an attitude completely at variance to the wishes of his district's people, as well as to that adopted by his counterpart in California — Munroe felt it his duty to deny any authority to elected state officials. Alvarez knew of the events in California and seems to have used that territory as an example for New Mexico; but the similarities ended when Munroe refused to acquiesce, arguing that the postelection proceedings were entirely extralegal and without congressional approval. He could not recognize Alvarez's attempts to put the government into full operating force.[42] How Munroe might have reacted had his party won the elections is conjecture. Nevertheless, he gave one reason for his opposition to Alvarez and the rest of the statehood advocates: He felt the Mexican character was unstable and the people were ignorant. Not only that, they also manifested a dislike for Americans. Munroe's opinion was not unlike McCall's.[43]

Munroe and Alvarez did not hesitate to address each other directly. Munroe dispatched a letter to Alvarez, reminding the acting governor that all was to remain inoperative until Congress should act, as per Munroe's previous pronouncements, and that the current actions of the state legislature appeared to have as an obvious goal subverting the military government. Such actions, he continued, could only be deemed treason. And how did Munroe know of the actions that the government wished to carry out? Alvarez had told him in fulfillment of a voluntary promise to inform Munroe of any important steps he planned to take.[44] In his reply dated the next day, Alvarez listed answers to Munroe's objections. The acting governor cited, among other things, the people's "undoubted right" to form their own government, with or without the commander's permission, because the people's wishes are the highest authority. He did not deny Congress's right to legislate over the state or territory of New Mexico, as Munroe had asserted in an earlier communication. However, Congress had done nothing and, he stressed, "has not declared us a territory, nor extended over us the laws of the United States."[45]

A determined — his opponents would say stubborn — man, Alvarez persisted, and the legislature cooperated. Almost immediately they passed an act aimed at destroying the strength of their opponents. The new law required an election of all prefects and alcaldes on August 15. Munroe protested loudly, instructing the public and his officials not to recognize the illegal act. Undoubtedly at Munroe's request, Donaciano Vigil also sent out a circular, written in Spanish, to all the county prefects, reiterating Munroe's reasoning that the state government had no legal basis for holding elections — or for doing anything else — until New Mexico had been admitted into the Union by Congress. Until then, he continued, the present government headed by Munroe should continue, and the prefects should ignore Alvarez's call for elections because it or any future, similar act was null and void. Only John Munroe had authority to institute elections.[46] If any of Alvarez's nominees tried to take their positions, Vigil would consider such attempts violations of their duties as citizens of the United States.

Federal appointee James S. Calhoun commented that Munroe was trying to impose his own people on the populace after they had adopted the new government at a constitutional convention and election Munroe himself had called. A feud had developed between the commander and Alvarez, and "the minority [Munroe] charge the majority with revolutionary and treasonable designs, a charge that I do not think can be dignified as a hallucination."[47] Munroe's determination to call the state government's activities unwarranted and revolutionary brought a quick response from Alvarez, who cited President Polk's 1848 inaugural address in which he called the military regimes of occupied territories "de facto governments" that existed "by the presumed consent" of the inhabitants. He bolstered his point with quotations from Polk again, and from the secretary of war, who had stated that military regulations established during the war "were superseded by the return to peace."[48]

Both men had good arguments to support their respective views: Munroe, a more legalistic technical view; Alvarez, a philosophical answer. The former felt that congressional action had to initiate any legitimate government, and the latter argued that the people's mandate was good enough, at least until Congress should refuse to sanction the territorial institutions, and at least one historian felt that Munroe and Alvarez were about to lead their followers into a violent conflict over the issue.[49] However, both men had enough common sense to avoid violence, and thus they compromised. Rather than interfere, Munroe asked his prefects neither to aid nor to hinder — in other words ignore — the elections. For his part, Alvarez wrote on August 8 that elected officials should not attempt to take any authority under the state government until November 1, 1850, or when commissioned to do so.[50] The acting governor had received a lukewarm response from his own people in pressing the matter —

Tomás Cabeza de Baca, unsuccessful candidate for governor, at once endorsed the proposed election and questioned its legality[51] — and the issue was of too minor a consequence to press in the face of violence that might ruin everything. This was nothing new; Alvarez had lived a life of such maneuvering — in New Mexico it was a means of existence. The proposed elections never occurred, the goal of replacing appointed county officials was never achieved, and Alvarez and Munroe — despite their compromise — never agreed on their respective legitimate authority.

On July 15, the New Mexican Senate and House of Representatives passed a joint resolution reiterating Alvarez's stand, stating that the military regime had become null and void because the present state government rested on higher authority than Munroe's. The "indisputable right of the people," in absence of congressional action, superseded "the right of exercising any civil function" by the commander of the Ninth Military Department. The two bodies of the legislature added their complete approval of Alvarez's communications to Munroe and of the vice-governor's intent "to establish and maintain in operation" the recently organized government.[52] The legislature maintained its mandate, selecting Richard Weightman and Major Francis A. Cunningham as senators.

Weightman, especially, took a strong stand in Alvarez's and statehood's support. His initial task was to take a sheaf of papers to the powers in Washington, including the legislature's joint resolution, Alvarez's inaugural address and a message, and the senator's own message. All this was delivered to the president and vice-president,[53] but Weightman's efforts met disappointment partly because President Taylor died before the newly proposed senator could see him. The president's death bode ill for Alvarez's efforts, and Weightman knew it: "I receive very little to encourage me in the prospect of New Mexico being admitted."[54] Millard Fillmore did not have his predecessor's sympathy for New Mexico's statehood efforts. Indeed, Clay's famous compromise had won presidential as well as congressional backing, and statehood met a resounding defeat in a vote called by Senator William Seward. It was abandoned in a series of votes that have come to be known as the Compromise of 1850.[55]

New Mexico did not officially become a territory until the Texas legislature voted acceptance of a congressional border proposal and received a US government payment of $10 million in return for giving up claims to territory up to the Río Grande. The delay coincided with the end of the current congressional session and the beginning of the next, and with renewed vigor, Weightman suggested a new strategy: If Alvarez could arrange another referendum wherein the New Mexican people overwhelmingly demonstrated their preference for statehood, the aspiring senator felt sure Congress would acquiesce.[56] In addition, Congress had to be made aware of the unjust military regimes under which the people of New Mexico suffered, and Colonel Munroe's activities would be an excellent illustration. When Munroe had complained to Secretary of War Charles M. Conrad, the secretary sided with Alvarez and instructed his commander to refrain from all interference in civil affairs.[57] Neither the president nor Conrad would entertain Munroe's charge of treason; indeed, Washington seemed to believe that all the problems stemmed from Munroe: "The opinion is," Weightman wrote to Alvarez, "that Munroe the *Anglo-American* in his correspondence with you sir, has suffered at the hands of the *Anglo-Mexican*."[58] With Munroe in disfavor and receiving instructions not to interfere, the state government had an opportunity really to operate and possibly even completely oust the military government "if only for a month."[59]

With Alvarez keeping him informed of local activities, Weightman did everything he could to agitate on behalf of statehood. Although Weightman informed Alvarez that a territorial government was being formed, he kept up his plan relative to the military, and Munroe, who had no intention of quitting the fight, played right into his hands by disobeying his instructions and not cooperating with the Indian agent Calhoun. He would not give up the "governor's house" until the presidential appointee — Calhoun — eventually took over as territorial governor.[60] Meanwhile, Weightman stayed in Washington, using every opportunity to report Munroe's misbehavior. He finally received a letter from Secretary of War Conrad that at once denied Weightman's allegations that Munroe had violated his instructions and announced that the colonel had been relieved. Any acts of interference, he stressed, with civil and political affairs subsequent to his orders of September 10, would be investigated.[61]

Congress had decided to act on the resolution of the 1849 New Mexico Convention, and with mixed feelings, Alvarez accepted the fact that New Mexico would become a territory. Possibly because he had a sense of the situation's reality, he had never followed up on Weightman's call for a second referendum. The Compromise of 1850 was much too big an event for New Mexico to fight, and within the national picture, the new territory mattered very little. Indeed, Daniel Webster, the new secretary of state as of August 1, 1850, was one of many Washington officials who felt the area worthless and the people not much better. Webster's New England provincialism was well known and probably kept him from his coveted goal, the presidency of the United States.[62]

Although the various factions in New Mexico took up seemingly different causes, their motives seem twofold: All saw the pending decline of military authority and, indeed, sought to hasten that trend; given that premise, each side desired to secure its own positions in whatever government replaced the army. To this end, the combination of Alvarez in Santa Fe and Weightman in Washington proved somewhat beneficial. No words were more telling than those Weightman wrote to Alvarez when he said that he was taking "such care of my friends as I may be able." Primary goals were the offices of governor, secretary of state, and federal marshal, and seats in the judiciary. It appeared that Calhoun would be governor and Alvarez secretary — "certain, I think."[63] Although Alvarez never actively took part in the campaign to make him secretary of the territory, the fight to have the old Spaniard appointed plunged him into a debate that carried from Capitol Hill to Santa Fe's plaza.

There were many reasons why Alvarez should have received the appointment. Friends pointed out that he was "peculiarly fitted" as well as the people's choice for the job. Actually, demonstrating a lack of coordination, David Waldo recommended Alvarez for governor on the basis of his experience, intellect, honesty, and popularity, and also as a man whose feelings are in tune with those of New Mexico.[64] Waldo was a little late with his recommendation. Calhoun had already been put forth for the governor's position and his candidacy proved no problem. For one reason, the position included the duties of Indian agent, a job he already held, and he thus brought experience and the promise of a smooth transition to the top office in a new government. Calhoun had proved himself a staunch local-rule advocate and his appointment pleased Alvarez's group. Diego Archuleta, a key Mexican leader, asked Alvarez to express his and his friends' congratulations to Calhoun.[65]

The second position, however, became a competitive focal point, and Alvarez's prospects looked bleak. He had been treated with a still-inexplicable lack of gratitude in 1846, and this time his activities in opposition to the military and in favor of home rule could give the federal authorities reason to ignore him. It seemed the Spaniard's conscience always brought him into dispute with authority, be it Mexican or American. In addition, as secretary of state, Daniel Webster would handle all territorial appointments, at least on paper, and Webster would hardly have forgotten the letters and audacity of the vibrant consul. Receiving some credit for Clay's compromises while championing nationalism would only direct him away from seeing New Mexico's problems from Alvarez's point of view. All in all, the new secretary was not one of the best officials to go to for procuring Alvarez's appointment. So far as Webster was concerned, the primary candidates had to be Hugh Smith, ex–territorial delegate, and William S. Allen, who had been considered for the same position in Utah.[66]

Weightman, like Waldo, did his best to influence the officials in favor of Alvarez, but he apparently believed that his old political opponent, Hugh Smith, presented Alvarez's only opposition, for he concentrated solely on defeating that candidate. Early in December, Weightman and Messervy recommended Alvarez to the president. Not to be outdone, the opposition started spreading false information that Alvarez's political affiliation could best be described as that of a "loco foco": a Whig with democratic tendencies. The *Louisville Courier* and *St. Louis Republican* both cast doubts on Alvarez's loyalty to the Fillmore administration by indirectly labeling him a loco foco, and the *Republican* additionally campaigned for Smith, a native of St. Louis.[67] The ensuing battle lasted three months. Weightman's and Messervy's arguments reasoned the advantages of appointing their friend: He had both the people's confidence and a record demonstrating his concern to do a good job. Weightman echoed David Waldo by insinuating that Alvarez's appointment would give the Mexican population, in their gratitude, a good reason for joining the Whig party. Although Alvarez seems to have given no indication of his political preferences, others were making grandiose claims.[68]

On the last day of December, Weightman dashed off a letter to the president and secretary of state. In direct answer to Houghton and others who had decided to countermand Weightman and Messervy by relocating in Washington, he stressed that Alvarez's activities in New Mexico had indeed made political enemies. However, he pointed out, at no time had the opposition attempted in any way to undermine Alvarez's "honor and high character"[69] — in spite of the use of the derogatory term *gachupín* (native Spaniard), used both to stress Alvarez's foreign origins and as an attempt — which failed — to turn the Mexican population against him. All correspondence, pro- and anti-Alvarez, ended at Webster's desk. The subject of Alvarez's nationality and the accompanying implication that he was not an American citizen may have struck a responsive chord with the aging, ailing secretary of state, whose previous encounter with the Spaniard had ended on such a note.

By January, Calhoun had been confirmed as governor, and Smith's name had been put before the Senate. Weightman still felt Alvarez would get the appointment because Calhoun's friends were working for Alvarez and against Smith. Back in New Mexico, Father José Manuel Gallegos was suggesting that "we organize . . . correspondence so that our friends" receive positions in the government. He later added that "the works of the enemy will remain confirmed in depression" and expressed his sentiments in favor of Alvarez's appointment and for statehood.[70] In Washington, Weightman carried on a virtual one-man campaign. He took his argument directly to Webster when, during a private audience with the legendary man on the morning of January 18, he asked the secretary to replace Smith's nomination with Alvarez's. This meeting was followed by a scathing written attack on Smith, plus the reiteration that Messervy, "the Representative elected by the people of New Mexico," concurred in Alvarez's nomination.[71] Alvarez apparently complained about some of the exaggerated things his friends had claimed while in the heat of campaigning. Weightman stressed that there was no secrecy involved, the motive for his actions being his *"own satisfaction only,"* and assured

Alvarez that his integrity had not been compromised.[72] Possibly Alvarez had tired of American political life.

In the end, the effort was for naught, for neither faction had their favorite son selected. Both Alvarez and Smith were passed over for William Allen. No doubt Webster was somewhat influenced by Allen's New England background — the appointee was a native of Essex and a graduate of Dartmouth[73] — and Allen had not been above helping himself: He had seen fit to send Webster the article in the *St. Louis Republican* that falsely cast Alvarez in a derogatory light. Allen favored the argument that New Mexico had proved itself so chaotic that some new, outside influence was needed, and he was backed by some influential people in Missouri and elsewhere, not the least of whom was Colonel Munroe's replacement, Colonel Edwin V. Sumner.[74] By the middle of February, the campaign had ended, and Weightman readied himself for his return to New Mexico, dejected, it seems, over Congress's refusal to vote him pay and by "the unprotected state of New Mexico."[75]

Although Alvarez was not appointed secretary, he had played integral roles in the transition to and from American occupation and, on a larger scale, had achieved his goals, both in preparing the way for a successful American takeover and in clearing the way for a more equitable government. His followers did not succumb in defeat to either the military or the opposing faction. They did not achieve statehood, true; but they did accomplish a form of local rule under which New Mexicans could enjoy their constitutional rights. New Mexico became a territory with an Alvarez-faction governor and representatives, and the secretarial post went to an outsider who, in the local feuds, could only be classified as neutral. Alvarez served a very real and intricate function as a catalyst through whom many New Mexican politicos could adjust to similar positions in a new system. The fact that people such as Gallegos, Archuleta, and Armijo supported him politically once again demonstrates the trust and respect he commanded.[76] He led the way for the very people who had opposed his activity when he was consul. Indeed, a difficult job had been done, and Alvarez, now in his fifty-sixth year, was ready for semiretirement. He turned to local affairs, to his business, and to travel.

8

A Multifaceted Man

William Allen's appointment as territorial secretary seemed to create a lull in Alvarez's political life, leaving him free to embark on some intriguing business ventures, but New Mexican politics continued to boil with personal rivalries: Richard Weightman found out that William Messervy, a longtime Alvarez ally and friend, had inexplicably shifted his support to Allen.[1] A definite reason for Messervy's change has yet to come to light, but his move probably eliminated any chance for Alvarez's appointment. A group of "legitimate successors to the old military party" flooded Washington in a concerted attempt to countermand Weightman's influence and advance their own cause. James Collins led a viciously critical attack on Governor Calhoun.[2] By misplacing blame and utilizing appearances over reality, Collins and his group attempted to lay all of New Mexico's problems at the governor's feet in an eighteen-page petition as well as letters sent directly to the president.[3] Collins and friends expressed concern for New Mexico unless the Americans governed because they felt the "spirit" of Mexican rule "must be corrupt" and charged that the governor's party pandered to Mexican cupidity, rallying around itself a "corrupt Catholic Priesthood." With some reasoned cunning and

William S. Messervy, 1849. A trader on the Santa Fe Trail and interim territorial governor of New Mexico, 1853, who destroyed Alvarez's chances for appointment to territorial secretary. *Courtesy of the Museum of New Mexico, Santa Fe. MNM 88121.*

the time-honored technique of conveniently shuffling or reinterpreting figures, even Weightman's recent election was presented as telling against the legitimacy of the statehood party.

While neither Calhoun nor his supporters had to answer to such bigoted opinions, and the election spoke for itself, the governor labored under real difficulties — he had an understaffed, hostile military force with which to work, his health was rapidly deteriorating, and he had no governmental operating funds and no secretary.[4] He had to function under impossible circumstances, but though his critics tried unjustly to turn these against him, the territorial legislature and Weightman came to his aid.[5] Although nothing was achieved as far as removing Calhoun, New Mexico seems to have had more than its share of problems. The most unfounded assumptions about the territory and its people appeared confirmed. Even one of Alvarez's friends, noting that he kept up on New Mexican affairs by reading the *St. Louis Republican,* asked if the merchant had forsaken politics: "Can't you tame [the people] or are you [New Mexicans] always to be Revolutionizing?"[6] Overcoming this kind of popular mentality proved a very real uphill battle, and the statehood party by its actions at once debunked and fostered the outsiders' view.

Alvarez became especially interested when Weightman heard rumors of Secretary Allen's resignation. The old territorialists tried to keep the news from Weightman as long as possible, but Weightman proved a bit quicker than they expected, for he knew of the resignation when it happened. He later accused Allen of having played "a pretty trick" by resigning without telling any "of our friends not even the Governor" and writing a "cock and bull letter" that in effect covered up his action. Alvarez's friend surmised that Collins and his allies had known Allen's plans a month before he vacated his office,[7] and he seems to have been right about that. Allen's resignation put Alvarez's hat back into the ring. Weightman stressed that the Hispanic had been and would always be his first choice as territorial secretary, and even though President Fillmore again wanted to appoint a neutral candidate, he felt Alvarez's candidacy might be successful if the president's choice, a Mister Harris, refused the appointment. That confidence derived from a conversation with the president, or so Weightman claimed.[8] According to script, he formally nominated Alvarez when he heard that Harris had declined, stressing that Alvarez was "neither a Whig or a Democrat" but "a dignified gentleman of high character." From a practical point of view, Alvarez's nomination counterbalanced the opposition's candidate, Hugh Smith.

For his part, Collins tried to undo Weightman's plan by embarking on a short-lived campaign that both demonstrated his journalistic experience and tended to fall short of the truth. In a letter to President Fillmore, Collins, pointing to his twenty-year friendship with Alvarez, claimed that he had become a Democrat and volunteered to supply the evidence.[9] Alvarez, like most New Mexicans, in fact showed no preference for national political parties; nonetheless, he was again labeled a "rank loco-foco," an untruth that eventually made its way into the *New York Tribune*.[10] Although Messervy may have unknowingly backed the territorialist, "compromise" candidate in the first campaign, the second time around proved much different. Early in June he suggested to Fillmore that the president had an opportunity to improve New Mexico's political condition by replacing Governor Calhoun with James Collins and denying Allen's resignation.[11] Fillmore did not take Messervy's advice, but the letter leaves no doubt about which faction Messervy backed.

After Harris's declination, Fillmore seemed somewhat confused. Apparently, by this time neither Allen nor Smith were under consideration, for Fillmore asked a friend who was familiar with New Mexico about the quality of Alvarez and Henry C. Johnson. In reply, Edward H. Wingfield described the American inhabitants of New Mexico as being, for the most part, *"mere adventurers"* who degraded the Mexican population. In his opinion, both men had the qualifications "to discharge the duties of that office." He cited Alvarez's diplomatic career — "He is a man of ability" — as well as his recently published dialog with Colonel Munroe but went on to recommend Johnson primarily because he had "held himself aloof from the parties and factions" that had disturbed New Mexico.[12] As in the previous battle for the secretary's position, the two opposing factions managed to stalemate each other while Washington officialdom sought a neutral appointment.

Through all the maneuvering, all the half-truths, and all the so-called politics surrounding his second candidacy for territorial secretary, Alvarez's friends kept him visible, but he did not actively campaign, feeling that his record and his friends would speak well enough. Governor Calhoun kept Alvarez in the fore by initially appointing him to an unnamed commission and then to acting governor during an intended vacation[13] (unfortunately, illness prevented the governor from leaving New Mexico, so Alvarez never functioned in Calhoun's stead).[14] It is not without irony, then, that Weightman withdrew Alvarez's name. Because of Collins and company's slanderous campaign, he related to Fillmore that he did not wish "to subject so dignified and excellent a gentleman" as Alvarez "to *chance* of mortification"; compared to Alvarez's dignity, the office was "indifferent." Besides, an old Calhoun and Alvarez supporter named John Greiner appeared to be the new favorite for the position.[15]

Alvarez, of course, never retired from influencing some aspect of New Mexico's political scene. Although his career never again would reach Washington, he had, after all, helped develop and lead the early movement for local rule, and life never calmed down for an active, intelligent man

Letter of James S. Calhoun, territorial governor of New Mexico. This letter, dated March 29, 1852, and signed by Calhoun, appoints Alvarez acting governor during a trip Calhoun was planning. *Original in the Benjamin Read Collection, New Mexico State Records Center and Archives, Santa Fe.*

To all whom it may concern

Know ye, that. Whereas I, James S. Calhoun, Governor of the Territory of New Mexico in consequence of physical inability will not leave the Territory so soon as contemplated, but will continue in the discharge of my Executive duties as heretofore, therefore the order issued March 30th 1852. appointing Hon. Manuel Alvarez as acting Governor of the Territory is hereby revoked and I have the pleasure of informing the Honorable Manuel Alvarez that he will be relieved from the performance of the duties which he so kindly consented to perform at my earnest solicitation

Given under my hand and seal this second day of April 1852.

James S. Calhoun
Governor
by David V. Whiting

Letter of James S. Calhoun, territorial governor of New Mexico. This letter, dated April 2, 1852, revokes the appointment after the trip was canceled. Calhoun's shaky signature is an accurate reflection of his health. The governor eventually left for the States and died on the trail. *Original in the Benjamin Read Collection, New Mexico State Records Center and Archives, Santa Fe.*

living on a frontier. Change was a natural trait for such an area and neither New Mexico nor Alvarez deviated from the norm. Maintaining his good reputation, he continued actively to participate in New Mexico's history on, as was his custom, a less visible level. He was saddened by the death of Calhoun but pleased with William Carr Lane as his replacement. Again, Alvarez's influence was tapped when he received the job of introducing the new chief executive to the Mexican gentlemen of the territory, even interpreting Governor Lane's inaugural speech.[16] Alvarez also made himself responsible for getting 2,000 ballots each printed for the Río Arriba, Santa Fe, and San Miguel county elections, underlining the significance he placed on local politics. His act also may have helped justify the opposition's criticism that the "Alvarez faction" catered to the Mexican population, for not only were the three counties primarily Mexican in ethnic makeup but Alvarez himself had paid to have the ballots printed in Independence.[17] Politics notwithstanding, Alvarez enjoyed the personal respect of his enemies. It is a telltale sign that Calhoun's and, by implication at least, also Alvarez's harshest critic, James Collins, when writing to Governor Lane and relating the story of Alvarez's 1841 trip across the plains, minced no words in praising the old merchant.

The old political feuds ground on, racial bias made its ugly presence felt, lawlessness seemed rife, and Indian attacks continued, but none deterred Alvarez from pursuing, as he always had, his life as a merchant. A thread of consistency, his profession flourished, and an occasional notice appeared in the local newspaper when he started legal proceedings against a delinquent customer.[18] Alvarez's correspondence continued to reveal the business community's confidence in him, and Indian hostilities did not prevent him from investing in trading ventures. In 1850, he and two partners, Miguel Griego and Diego Archuleta, bonded themselves for $5,000 to receive an Indian trading license from the government.[19] He expanded his trade through Peter Harmony, Nephews and Company and even introduced his old adversary, Manuel Armijo, to the New York firm.[20] Meanwhile, the old business of collecting debts increased. A good portion of Santa Fe's merchants' customers belonged to the army and their debts moved with them: For example, a soldier in Missouri destined for Santa Fe would buy on credit at the former place and pay at the latter.

Kearny's success had encouraged a new wave of Americans to venture into the Southwest, and prosperity spread to and from Santa Fe like spokes on a wheel. Business not only increased between New Mexico and Missouri, it also followed the US Army to show a marked improvement in the southern markets at Mesilla, El Paso, and Chihuahua, as well as in the virtually new market of California. Alvarez's business reflected the changes, and he acted as "attorney" for various people and firms — it proved to be a multifaceted line of work. Many of the new people Alvarez dealt with had probably put their trust in the experienced merchant on the recommendation of third parties. He usually received instructions to take a percentage of the debts he collected for his "trouble," but on other occasions he acted with the understanding that the favor would be "cheerfully reciprocated"[21] — the customarily informal basis.

Some companies drew up contracts specifically designating Alvarez their "true and lawful attorney" — Manifest Destiny starting to show its legalistic head.[22] This system of payment became quite complicated, providing for a flow of cash through many hands and an opportunity for each person involved to utilize the available capital for a quick return. Such investments were accepted, but there was a premium on honesty and a proliferation of acknowledgments of payment.[23] William McCoy, bookkeeper to David Waldo and Company, wrote to Alvarez from Independence: "I have received from M.W.E. Ewing your favor of 18th February covering

remittances to amount of $1086.95/100 and have . . . passed
the same credit to David Waldo."[24] On the other hand, many
debtors or merchants found it much harder to raise money
than expected, and Alvarez also received letters requesting
an extension of time: One could not pay for his current order
for supplies because he had not yet sold his corn and owed
some money to the "soldiers of L. M. Valdez' company in Las
Vegas"; Alvarez was assured that he would be paid within
two months.[25] Another friend collecting for Alvarez confronted a nonpayer and found him seriously ill; the man,
however, had covered his debt to Alvarez in his will. A few
years later, in 1853, Alvarez received an excuse from Las
Cruces that was becoming more commonplace: "Bad luck and
hard times has compelled me to disappoint you"; as soon as
business improved the money would be sent.[26] Another poor
fellow that same year had fallen on such hard luck he decided
to relocate to California; he assured Alvarez that "should the
Almighty give me a hand, I shall be most happy to return and
square up."[27] Alvarez could only gamble on the man's honesty
and possible good fortune. Aside from documenting that not
everyone benefited from recent geographic increases of trade
and flow of money, such letters singled out the La Mesilla–
Las Cruces area as an especially difficult locale in which to
run a business.

In 1851, Alvarez's account with David Waldo and Company showed that he sent them $850 in September and
$879.02 in December; from September 1851 through August
1852, he paid a total of $9,312.99. Waldo and Company
merely listed everything they felt Alvarez owed, including
debts of people from whom he had to collect: Thus, debts of
such men as Hugh Stevenson, José Chaves, Judge Baird, and
Diego "Escavel" were listed for collection and considered
Alvarez's debt. This was all informally done, and an accompanying letter concluded that Alvarez should not collect the
"whole account" of one José "Chaviz" because it was, overall,

possible that the account "may not compare strictly with" Alvarez's books; McCoy felt it would be best for Alvarez "to examine the account" and send a correction.[28] Meanwhile, Alvarez kept accounts on his own agents, not the least of whom was William S. McKnight. McKnight turned in a batch of paid notes on September 30, 1852, and among the payees was the same Diego Esquivel who owed Waldo and Company $1,380. He paid Alvarez, through McKnight, $778.13. In total, McKnight turned in over $20,000.[29]

Alvarez, of course, took advantage of the new opportunities. His experience and honesty worked in his favor, and from his store he had spun a web of financial maneuverings built upon debt collection, an activity that could pay off because a good proportion of the outstanding debts involved some very large sums — from 1847 through 1850, Alvarez had collected and paid out at least $20,000, and the amounts flowing through the merchant's hands increased, as McKnight's collections attest. Being essentially a frontier collection agency and money changer required a good sense of organization. Nothing was uniform, and Alvarez not only kept track of small amounts — for example, a $5 loan that was repaid five days later[30] — he still maintained business with some of his regular customers and friends, such as José Ignacio Gonzales, who in 1849 paid the Spaniard eight pesos after he had sold the merchandise Alvarez gave him.[31] The next month Julian Tenorio of Ranchos de Taos acknowledged receiving four pesos from Manuel Chaves "de Sebolleta" in an arrangement that somehow involved Alvarez.[32]

In contrast, dealings with such merchants as Waldo and McCoy were huge. It appears that Waldo's firm became Alvarez's main contact in Missouri, and it, in turn, depended on him in New Mexico. In 1847, Alvarez had sent $1,086.95 to Waldo through McCoy, and that seems to have become a regular payment; he paid that amount again in 1850, and the only variance in the sum was the loose change. During that same year he collected $1,036 for Waldo from Thomas Day,[33] and toward the end of 1848, McCoy asked Alvarez to collect $9,500 from, of all people, Joab Houghton and associates.[34]

Houghton's and Alvarez's political jousts took a backseat to financial matters (although in this case the pleasure was Alvarez's and the pain Houghton's), but not everyone wanted the experienced merchant to handle his business nor did everything run smoothly.

It smacks of the current political contests that, after David Waldo had subdelegated business to him, the firm of Lewis and Courtney canceled Alvarez's services, asking that he "hand the power of attorney" to Hugh N. Smith, whom they had "made our regular attorney for Mexico."[35] A year later, in 1849, Alvarez took possession, as collateral, of goods belonging to Solomon Sublette, a prominent old mountain man and merchant, but on April 3, the sheriff ordered him to deliver the key to the storage room containing Sublette's goods.[36] A few weeks later, Alvarez received two letters from T. A. Hereford, another merchant and old acquaintance, that shed some light on this mystery: The goods apparently belonged to Hereford, who had used them as collateral with Sublette, from whom, in turn, Alvarez had attached them. Feeling "it better to have my goods free than to be tied up," Hereford decided to pay off the "mortgage" to Alvarez and asked Alvarez to put the merchandise in possession of Messervy; Hereford would meanwhile inform Sublette of the transaction. He expressed the wish that Sublette would personally settle the matter when he visited Santa Fe in the summer.[37]

Hereford typified a universal problem for merchants: Many times payment became contingent on the ability to raise the necessary sum. Hereford wrote that he would pay off a $9,000 note "as soon as I can sell goods enough,"[38] and another acquaintance begged off in French, saying that he had lost fifty-eight mules — "abducted by water, Indians, and

Mexicans."[39] Despite such misfortunes, Alvarez's ventures, apparently, usually paid off. A customer who had sold "a lot of wheat" wrote that he would, on payment, "go down [to Santa Fe] to complete arrangements."[40] The Santa Fe merchant dealt with a lot of money in different forms and denominations, and hard specie continued to show up in his coffers. In November 1849, a bag containing $1,000 in silver and $249.38 in gold arrived from Chihuahua for transport to Independence,[41] and in April 1849, Alvarez had cashed in $1,626.29 worth of precious metal at the Philadelphia mint.[42]

Many of the old-timers who were familiar with New Mexico and northern Mexico sought either to go into business on their own or to encourage others, and Alvarez's experience was an asset to both purposes. Many of his friends became anxious for him to open another base of operations in Chihuahua: He had been such a positive force in Santa Fe when it was the northernmost Mexican trading center, it seemed logical that he would likewise bring benefit to the Chihuahuan community.[43] And in 1850, both George Wethered from Independence and Juan Bautista Beaubien sought Alvarez's mental and financial aid. Wethered, who planned to open a store in Santa Fe, asked the Hispanic to find a suitable building that he could rent for six months with an option to continue occupancy. Beaubien could not make ends meet on the "Rio Colorado" because Taos charged too much to keep his store stocked; he needed to get lower rates and better credit. Alvarez "would oblige [him] very much" if he could allow him to buy goods at six months' credit — if not, perhaps "from another merchant in Santa Fe."[44] People not only expected Alvarez to aid potential competitors but to give special rates or arrange such advantageous conditions through other merchants.

New opportunities developed for Alvarez with the beginning of the second half of the nineteenth century, and he may have been one of the initially few men to become aware of the lucrative potential of herding sheep to the California mining fields. New Mexican sheep had helped feed Mexico's population for decades, especially in the north central mining areas, and turning a profit in sheep would be a natural risk for Alvarez, who had considered grazing them on his Ocaté grant back in 1839. He had even toyed with introducing the more durable and thus potentially more profitable merino sheep to New Mexico but, unfortunately, apparently never followed through. Mules also were a normal part of Alvarez's business.[45] They had always been a popular commodity with Missouri farmers, who provided a lucrative market for draft animals, and Alvarez had risked his life trying to get a herd of them to Missouri in 1841. Merchants who traded down to Chihuahua also had found them a convenient item, which could be bought in Durango for around $30 a head and sold in California for as much as $300. People such as T. A. Hereford, an adventurous sort of businessman, had had no qualms about investing up to $6,000 in the California mule trade,[46] but with the discovery of gold in 1849 and the subsequent rush of miners, sheep became a more alluring animal — the main source of meat for a population concentrating on things other than food.

William Z. "Captain" Angney, lawyer, local-rule advocate, and Alvarez's old ally in the general assembly, had turned from politics to business. He was a little more compulsive than his friend and became one of the first New Mexicans to invest heavily in the new market. Apparently convincing others with his scheme, he raised enough money to take 6,000 sheep to California. After his arrival on the West Coast, he turned down an offer of $40,000 for 5,000 head because he rather confidently felt he could get $4 to $8 more per head at "the mines." Writing the details to Alvarez, he expressed a seemingly infinite potential for the California market: Huge profits could be made with a low investment of $2 per animal in New Mexico, and who, Angney inquired, would be more adept at arranging a major transaction of 20,000 head of sheep than Alvarez? But Angney and his partners did not want to launch Alvarez in the business — that would be self-defeating. They needed a trustworthy purchasing agent, a person who could "be low and keep the people in ignorance of" the new opportunity, who knew sheep and had experience in fiscal matters.[47] Alvarez could have done very little about keeping "low" — everyone soon knew of the sheep market's high potential on the West Coast — but he fulfilled the last two requirements nicely. So, at no risk to himself, he became an agent for yet another business venture.

"The mines" actually meant San Francisco, and, upon his arrival there in late January 1851, Angney became even more excited. He had been offered nothing less than $16 an animal; in hungry San Francisco, butchers could retail them for as much as $28 each. If things went as planned, Angney expected to make $100,000 with the next flock and could hardly wait to get back to Santa Fe to start a return trip to California with more sheep. Indeed, unless another partner, an elderly Frenchman named Jean Baptiste Fournier, arrived with more sheep, Angney had sole control of a limited commodity in a seller's market,[48] but he quickly encountered a major problem: He could not find anyone with a sufficient amount of cash to pay for the animals. He refused to deal with notes drawn on eastern banking houses because he had no faith in written promises so far away from their financial backing, and — although he felt confident, for "the market cannot be glutted" and remained the best investment "of the times" — he was worried.[49] He had instructed Alvarez to raise funds, sheep, or both for the next season; he had even suggested that Alvarez solicit his "old, true and kind hearted friend," Antonio Sandoval, to invest; and now, in December, he was impatient for Alvarez's response.[50]

In 1852, Alvarez entrusted his longtime partner and countryman, Damaso López, with 4,000 sheep,[51] his own investment. In January of that year, Angney, deeply in debt and apparently still unsuccessful in collecting enough money to repay the debts incurred on his initial investment, appointed Alvarez his attorney "to superintend" and "transact" all his business "of every sort and description" in New Mexico, with authority to sell any or all of Angney's personal property to pay his debts.[52] He wrote from Chihuahua, two days later, explaining that until his arrival in Durango, he had not realized that Alvarez was gathering sheep for him. With his usual efficiency, Alvarez had already sent the sheep on their way to California while Angney was en route east to Durango. Angney, facing the bittersweet necessity of returning to the West Coast, seemed happy with Alvarez's actions yet regretted not having the time to visit his family and friends in Santa Fe.[53]

Angney went into partnership with Fournier, who invested $6,000 in 3,000 sheep, and decided to make his permanent residence in California, maintaining his enthusiasm because he felt his "plan was not badly conceived" and would "yet be executed."[54] In the meantime, Alvarez had secured a big financial commitment from wealthy and respected New Mexican Antonio Sandoval, and Angney and Fournier, to their embarrassment, had trouble repaying him. The partners suffered from their 1852 investment for a number of reasons: Indians stole some of the animals they were herding from Chihuahua to California; business had "been unfortunately managed" in Mexico, and Fournier blamed Angney for his poor judgment in picking a man "incapable" of maintaining their interests.[55] After a series of apologetic promises, Alvarez received Angney's hesitant permission to sell his house to Sandoval and thus square the account. This incident, coupled with Fournier's complaints that Angney had not paid his debt or kept deadlines, indicates that Angney's business acumen fell short of his vision. Nevertheless, he had assessed the California market accurately — others were enjoying its advantages[56] — and the two partners hit upon another imaginative idea while in San Francisco. They would revive the "ancient philosophy" of Chinese theater, complete with a *comédien chinois* — a Chinese comedian! After an initial investment, they scheduled a company of forty-three people to go to New York for an industrial exposition. From there, the partners planned to take the company to London and Paris, but, unfortunately, Fournier's health and age, and Angney's inattention caused the former to abandon the enterprise in New York.[57]

In contrast to these almost farcical escapades, Alvarez had to deal both with the death of his *paisano,* fellow Spaniard Damaso López, and with a potential total loss of his own sheep venture. The cause of López's death is not given. Angney and another man had met with him on the trail, and in answer to their inquiries, López had stressed that the sheep belonged to Alvarez, not to Angney.[58] He had safely crossed the Colorado River and traversed the Mojave Desert when, suddenly, he died. The owner of the ferry at the river, who had been traveling with López, took over and herded the sheep to San Diego, where he remained as special administrator until a replacement was appointed.[59] Alvarez heard of López's death on September 12, 1852. Sympathy with Alvarez's personal loss as well as concern for his financial affairs can be measured in the number of people who took the time to write him of the sad news. William Dryden and John Rowland advised him to travel to California if he wanted to save his investment;[60] Angney reported that the new administrator, William St. Moon, had aborted an attempt to sell the sheep at Alvarez's expense, but Alvarez, he felt, would "be fortunate if [he] escaped being made a victim."[61] A week later Angney reported that Rowland had heard that 1,000 of the sheep were sold to cover expenses and added, "Your business has been shamefully mismanaged."[62]

A couple of days after Angney's second letter, Alvarez

received another report via Chihuahua with an account of
López's death and a narrative of his sheep business; this
writer also concluded that Alvarez should go to California. By
the end of January, a concerned Alvarez had received more
particulars from Fournier and Angney. Angney still painted a
pessimistic picture and reiterated that the business "had
fallen into bad hands": Alvarez's sheep were sold at $6.25
each; the going rate hovered at $8.[63] Fournier had a different
opinion: In April 1852, he wrote that he had "no fear" for
Alvarez's sheep venture. Although his previous letter, as described by Angney, had given some details and expressed
disgust, it also had ended on the positive note that Alvarez
would not lose all his capital. Expenses included the first
administrator and twelve shepherds, all of whom were paid
from the aforementioned sale of sheep along with some mules
López and Alvarez owned.[64]

The conflicting reports of the fate of a $6,000 to $8,000
investment necessitated some action. Angney seemed too
emotional to handle matters, so Alvarez turned to an experienced frontiersman, François X. Aubry, who was even then
famous for the speed and endurance with which he traveled
around the West. Aubry was conveniently preparing to conduct a drive to the coast, and the added burden of power of
attorney over Alvarez's money would be no problem for him.
As it turned out, he allayed Alvarez's fears when he reported
from California — Aubry wrote that St. Moon was an "honest
man" who had collected $26,633.12 at a public sale of
Alvarez's sheep. Various expenses — including over $1,300 (5
percent) for the auctioneer — had to be paid, but Aubry
surmised that Alvarez would have a balance of over $20,000.
Aubry would try to have it sent but warned against expecting
the money quickly because he believed the law required a
one-year lapse to allow settlement of all claims.[65]

Aubrey's next report had more detail, including the good
news that St. Moon would recommend that the money be

turned over to Alvarez's agent. The expenses were $1,200 for crossing the Colorado River at the ferry, $1,500 for the shepherds, the $1,300 for the auctioneer, and 5 percent for the administrator. Finally, a "Mexican peon" associated with the affair had made an "unjust" claim that nonetheless had to be paid. There was still some doubt about the exact amount Alvarez could expect to net because St. Moon had entered a suit against the auctioneer; nevertheless, Alvarez was coming out ahead and, advised Aubry, should write a letter thanking St. Moon for his fine job. Aubry credited Alvarez's good fortune to St. Moon, Rowland, and one of the Robidoux brothers. He said nothing of Angney or Fournier, perhaps implying criticism. Angney, however, penned a letter the same day, echoing Aubry's report; he had received the news from the first administrator, who also had a good opinion of St. Moon.[66]

One minor problem remained. Because of the high interest rates in California, Aubrey thought that Alvarez's money had been collecting an 8 to 10 percent interest that had not been mentioned: Rather than risk a delay in payment, Alvarez should enter a suit against St. Moon after the initial money had been paid. Aubrey tried to leave this job to Rowland, who refused, and whether or not the scheme worked is unknown.[67] Suffice it to say that Alvarez eventually received a profit from his investment and it was a nice sum for his initial venture in the California sheep business.

Aubry was so impressed with California he decided to outfit another herd of sheep. He wrote Alvarez that more could be made in a month on the coast than in three years in New Mexico; could the Hispanic start making arrangements for a major herd? Aubry initially bought his sheep through Alvarez from a Don Santiago of San Miguel and from Antonio Sandoval, who must have been a major supplier. Unlike Ang-ney, Aubry returned to Santa Fe to pay his suppliers personally and, coincidentally, to pay off Angney's debt to

Sandoval.[68] Aubry and Alvarez eventually raised and gathered enough sheep to qualify this expedition as the major
venture of the 1850s. Other prominent New Mexicans such
as A. J. Otero, Francisco Perea, and José Francisco Chaves
joined in the enterprise, raising among them all a herd of
40,000 to 50,000 animals. With many of the proprietors
choosing to accompany Aubry and the livestock, they
started their journey over the Old Spanish Trail in early
October 1853.[69]

Alvarez, now in his late fifties, had played an integral
role in the New Mexico–California sheep industry, helping
to raise capital as well as buy sheep for three major drives,
including his own. In addition to the difficulties and uncer-
tainties of these widespread ventures, his land in New
Mexico was demanding a good deal of time and attention.
Why Alvarez kept his land at Ocaté has always been a
mystery of sorts. He never really used or even seemed to
care about it until the grant attracted another's interest.
Brevet Colonel Edwin V. Sumner, the newly appointed military commander, had instructions to economize. He decided to establish forts outside of population centers and to
develop experimental farms, reasoning that this would cut
food expenses for both men and animals. He was so set on
this idea that he personally brought farm equipment to
New Mexico and established Fort Union, located outside of
Las Vegas, as his headquarters. The fort's farm became
controversial when the colonel chose Alvarez's land on the
Ocaté River for one of his farm locations[70] and, apparently,
tried to farm it before he secured permission. Alvarez, who
seemed to have heard of the contemplated move, sent H. H.
Green to "warn off" all trespassers. Green encountered an
army detail led by Sergeant Thomas Pollock and succeeded
in fulfilling Alvarez's wishes.[71]

Once again at odds with a military commander, the experienced Hispanic wrote to Sumner on March 1, 1852, describ-

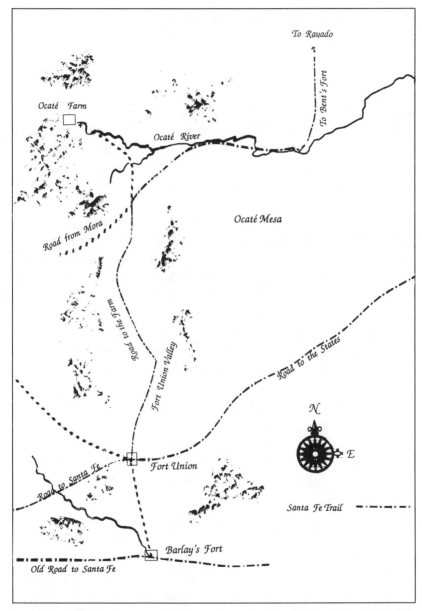

Alvarez's Ocaté and surrounding area, based on General T.K.F. Mansfield's report, Records of the War Department, FUA.

ing the boundaries of his land and saying that his Mexican grant had been properly filed with the office of the territorial secretary. He informed Sumner that he wished to forgo a lawsuit, "which is at all times to be avoided when convenient."[72] The letter reached Fort William, where the superintendent replied to Alvarez that the matter had been passed to headquarters and Colonel Sumner would probably write an answer. The reply, if any, is unknown, but, apparently, Sumner was not totally convinced of Alvarez's legal possession, nor did Alvarez feel confident, for he quickly had Weightman file his petition to validate and record the grant through the US government. Weightman at first seemed optimistic, then later felt the chances were slim because Congress was so cumbersome and had approved such a small number of such grants.[73] Alvarez's Ocaté claim was filed as "number one" and became the first case presented under Congress's Act of 1854 and the Treaty of Guadalupe Hidalgo.[74] Subsequent events indicate that Alvarez's petition was successful.

Sumner eventually made arrangements with the Spaniard to rent the land and open up his farm.[75] Situated approximately twenty-five miles directly north of Fort Union, the farm in 1853 yielded about fifty acres of corn and about seventy-five tons of hay, but the army's Ocaté experiment fell $14,000 in debt.[76] Although a military inspector recommended that the experiment continue, the soldiers soon quit farming and used the land for grazing and cutting grass, paying Alvarez a small annual sum for the privilege.[77] Many soldiers familiar with the area attempted to purchase or rent land at Ocaté, but Alvarez refused. The property was and is prime fertile land, and homesteaders soon became another problem. On one occasion, Samuel B. Watrous of Las Vegas reported a discharged soldier homesteading on the Ocaté. Watrous, whose "servant" had discovered the illegal settler, relayed the information to Alvarez "because I like to do as I would be done by."[78] Evidently, by the time of his death,

Alvarez had become more open to offers because he arranged rental to Captain William Shoemaker, Fort Union's ordnance officer.[79]

Alvarez's hesitancy to rent and refusal to sell his real estate on the Ocaté contrasted with his fast-paced real estate activities around Santa Fe's plaza. Alvarez rented out rooms for varying periods of time and in different buildings on at least fourteen different occasions from 1850 to June 1856[80] and apparently invested in property around the plaza. He came into possession of Damaso López's house, a dwelling that had formerly belonged to José Ortiz, and a place on the northeast corner of the public square, known as the Weaverly House.[81] The rents varied from "free" to as much as $57 per month, and, on the whole, Alvarez seems to have received a fairly steady income from his rentals,[82] which included everything from four rooms and a corral to a "beer house" that comprised a storeroom, kitchen, and saloon.

His property on the public square may have made him, by 1856, the biggest real estate owner in the central part of town.[83] All the property fronted the northeast and north sides of the plaza, but the exact locations of all his buildings are somewhat unclear, because the actual layout of the square's adjoining property — even the size of the square in the early 1850s — is very hazy. Although certain streets and properties are mentioned, Alvarez's original residence and his last place of occupation, the Weaverly House, can be located in the general area east of the Governor's Palace. Whether the buildings were on the plaza's north side facing south or on the north end of the east side facing west is not clear from Alvarez's rental contracts. A map drawn up for Kearny in August 1846 shows the palace and buildings directly all occupied by the military. Alvarez's property, therefore, must have been located on the plaza's east side. The buildings faced west and were, at least, at the north end of that side. In October 1849, he also purchased a house in Santa Cruz from two

Americans listed as J. B. Smith and P. B. Shelby. The house was located on the north side of Santa Cruz's plaza, and Alvarez apparently bought it for rental purposes; there is no account of his ever residing in Santa Cruz even though he kept the property until his death.[84]

When Congress appropriated $20,000 to the territorial government, earmarked for public building, the legislature approved a law on January 12, 1853, forming a Public Building Commission that would be made up of three men, each bonded for $10,000 and with authority to disperse federal money. Governor Lane wasted no time filling the positions, and Alvarez was one of the appointees. He recited the oath of office as public building commissioner before Judge Tolen Watts on January 17, 1853.[85] In vintage Alvarez fashion, he served his relatively short term of roughly a year until January 13, 1854, on a commission embroiled in activity.[86]

Alvarez's old adversary, Joab Houghton, became Acting Governor Messervy's appointed superintendent of public buildings. As such, Houghton oversaw all construction of public buildings but had no part in contractual arrangements, or so it seemed. Alvarez and the two other commissioners, Preston Beck and Francisco Ortiz y Delgado, voted Houghton's salary at an annual rate of $1,500; Houghton felt such compensation far too low but would not resign.[87] When, shortly thereafter, David Merriwether — an old Santa Fe trapper and trader and a distant ally of Houghton's old territorial party — took over as the new governor, he immediately requested a detailed report of the commission's activities.[88] The commissioners promptly answered with a preliminary and final report that indicated they were pretty adept at getting things done efficiently.

A new territorial capitol building had been started on land 200 yards north of the plaza, an area formerly used by Spain and Mexico "as an appendage to the Palacio for civil and military purposes." Contracts for woodcutting and rock-quarrying had been put out to bid, and by the fall of 1853, the basement level of the future capitol had been completed. The projected final cost would be $68,164.[89] Both the commission and Houghton counted on another federal appropriation, guessing that Congress would do as it had elsewhere,[90] but they misjudged the federal politicians. Either Congress or the Treasury Department had become disappointed, and the federal comptroller adjusted the commission's allocation, leaving a deficit of $16,729.16 "found to be due . . . to the United States."[91] Because the expected new appropriation never received federal approval, Governor Merriwether disbanded the Public Building Commission.[92]

On the face of the record, all seems simple enough: The territory received one allocation for public buildings, overspent while expecting a second grant, and then received nothing more. Behind the scenes, however, a whole different story may have given just cause for the Treasury Department's show of no confidence. Joab Houghton took the job of superintendent of public buildings after he had run into financial difficulties — he was no longer a judge and had failed as a merchant. As the handpicked superintendent, he had been criticized for trying to turn the position to his financial advantage and, in the process, alienating Washington, but Houghton persisted in his position and became involved in further overruns long after Alvarez had left the commission. For the period of Alvarez's tenure, however, Houghton appears innocent of any intentional wrongdoing,[93] and the government later retracted its stand and allocated more funds. In fact, Collins informed Alvarez, by then an ex–building commissioner, that New Mexico's delegate, José Manuel Gallegos, had secured an appropriation of $50,000.[94] Collins's correspondence included other letters that by their very nature precluded any continuing rift from the local-rule fight, and any alleged break between Alvarez and Houghton over public building funds would have been even less likely. Nevertheless, Houghton remained active, Alvarez did not, and the problem of increasing expenses and overruns delayed completion of the capitol building for over twenty years.[95]

By 1854, Alvarez had become one of the elder statesmen of Santa Fe; with age he began to have problems with rheumatism,[96] but this did not stop him from continuing with as many or more activities than anyone else. The 1853 congressional election between Lane and Gallegos had been hotly contested, although not quite along the old factional lines. Both men were Alvarez's friends, and he therefore became a trusted source of information and a political prognosticator. Alvarez kept up on current events, even if he had retired from public life. Lane sought his advice and Martínez complained to him of fraud while Weightman and others predicted a civil war between the states. Alvarez is mentioned for his support of southern New Mexico's attempt to become a separate territory; he suggested it be named Cibola.[97] On the local scene, he dealt with and supported the Catholic church in New Mexico.[98] One of the reasons for this was the arrival of Father Damaso Taladrid, who had been recruited from Spain by Jean Baptiste Lamy, the titular leader of New Mexico's Catholics since 1851. As paisanos, the priest and merchant became fairly good friends and kept each other informed of their respective activities. Taladrid apparently arranged loans from Alvarez for the archbishop,[99] and after the merchant's death, Taladrid wrote to Lamy about his contributions to the church.

Alvarez also continued to function as a business agent, dealing with, and for, William McKnight, Waldo and Company, María Barceló, Lane, Fournier, and Weightman, among others.[100] Notably absent from the records for 1852 through 1856 is any indication that he continued business through New York and London firms, but in New Mexico, one of his principal clients was Solomon Houck. Houck, who — like Angney earlier — left all his New Mexican business in

Alvarez's hands, instructed him to pay himself for his "trouble" — a normal practice for the time. Although Alvarez collected as much as $7,000 for Houck, he apparently refused or forgot to keep a commission. Houck reminded his agent of the oversight, insisting that he felt "under many obligations" to Alvarez for his prompt "attention to" business.[101] Houck and Alvarez had been friends for a long time, so when a minor crisis arose, Houck did not hesitate to call on him. Uncomfortably for Alvarez, the controversy pitted Houck against Preston Beck, who had served on the Public Building Commission with Alvarez. Houck and Beck became angered over a coffee deal: Things were said and each accused the other of slander. Perhaps as a result of Alvarez's longevity, the ticklish situation of finding himself caught between mutual acquaintances seemed to be happening with more regularity.[102]

Epilog

It Ended As It Began

Age, recurring sickness, and a growing desire to see his family convinced Alvarez to plan a second trip to Europe. He had been corresponding regularly with the Frenchman, Fournier, who wanted to meet him in France. Fournier had become fond of Alvarez and the latter reciprocated; both men were native Europeans and about the same age. Fournier, perhaps reflecting Alvarez's sentiments, wrote philosophically: Although men of their years should think of retirement because they cannot "resist strong tiredness," a life of activity was much more enticing.[1] Ironically, both men became ill at the same time. Alvarez suffered painful rheumatism and was unable to write his friend, who was laid up in New York with a bad ear infection. Alvarez's silence worried Fournier, for the New Mexican had sent only a short letter that described his suffering,[2] and both men knew that sickness could become serious very easily at their age. Fournier succinctly summed up their plight when he wrote that they must hope for better and thus endure.[3]

By the end of October, Alvarez had recovered enough to plan for his trip. He wrote Fournier that he wanted to see the Paris Exposition and would leave sometime around the end of March 1855. By this time, Alvarez had received a number of travel journals and newspapers from his friend and, judging by Fournier's lively correspondence on French affairs, must have been well versed in that country's politics.[4] Alvarez planned to sail from New York to London after a brief stop in Philadelphia. He took with him a letter of introduction from W.W.H. Davis that stated he would board at a place called the Quarters in the Quaker City. Meanwhile, Father Taladrid had asked his compatriot to bring him some religious books from Barcelona, Spain. Taladrid's request is the only tangible evidence of Alvarez's intention to visit his native country.[5]

Tiring of New York, Fournier left word with an M. A. Mataran explaining where and how he could be found. Although he dearly wished to meet his longtime pen pal and had intended to wait, he had decided to sail from Boston.[6] Alvarez arrived in New York with some friends and apparently sailed to England aboard the steamer *Asia,* which arrived in Liverpool on April 21. Fournier wrote from Paris that the exposition would open on May 15; perhaps the two of them could meet there. Alvarez traveled to Paris, arriving by May 6 — within two days of the date of Fournier's last letter — yet they missed connections![7] Fournier was crestfallen that he "did not have the pleasure of embracing" his friend and feared that he might have lost the opportunity. Could Alvarez, he asked, "make a sacrifice to see an old friend?"[8] Alvarez answered that he could, but only after he had returned from Italy around the first of August. Fournier waited at the Mau Monde Hotel in Paris, but again he tired of the city and left around August 10, missing Alvarez once more. Fournier jealously feared that "that beautiful Italy" had delayed his friend, but he found that Alvarez had an excuse quite to the contrary: Italy's "heat and pollen" had proved harmful to him. Fournier was very much relieved that Alvarez had recovered and had arrived safely back in Paris.[9] There is no further correspondence from Fournier, so whether the two men ever formally embraced is unknown; also unknown is whether or not Alvarez, obviously fatigued, ever made it back to Spain.[10]

Battery Place, New York, 1853, looking north. Photograph by Victor Prevost. The steeples are of Trinity Church, nearby, and, in the distance, Saint Paul's Chapel. Ships are docked to the left. *Courtesy of the New York Historical Society, New York City.*

By the end of November, Alvarez had recrossed the Atlantic Ocean and was traveling back to Santa Fe but, typically, not fast enough to avoid William McKnight's request for a $5,000 to $6,000 loan.[11] After returning to his old home, he continued business as usual, and on February 26, 1856, a little over four months before his death, he received an appointment to what some people would consider a minor position. Yet, in some ways it was an honor that most fitted the man: Judge Miguel F. Pino named Alvarez to the Santa Fe County Board of Education.[12]

Late in Alvarez's life, his friend Fournier had complained that everything had become upsetting in the world: People "have become serious, taciturn, hypocritical and selfish. . . . They think of nothing but money."[13] France, and by implication Europe, had become Americanized; Fournier and his friend had grown out of place; their world had passed. Fournier may have been correct in one way, but he was wrong in another sense, for such men as Alvarez always have a place.

There is a dichotomy in the history of the United States: The founding fathers devised a system in which they intended the smartest man, a philosopher king, to become leader or president; but where once such men as Adams and Jefferson ruled as they were intended, Jacksonian democracy, developed by, among others, Andrew Jackson and Martin Van Buren, introduced the modern political campaign. Inherent to that system is a complete rejection of the intellectual who will not stoop so low as to "glad-hand, back-slap," or speak down to folk on the premise that otherwise they "could not understand." The intellectual has no use for "political expediency" and little room for compromise. Thus, in a mutual rejection, the new political order saw the intellectual as a threat and the intellectual saw the politician as a hypocrite.

Alvarez lived with this dichotomy. Educated, intellectual, and somewhat aristocratic, he took stands on which he would not compromise. Many times, unfortunately, his position was contrary to that of his superiors, both in Washington and in Santa Fe. He had arrived on the New Mexican frontier with the beginning of Jacksonian democracy, and by the time he had become a diplomat, the art of political expediency had been refined for some twenty years. An anachronism, Alvarez did not fit comfortably into the new political sphere; perhaps this is why the federal government bypassed him in favor of less qualified people after New Mexico became a territory. Alvarez's arguments with Daniel Webster and John Munroe make an interesting dialog in US intellectual history. Alvarez, like the more famous Henry Adams, was a man of an outdated mold; like Adams, he became frustrated when not called to serve. Yet, his obituary reads, in part, that he was "highly esteemed for his intelligence and integrity of character, as well as his social qualities." Although a "devoted friend," he "never allowed his position to be misunderstood." He would be missed by those "who understood him, and had learned to appreciate his worth."[14]

Among Alvarez's papers is a notebook in which he hand-wrote a copy of a letter written by Benjamin Franklin in 1765 — a tract on thoughts of religion.[15] The ledger book containing this letter is dated 1834, a year after Alvarez retired from the fur trade, and how he came to know of Franklin's letter is obscure. What is more important is that he bothered to copy it. Perhaps he was responding to the similarities between his life and aspirations and Franklin's life: Alvarez published,[16] traveled, and had a personal code by which he conducted himself; he was not afraid to take unpopular stands; he clearly believed in human rights, and he saw the value of education. With the help of his friend Richard Weightman, Alvarez arranged to have the federal government purchase "26 volumes by distinguished authors ancient and modern" and send them to New Mexico, where he presented them to the territorial legislature.[17] He even kept a "poor Richard's almanac." Both Alvarez and Franklin were fated to live in times and places that needed their talents: one to aid the birth of a nation; the other to help prepare a cosmopolitan society for a new political and cultural regime. Certainly, Alvarez commanded the respect and trust of everyone who knew him. In all the archives, letters, and diaries, not one aspersion of his integrity is to be found.

Quite obviously, Alvarez had ambition and confidence. He did not hesitate to embark on new adventures; indeed, he seemed to enjoy the challenge. In one way or another, he managed to succeed in an astonishing array of callings, but he was above all a merchant — the occupation for which he apparently had left his native Spain for the New World and Santa Fe. He built his business into one of the major mercantile establishments in the Southwest, and he always managed to do some business on his trips to the States. Everyone in the Southwest, even the inarticulate, did business with Alvarez, but while most other merchants took advantage of newspaper ads, none appears for his store. When others carried on personal feuds, Alvarez maintained his dignity and his competitors' respect. Indeed, he seems to have received more than enough requests to act as a disinterested third party.

There is no question that Alvarez accepted all the challenges life brought him with the same forthright determination. He gained his colleagues' admiration, and they demonstrated their feelings in their generous support and gratitude, freely expressed on so many occasions. No man was more qualified than Alvarez to embody the aspirations of a new frontier, and the recognition of his worth is evident in David Waldo's simple statement that "no gentleman stands higher" in esteem than Alvarez. In a petition carrying over 140 signatures, he was described as a man of "inprochable [sic] integrity" in whom men and women could place their "utmost confidence."[18]

Alvarez won the respect of the Hispanic population, too, even though he worked as an adversary of the Mexican government. He never let himself be drawn into the bigotry many of his colleagues displayed, and many a Mexican recognized him for the intelligent, fair man he was. Colonel Francisco Perea, writing in the late 1830s, called Alvarez a prominent man, a scholar of "considerable note," a strict observer of national affairs, beloved by the people of Santa Fe. Alvarez, he noted, received the same kind of reaction wherever he went.[19]

A foreigner himself, Alvarez made some observations about the Mexican people and, as he did with many of his thoughts, wrote them down, almost as if writing was necessary to articulate his ideas. He saw only one fault in Mexicans: They were too gullible, especially to the polished chicanery of American merchants. Otherwise, he found the people wise and persistent; their survival in "this land" indicated such traits. His colleagues many times confused the inability to speak or write English with illiteracy — the irony is that most of the critics had trouble enough scrawling their own names — but Alvarez found Mexican people intelligent and gentle, praising the Spanish "transplants" for their "love and taste" for the "beautiful science" of music. The Mexicans, he proclaimed, have excellent bands.[20] He also readily acknowledged that as mounted soldiers they became a most efficient fighting force — a fact Kearny learned at the battle of San Pascual, California, during the Mexican War. Even Texans, Alvarez commented, spoke with high regard of these soldiers.[21]

Alvarez had no hatred for his adopted country, but Mexico came in for some criticism: It must come to realize that its wealth lay not in gold and silver, and it must recognize its poverty amid precious metals while the wealthiest countries, England and Holland, had no such natural resources. In 1834, he felt that Mexico would not achieve any degree of greatness without an influx of foreign immigration, and to achieve that it must destroy the prevalent picture of an ill-regulated and quarrelsome household. Instead, Mexico must embark on a "peaceful and prosperous course."[22] Alvarez's earlier reports, like the memorial in 1841, pretty much state his opinion of government at the local level: rife with neglect, corruption, and inefficient organization. The foreigner was handicapped by many regulations: no freedom of worship; meticulous and cumbersome naturalization laws; legal obstacles to marriages and burials; and prohibition of freehold landownership. Alvarez, an artful dodger and a pragmatist of the highest order, managed to avoid all the regulations; he became a landowner simply by allowing Mexican officials to believe he was a naturalized citizen. The system had an elasticity about it, and, as Alvarez pointed out, most foreigners could take advantage because their hosts were most "easily subdued by kindness."[23]

Alvarez could be painfully accurate; that was his style. He dealt with the large philosophical picture and studied to keep himself at that level, not only reading great thinkers but carrying on a dialog with them. His notebook is strewn with notes and arguments, his own and those of others, about, against, and for the writings of such men. Thomas Jefferson would have appreciated this frontier philosopher-king, a Spaniard with *castizo* — a concept that combines, as nearly as it can be translated, intellect and dignity. Castizo had its place in the North American Southwest, for the final meeting of the northbound Latin tradition with the westward expansion of the Anglo-American culture needed such a man. In the final analysis, he was perhaps more important than the more obvious Houghtons, Weightmans, Carsons, Armijos, and Kearnys. He was not simple enough for the new way of things, yet he was necessary. In his 1834 ledger book, Alvarez wrote: "*A great man* had an extraordinary mark of distinction sent him by his prince, as he lay on his death bed. 'Alas!' said he looking coldly upon it, 'This is of immense value in this country, but I am just going to a country where it will be of no service to me.' "[24] In August, the *Missouri Republican* noted that the last mail from New Mexico brought news that after a very short illness, Manuel Alvarez had died on the morning of July 5, 1856. He was sixty-two years old.[25] He was laid to rest, with no "extraordinary mark of distinction" save that of a life fully lived, at Santa Fe's Parroquia, which was then just beginning to be transformed into a cathedral.[26] His life in New Mexico had ended, as it had begun, quietly.

Alvarez has remained a somewhat anonymous historical figure. No photographs or contemporary images of him are known to exist, and while many of his contemporaries have streets, buildings, parks, and sites named in their honor, Alvarez has none; and that is in keeping with his legacy.

Alvarez probably would have held that his appearance, along with worldly honors, are not important. Nonetheless, the traveler "de las Abelgas" lived a life of accomplishment far from his birthplace in north central Spain. I hope that this biography will be of value, not to him but to others who have a continuing curiosity about the history of the North American continent.

Notes

The following abbreviations for archives and manuscript collections are used throughout the notes, for the convenience of both author and reader.

AASF   Archives of the Archdiocese of Santa Fe

AD   Andrew Drips Papers

AGN   Archivo General de la Nación

ALC   Abiel Leonard Collection

ALP   Abiel Leonard Papers

AP   Manuel Alvarez Papers

APUNM   Manuel Alvarez Papers, microfilm

ARPO   Applications and Recommendations for Public Office

BR   Benjamin Read Collection

CD   Consular Dispatches

CL   Charles Lucas Collection

DSMM   Dispatches from US Ministers to Mexico

DSTP   Department of State Territorial Papers

FUA   Fort Union Archives

GRDB   St. Louis General Records, Deed Books

GSA   Papers of the US General Services Administration

JWA   James W. Arrott Collection

LGF   Land Grant File

MANM   Mexican Archives of New Mexico

MNM/HL   Museum of New Mexico, History Library

MWF   Mexican War File

NMSRC   New Mexico State Records Center and Archives, Santa Fe, NM

PC-M   Pierre Chouteau-Maffitt Collection

SFTP   Santa Fe Trade Papers

TPUSS   Territorial Papers of the US Senate

WGR   William G. Ritch Papers

Introduction

1. Eugene T. Wells, "The Growth of Independence, Missouri, 1827–1850," *Missouri Historical Society Bulletin* 41, no. 1 (October 1959): 42; R. L. Duffus, *The Santa Fe Trail* (New York: Longmans, Green, 1930), p. 184.

2. Some historians argue that poverty did not reign, pointing out that many New

Mexicans made fortunes through sheep and the Santa Fe Trail. While this may be true, the reality of New Mexico's distance more than offsets such wealth. A cursory look at the kinds of furniture, toys, utensils, and so on used by New Mexicans amply demonstrates the effects of distance, even upon the relatively well-off.

Chapter 1

1. Last will and testament of Manuel Alvarez, MNM/HL.

2. Walter D. Sadlowski, Jr., "Manuel Alvarez: Merchant and Trader, Consul and Commercial Agent Politico" (unpublished paper (unpaginated), MNM/HL, first page; Francisco Perea, "Santa Fe As It Appeared During the Winter of 1837 and 1838," ed. W.H.H. Allison, *Old Santa Fe* 2 (October 1914): 182–83. The *Historia* is a monumental as well as landmark work. Clavijero, born in Veracruz in 1731, was expelled from Mexico with all his Jesuit brethren in 1767 and died in Bologna, Italy, in 1787. *La Historia Antiqua de México* was published in four volumes in 1780–1781. Humboldt, born in Berlin, Germany, in 1769, received permission from King Carlos IV of Spain to tour New Spain. He spent most of 1803 and 1804 in Mexico and published his enormous *Political Essay* with a grateful preface to Carlos IV in 1808. Alvarez had both books in Santa Fe by, at least, the 1830s.

3. AP/Ledger Book, 1834.

4. Ibid.

5. Ibid.

6. Louis Houck, *The Spanish Regime in Missouri: A Collection of Papers . . .* , vol. 2 (Chicago: R. R. Donnelley & Sons, 1909), p. 376. Eugenio Alvarez is listed as head of a six-member family; he lived in St. Louis from, at least, 1779. Houck, *History of Missouri,* vol. 2 (Chicago: R. R. Donnelley & Sons, 1908), p. 21, has Alvarez arriving on the continent in 1768. John Barber White, "The Missouri Merchant One Hundred Years Ago," *Missouri Historical Review* 13, no. 2 (1919): 100–101, lists Eugenio Alvarez as one of the principal St. Louis merchants at the time of Missouri's cession to the United States. Manuel's acquaintance with Eugenio is, at this point, conjecture. The past is somewhat muddied because Eugenio had a son also named Manuel. Houck, *History,* p. 21, mentions a Manuel Alvarez but is unclear about his identification. A choice parcel of land next to St. Louis's main church was conferred to Manuel the son, who immediately sold it. The lot is shown on a map I found in the holdings of the Missouri Historical Society, St. Louis. See also the contract between Charles Lucas and Christopher M. Price, June 18, 1817, CL. Just exactly how much other land went to the son, and how it was conveyed, is unclear. He did purchase 150 river frontage acres for $250 in March 1820. This land, however, was not a valuable city lot; that may have been the lot for which he paid his father $100 on May 27, 1816; GRDB, I and J, nos. 99k–100, March 6, 1820. A curious fact is that the land was surveyed by Silas Bent, the father of the Bent brothers who will be noted later. See also GRDB, E, no. 496, May 28, 1816. Documentation establishing Manuel the son as landowner are GRDB, E, no. 496, May 27, 1816, and J, nos. 100–101, March 9, 1820. The son died sometime in mid-1840, thus definitely establishing him as a different Manuel Alvarez. See GRDB, O^2, no. 60, September 15, 1840 and nos. 60–61, October 19, 1840.

The auction of Alvarez's land is attested to by the city clerk, John Rowland, another person who will be noted later. It is my hope that this brief degression on the life of Manuel Alvarez, son of Eugenio, may help keep subsequent historians from falling into the trap of confusing the two Manuel Alvarezes.

7. LGF, passport, September 3, 1824, reel 6, frame 1132, no. 11. See also Harold H. Dunham, "Manuel Alvarez," in *The Mountain Men and the Fur Trade of the Far West*, vol. 1, ed. LeRoy Hafen (Glendale, CA: Arthur H. Clark, 1965), p. 182; David J. Weber, *The Taos Trappers: The Fur Trade in the Far Southwest, 1540–1846* (Norman: University of Oklahoma Press, 1971), p. 86; and passport, 1824, in Ralph Emerson Twitchell, *The Spanish Archives of New Mexico*, vol. 1 (Cedar Rapids, IA: The Torch Press, 1914), p. 342; and Sadlowski, "Manuel Alvarez," passim.

8. Weber, *Taos Trappers*, p. 94.

9. For example, see the "Plano de la Provincia interna de el Nuevo Mexico . . . , 1779" by Bernardo Miera y Pacheco, reproduced in Angélico Chávez and Elenore Adams, *The Missions of New Mexico* (Albuquerque: University of New Mexico Press, 1956), p. 4.

10. Zebulon Montgomery Pike, *The Southwestern Expedition of Zebulon M. Pike*, ed. Milo Quaife (Chicago: Lakeside Press, 1925), p. 136.

11. A good example of a contemporary impression of Santa Fe is "Journal of M. M. Marmaduke," SFTP; Marmaduke could accept Santa Fe but not the beggars and mud houses.

12. William Becknell, "Journal of Two Expeditions From Boon's Lick to Santa Fe," *Missouri Intelligencer* (Franklin), April 22, 1823; Thomas James, *Three Years Among the Mexicans and the Indians* (Chicago: Keystone Books, 1962); and David J. Weber, *The Mexican Frontier, 1821–1846: The American Southwest Under Mexico* (Albuquerque: University of New Mexico Press, 1982), pp. 128–29.

13. That Santa Fe trade was lucrative in its early years is demonstrated by a contemporary, G. C. Broadhead, who kept notes on caravans returning from New Mexico to St. Louis. On October 18, 1834, he reported a St. Vrain–Bent Company caravan that brought "upwards [of] $200,000 in specie." Broadhead, "Notes on Santa Fe Traders," p. 4, SFTP.

14. See Weber, *Taos Trappers*, for an excellent study on the role of the New Mexican fur trade.

15. *Missouri Intelligencer* (Fayette), July 19, 1827. Alvarez and Padilla went back to New Mexico under a permit to travel through the Indian territory issued by Governor William Clark; see Louise Barry, *The Beginning of the West: Annals of the Kansas Gateway to the American West, 1540–1854* (Topeka: Kansas State Historical Society, 1972), p. 146. See also David J. Weber, *The Extranjeros: Selected Documents from the Mexican Side of the Santa Fe Trail, 1825–1828* (Santa Fe, NM: Stagecoach Press, 1967), p. 43; here, Alvarez and party are noted by the Secretaría de Relaciones. They arrived on November 12. Alvarez is listed as a native of Leon, resident of Santa Fe, and a merchant by trade. In all, Alvarez made five treks across the plains.

16. Weber, *Taos Trappers*, p. 185.

17. Ibid., p. 164.

18. Dunham, "Manuel Alvarez," p. 185. Alvarez, mentioned in documents as Alvaris and Alvaripe, is alleged to have married an Indian woman who had three children by him; one died and the other two were purportedly sent to Spain. The undocumented story of marriage is contradicted both by Alvarez's will and a family tree apparently drawn by him.

19. Warren A. Ferris, *Life in the Rocky Mountains,* ed. P. C. Phillips (Denver, CO: Old West Publishing, 1940), pp. 192–94.

20. See Merrill J. Mattes, "Exploding Fur Trade Fairy Tales," in *Probing the American West,* ed. K. Ross Toole et al. (Santa Fe: Museum of New Mexico Press, 1962), p. 96. The chapter is based on Mattes's paper, read to the first annual meeting of the Western History Association, in which he discredits Colter's claim to the discovery of the natural wonders and gives qualified credit to Alvarez. See also Richard A. Bartlett, *Nature's Yellowstone: The Story of an American Wilderness That Became Yellowstone National Park in 1872* (Albuquerque: University of New Mexico Press, 1974), p. 103. I must refute Phillips's contentions, because Alvarez did not enter the mountain life until 1828. See Bartlett, *Nature's Yellowstone,* pp. 224–25, fn. 30, and Merrill J. Mattes, "Behind the Legend of Colter's Hell: The Early Exploration of Yellowstone National Park," *Mississippi Valley Historical Review* 36, no. 2 (September 1949): 258.

21. Daniel T. Potts to Robert T. Potts, July 8, 1827, Research Library, Yellowstone National Park, Wyoming.

22. Ferris, *Life,* p. 259; the story first appeared in 1842–1843 in the *Western Literary Messenger*. See also Mattes, "Behind the Legend," p. 269.

23. Mattes, "Behind the Legend," p. 271.

24. Dunham, "Manuel Alvarez," p. 186; draft for $1,325.98 to Manuel Alvarez, July 31, 1833, PC-M. Alvarez's old boss, Louis Papin, received payment for only $116.62; see Lansing Bloom, "Ledgers of a Santa Fe Trader," *El Palacio* 14, no. 9 (May 1923): 135.

25. Twitchell, *Spanish Archives,* vol. 2, p. 626.

26. For various versions of this incident, see LeBaron Bradford Prince, *Historical Sketches of New Mexico* (Kansas City, MO: Ramsey, Millet & Hudson, 1883), pp. 241–42; Rex Arrowsmith, ed., *Mines of the Old Southwest* (Santa Fe, NM: Stagecoach Press, 1963), p. 50; and John M. Townley, "El Placer: A New Mexico Mining Boom Before 1846," *Journal of the West* 10, no. 1 (January 1971): 108–10.

27. Sadlowski, "Manuel Alvarez," eighteenth page; Alvin R. Sunseri, "Sheep Ricos, Sheep Fortunes in the Aftermath of the American Conquest, 1846–1861," *El Palacio* 83, no. 1 (1977): 6.

28. Weber, *Taos Trappers,* p. 40.

29. The last big rendezvous was held on the Green River, near the mouth of Horse Creek, in 1840.

30. Bill signed by David Waldo, October 28, 1835, AP.

31. Smith left trapping to invest in trade on the Santa Fe Trail, where he died in a Comanche ambush.

32. Janet Lecompte, *Rebellion in Rio Arriba, 1837* (Albuquerque: Historical Soci-

ety of New Mexico — University of New Mexico Press, 1985), pp. 13, 19–20.

33. US Merchants of Santa Fe to the Honorable Powhatan Ellis, Minister Plenipotentiary and Envoy Extraordinary from the United States of America to the Republic of Mexico, September 7, 1837 (hereafter Merchants to Ellis), BR, no. 8, p. 3.

34. Ibid.

35. One historian has pointed out that the property of the deceased was disbursed according to law. See Philip Reno, "Rebellion in New Mexico–1837," *New Mexico Historical Review* 40, no. 3 (1965): 197–213. This may have been why, even after the victory of fresh government forces from the South, reparation to the merchants was not forthcoming.

36. Merchants to Ellis, September 7, 1837, BR, no. 8, p. 2.

37. Manuel Armijo to José Sutton, September 25, 1837, in Reno, "Rebellion," pp. 202–203. Alvarez was among those thanked on behalf of the president of Mexico.

38. Merchants to Ellis, September 7, 1837, BR, no. 2. For Alvarez's authorship, see Orral Messmore Robidoux, *Memorial to the Robidoux Brothers: A History of the Robidouxs in America* (Kansas City, MO: Smith-Grieves, 1924), pp. 205–208.

39. Lansing Bloom, "New Mexico Under Mexican Administration," *Old Santa Fe* 2 (October 1914): 141.

40. S. Vergara to Alvarez, August 17, 1838, BR, no. 298.

41. APUNM, reel 4 (not with the originals in AP).

42. US residents in Santa Fe to Alvarez, December 8, 1840, BR, no. 9.

43. APUNM, reel 4; original in BR Alvarez Letter Book (hereafter cited as BR/Letter Book).

44. Ocaté, claim no. 1; Dunham, "Manuel Alvarez," p. 193.

Chapter 2

1. For an interesting overview, see Norman A. Graebner, *Empire on the Pacific: A Study in American Continental Expansion* (New York: Ronald Press, 1955).

2. David Lavender, *Bent's Fort* (Garden City, NY: Doubleday, 1954; reprinted Lincoln: University of Nebraska Press, 1972), p. 220.

3. Juan Andrés Archuleta to Damaso López, prefect of the first district, January 15, 1841, BR, no. 171.

4. Guadalupe Miranda to Alvarez, January 28, 1841, AP.

5. Simeon Turley to Alvarez, January 28, 1841, AP.

6. For a sampling, see Luis G. Guevas to Manuel Armijo, March 10, 1840, WGR, no. 183; Guadalupe Miranda to Alvarez, April 23, 1849, BR, no. 203; Manuel Armijo, passport for Consul Manuel Alvarez, October 25, 1841, BR, no. 18; Dunham, "Manuel Alvarez," cites Alvarez as being treated as a Mexican citizen in the 1820s.

7. Memorial of Manual Alvarez, 1842 (hereafter Memorial), CD, M-199, roll 1, pp. 15–16; copy in MNM/HL. Weber, *Taos Trappers*, p. 176, correctly states that

there is no documented proof of Alvarez ever becoming naturalized. On the other hand, Dunham, "Manuel Alvarez," p. 182, concludes that Alvarez did indeed become a Mexican citizen, since Mexican officials began treating him as such.

8. See, for example, the petition for Mexican naturalization, 1825, LGF, no. 182, reel 6, frame 1132.

9. Dunham, "Manuel Alvarez," p. 182.

10. Memorial; list of Spanish citizens, November 20, 1829, MANM, governor's papers, 1929, Miscellaneous Documents.

11. Alvarez to Daniel Webster, March 4, 1842, CD.

12. Alvarez, official certificate of US naturalization, April 9, 1842, BR, no. 5; Alvarez to Webster, May 4, 1842, CD.

13. Passport, March 4, 1839, BR, no. 144.

14. Records of the US Department of State, 1842, US National Archives; official certificate of office, February 12, 1840, US National Archives, Washington, DC.

15. F. W. Hodge, ed. "Letter Dated Santa Fe, July 29, 1841, Reproduced from *Niles National Register,* December 4, 1841," *New Mexico Historical Review* 5, no. 3 (July 1930): 303; Daniel Tyler, "Governor Armijo's Moment of Truth," *Journal of the West* 11, no. 2 (April 1972): 310.

16. Armijo to minister of the interior, August 2, 1839, AGN, Justicia, vol. 159-1/2, pp. 302–303.

17. Letters to Armijo, August 21, 1839, APUNM, reel 4; Alvarez to Armijo, August 21, 1839, and Armijo recommendation, August 21, 1839: both in AGN, Justicia, p. 305; and Armijo recommendation, August 28, 1839, AGN, Justicia, p. 306. The last letter has a scribbled notation dated March 10, 1840, recommending concession of a license.

18. Ellis to Alvarez, November 2, 1839, BR, no. 142.

19. Unsigned letter to Alvarez, February 17, 1840, CD.

20. Miranda to Alvarez, February 18, 1840, BR, no. 201; a copy of this letter is attached to Memorial and lettered A.

21. Minister of the Interior Luis G. Guevas to Manuel Armijo, March 10, 1840, WGR, no. 183; Mexico, Ministerio de Relaciones Exteriores to Armijo, March 14, 1840, AGN, Justicia. The latter letter is a copy of one written by the Mexican president in which either he or the copier mistakes Nueva Leon for New Mexico.

22. Miranda to Alvarez, April 23, 1840, Memorial, copy lettered B; Miranda, circular to the prefects of the Department of New Mexico, March 20, 1840, BR, no. 202; Alvarez to Ellis, December 12, 1840, Memorial, copy numbered 8.

23. For salary, see official certificate of office, February 12, 1840, CD; for expense account, see John Forsyth to Alvarez, March 22, 1839, BR, no. 145; and Ellis to Alvarez, November 3, 1839, BR, no. 142.

24. Lavender, *Bent's Fort* pp. 191–92; Jack D. Rittenhouse, *The Santa Fe Trail: A Historical Bibliography* (Albuquerque: University of New Mexico Press, 1971), p. 199. Storrs did at least write detailed answers to questions asked by Senator Thomas Hart Benton, leading to a government survey of the Santa Fe Trail.

There seemed to be some initial doubt whether Storrs would take the diplomatic job; see G. C. Broadhead, "Notes on Santa Fe Trade," October 21, 1825, p. 4, SFTP.

25. Lavender, *Bent's Fort,* p. 207.

26. Alvarez to Forsyth, September 20, 1839, CD.

27. APUNM, reel 4. Alvarez had arrived with the "Walworth and Alvarez Party" in June 1839.

28. Forsyth to Alvarez, March 22, 1839, BR, no. 145.

29. John E. Sunder, ed., *Matt Field on the Santa Fe Trail* (Norman: University of Oklahoma Press, 1960), p. xix.

30. Specifically, Article I, ch. 1 of the general instructions; Forsyth to Alvarez, March 22, 1839, BR, no. 145.

31. Alvarez to Forsyth, September 20, 1839, CD.

32. Ellis to Alvarez, November 2, 1839, BR, no. 142.

33. Ellis to Gorostiza, July 11, 1839; Ellis to Forsyth, August 10, 1839: both in DSMM, June 12, 1837–July 28, 1840.

34. Gorostiza to Ellis, July 12, 1839, DSMM.

35. Ibid. A small sidelight to this correspondence is the translated copy of this letter wherein the translator substituted "Martínez" for "Alvarez." Also see Ellis to Forsyth, August 10, 1839, DSMM.

36. Memorial, p. 2.

37. Alvarez to Ellis, January 10, 1840, Memorial, copy numbered 4.

38. Alvarez to Secretary of State James Buchanan, June 18, 1845, CD.

39. Alvarez to Webster, July 1, 1843, CD.

40. Document dated August 1, 1840, ALC.

41. Alvarez, Memorial to the prefect of the first district, November 5, 1839, BR, no. 86.

42. Miranda to Alvarez, December 5, 1939, BR, no. 200.

43. Webster to Alvarez, March 3, 1842, BR, no. 308.

44. Alvarez to Webster, March 4, 1842, CD.

45. Webster to Alvarez, March 4, 1842, BR, no. 309.

46. Miranda to Alvarez, August 14, 1841, BR, no. 254, and August 20, 1841, BR, no. 212; a copy of no. 254 is attached to Memorial and lettered "P".

47. Alvarez, Memorial, p. 17.

48. Alvarez to Miranda, August 10, 1841, MANM, governor's papers received by secretary of government, January 15–December 2, 1841, reel 20, frames 1328–29; Alvarez, Memorial, numbered 20. Alvarez gives the date as August 16, 1841, even though the copy of the cited letter has the correct date of August 10. The memorial gives a straightforward account of the events, replete with citations for each pertinent document. For my purposes, the originals of those letters are used, the only discrepancy being the date.

49. Miranda to Alvarez, August 10, 1841, BR, no. 212. The copy attached to Memorial is labeled O. The date is incorrectly given as August 1, 1841, in the

calendar to the Read Collection. Internal evidence, the document itself, and the copy in Alvarez's hand attached to the memorial all attest to the correct date — August 10, 1841.

50. Alvarez, Memorial, p. 16.

51. Alvarez to Armijo, August 21, 1839, APUNM, reel 4.

52. Alvarez to Miranda, August 11, 1841, MANM, governor's papers, reel 28, frame 1330. The copy attached to Memorial is numbered 21.

53. Jorge Ramírez to Alvarez, August 14, 1841, BR, no. 254. The copy attached to Memorial is lettered P.

54. Alvarez, Memorial, p. 16.

55. Ibid.

56. Alvarez to Miranda, August 23, 1841, MANM, governor's papers, reel 28, frames 1332–33. The copy attached to Memorial is numbered 22.

57. Miranda to Alvarez, August 25, 1841, BR, no. 213. The copy attached to Memorial is lettered Q.

58. Alvarez to Webster, March 2, 1842, CD.

59. Alvarez to Webster, July 1, 1843, CD.

60. Charles Bent to Alvarez, April 29, 1843, CD.

Chapter 3

1. Forsyth to Alvarez, March 22, 1839, BR, no. 145.

2. Thompson to Alvarez, dated only 1838, AP/Business.

3. Litigated suit prosecuted by Waldo as attorney of Powell, Lamont and Company vs. Philip W. Thompson, November 9, 1839, pp. 1–14, ALC; Contested action — David Waldo as attorney of Powell, Lamont and Company vs. Philip W. Thompson for $8,000.00, n.d., ALP; and James W. Goodrich, "In the Earnest Pursuit of Wealth: David Waldo in Missouri and Southwest, 1820–1878," *Missouri Historical Review* 46, no. 2 (1972): 166. Both litigants had done business with and knew Alvarez.

4. A. Leonard to A. W. Turner, April 7, 1840, ALP.

5. E. Stanley to Leonard, December 21, 1839, ALP; Leonard to A. W. Turner, April 7, 1840, ALP.

6. Leonard to Turner, April 7 and 9, 1840, ALP.

7. Powell, Lamont and Company vs. Thompson, November 9, 1839, ALP.

8. Bent to Alvarez, November 11, 1839, BR, no. 40.

9. Barry, *Beginning of the West*, p. 271.

10. Armijo to minister of war, February 4, 1840, AGN, Guerra y Marina, correspondence of Armijo regarding the Santa Fe expedition.

11. Lavender, *Bent's Fort*, pp. 228–29; and Janet Lecompte, *Pueblo, Hardscrabble, Greenhorn: The Upper Arkansas, 1832–1856* (Norman: University of Oklahoma Press, 1978), pp. 91, 95. Francis Parkman, who visited Bent's Fort in 1846, described it as wretched, with a cracked mud wall and a gate that dangled on wooden hinges with half-broken-down pickets; *The Oregon Trail*, (1849; re-

printed Clinton, MA: Airmont, 1964), p. 203.

12. Lavender, *Bent's Fort,* pp. 228–29; Bent to Alvarez, September 19, 1842, BR, no. 57; Bent relates that he received an inquiry from Doctor Frank Lane. Lecompte, *Pueblo,* p. 95, states that Missouri Senator Lewis F. Linn inquired of Alvarez, who passed the word to Bent.

13. Alvarez to Buchanan, July 1, 1843, CD.

14. Bent to Alvarez, January 16, 1841, BR, no. 44.

15. Two other interesting facts were the presence of Mexican guides with the Indians and the claim that the Arapaho prisoners were originally taken by "easterners"; Bent to Alvarez, January 30, 1841, BR, no. 46. One historian identifies the "easterners" as the Utes; see Charles L. Kenner, *A History of New Mexican–Plains Indian Relations* (Norman: University of Oklahoma Press, 1969), pp. 76–77.

16. Bent to Alvarez, n.d., BR, no. 48; Bent to Alvarez, March 15, 1841, BR, no. 50; and Bent to Alvarez, March 22, 1841, BR, no. 51.

17. Bent to Alvarez, March 29, 1841, BR, no. 52.

18. Bent to Alvarez, April 30, 1841, BR, no. 53; quoted in Kenner, *New Mexican–Plains Indians Relations,* p. 77. The Las Animas River is now called the Purgatory River.

19. Barry, *Beginning of the West,* p. 460.

20. T. Hartly Crawford, Office of Indian Affairs, to Major T.F.A. Langford, July 2, 1842, and Langford to Andrew Drips, July 10, 1842, AD; Barry, *Beginning of the West,* p. 460, paraphrases Chittenden's theory that Drips's appointment was a shrewd move by the American Fur Company, old rival to the Bent–St. Vrain Company — an appointment of one of its employees could only strengthen its position vis-à-vis opposition traders. Yet, the Langford letter reveals that the opposition seemed quite satisfied with the designated agent. Frankly, Bent could not expect the government to appoint one of his own employees, for he had made the suggestion for such a position. See also David D. Mitchell, superintendent of Indian affairs at St. Louis to Agent R. W. Cummins, July 11, 1842, AD.

21. Barry, *Beginning of the West,* p. 460; Mitchell to Drips, April 20, 1843, AD.

22. Alvarez to Buchanan, July 1, 1843, CD. Much of the Taos liquor was made at Turley's distillery in Arroyo Hondo, just north of Taos. Historian David Weber, *Taos Trappers,* pp. 226–27, describes the population at Pueblo as retired mountain men and Mexicans, the latter in the majority.

23. Alvarez to Buchanan, July 1, 1843, CD.

24. Ibid.

25. Drips to Jos. V. Hamilton, November 4, 1843, and Drips to Antoine Raynald, December 14, 1843, AD.

26. Alvarez to Guadalupe Miranda, October 2, 1841, BR/Letter Book, pp. 37–38.

27. Bent to Alvarez, December 10, 1839, BR, no. 39.

28. Memorial, pp. 7–9, 26; Bent to Alvarez, January 30, 1841, BR, no. 46.

29. Bent to Alvarez, December 1, 1840, BR, no. 42.

30. Alvarez to Ellis, December 14, 1840, BR/Letter Book, p. 11; Alvarez to Guada-

lupe Miranda, March 12, 1841, BR/Letter Book, p. 21.

31. Alvarez to Albino Chacón, second alcalde of Santa Fe, July 7, 1841, BR/Letter Book, p. 21.

32. Alvarez to Waddy Thompson, August 25, 1842, and December 14, 1842, BR/ Letter Book, pp. 40, 42.

33. Memorial, p. 9.

34. Alvarez to Ellis, December 14, 1840, BR/Letter Book, p. 12.

35. Inventory of the goods and effects belonging to David White, March 27 and 28, 1841, AP/Business.

36. Alvarez to Guadalupe Miranda, December 24, 1840, BR/Letter Book, p. 12, January 25, 1841, BR/Letter Book, p. 13, September 29, 1841, BR/Letter Book, pp. 36–37, and October 2, 1841, BR/Letter Book, pp. 38–39.

37. Alvarez to Honorable Wilson Shannon, December 14, 1844, BR, AP/Letter Book, p. 98.

38. John H. Lyman to Alvarez, December 7, 1840, BR, no. 174; Lyman to Alvarez, November 29, 1840, BR, no. 173. Lyman had the cash in hand from a draft he had exchanged with Alvarez, who, in turn, had exchanged it on his account with L. L. Waldo; Alvarez account with L. L. Waldo, September 14, 1840, AP/Business.

39. Lyman to Alvarez, December 7, 1840, BR, no. 174; Memorial, p. 9.

40. Memorial, p. 9.

41. Lyman to Alvarez, December 7, 1840, BR, no. 174 (emphasis in the original).

42. Lyman to Alvarez, October 9, 1842, cited in *The Thomas O. Larkin Papers,* vol. 1, ed. George P. Hammond (1951; reprinted Berkeley: University of California Press, 1953), p. 298; Leroy R. and Ann W. Hafen, *The Old Spanish Trail: Santa Fe to Los Angeles,* Far West and the Rockies Historical Series, 1820–1875 (Glendale, CA: Arthur H. Clark, 1954), p. 298.

43. Memorial, pp. 10–11; Alvarez to Miranda, May 22, 1841, MANM, reel 28, frames 1291–93, and in BR/Letter Book, pp. 13–14; Alvarez to Miranda, June 14, 1841, MANM, reel 28, frames 1647–48, and in BR/Letter Book, pp. 19–20; Jorge Ramírez to Alvarez, May 24, 1841, BR, no. 253; Miranda to Alvarez, June 11, 1841, BR, no. 210; Vicar Juan Felipe Ortiz to Alvarez, June 12, 1841, BR, no. 231; Daniel Tyler, "Gringo Views of Governor Manuel Armijo," *New Mexico Historical Review* 45, no. 1 (January 1970): 29; Alvarez to Guadalupe Miranda, June 3, 1841, BR/Letter Book, pp. 15–16; and Alvarez to Ortiz, June 11, 1841, BR/Letter Book, pp. 18–19.

44. Memorial, p. 5.

45. Lavender, *Bent's Fort,* p. 205; Memorial, p. 4; Alvarez to Ellis, December 13, 1840, BR/Letter Book, p. 9.

46. Alvarez to Ellis, January 10, 1840, CD, and BR/Letter Book, pp. 3–4.

47. Memorial, p. 6.

48. Tyler, "Gringo Views," p. 36. Armijo's ploy worked, for Mexican activity in the Santa Fe trade increased tremendously from the time the governor's landmark tax was imposed.

49. Alvarez to Ellis, January 10, 1840, CD.

50. Memorial, pp. 5–7.

51. Alvarez account with L. L. Waldo, May 27, 1839 – March 20, 1840, AP/Business.

52. Ibid., June 1, 1839 – January 12, 1841.

53. Bill of sale, Waldo to Alvarez, October 16, 1839, AP/Business.

54. Receipt for Chaves, October 27, 1841, AP/Business.

55. Receipt from Giddings and Gentry, October 23, 1841, AP/Business.

56. Lists of debtors, October 25, 1841, AP/Business (two separate copies).

57. For example, see lists of debtors, October 25, 1841, AP/Business.

58. Manuela Antonio Jaramillo to Alvarez, March 20, 1840, and July 19, 1840, AP/Business.

59. Lists of debtors, October 25, 1841, AP/Business. Guadalupe García to Alvarez, April 23, 1841, and María Rosalía Baca to Alvarez, April 27, 1840, AP/Business, provide good examples of women fending for themselves during the late 1830s and early 1840s.

60. Turley to Alvarez, June 23, 1840, and October 16, 1840, AP/Business.

61. Account of Alvarez with L. L. Waldo, May 23, 1839, AP/Business; the ledger citation is May 27, 1840.

62. Account of Alvarez with David Waldo, May 10, 1840, AP/Business; the ledger citation is June 6, 1840.

63. Receipt with L. A. [Blount] and Company, October 29, 1838, AP/Business (the entry is unclear, but the name appears to be Blount).

64. Juan Rowland to Alvarez, May 3, 1840, AP/Business.

65. Alvarez account with L. L. Waldo, 1840, citations dated May 8 and September 14, 1840, AP/Business; account with David Waldo, 1840, citation dated May 8, 1840, AP/Business.

66. Memorandum of gold bullion, October 19, 1840, AP/Business; D. Waldo to Alvarez, April 20, 1841, AP/Business. Waldo went to New Orleans rather than to the Philadelphia mint because the Ohio River was "so low as to prevent travel east."

67. Receipt with Blount, October 29, 1838, AP/Business. This document is an excellent example of such an agreement.

68. David Waldo to Alvarez, April 20, 1841, AP/Business.

69. Alvarez account with Giddings and Gentry, 1840, AP/Business; the ledger citation is October 24, 1841.

70. I am here in disagreement with William J. Parrish, "The German Jew and the Commercial Revolution in Territorial New Mexico, 1850–1900," *New Mexico Historical Review* 45, no. 1 (1960): 5. Parrish, who credits Alvarez with some bartering in Taos and Abiquiú and "but three Eastern trips," based his conclusion on Lansing Bloom's "Ledgers of a Santa Fe Trader," *El Palacio* 14, no. 9 (May 1923): 133–36, and did not utilize or have access to the primary source: Alvarez's business papers.

71. These mules were eventually sold in Louisiana. D. Waldo to Alvarez, April 20, 1841, AP/Business; Michael Cox, "Through the Governor's Window, 1821–

1846," *El Palacio* 80, no. 3 (1974): 23.

72. Alvarez to Webster, December 18, 1842, CD.

73. Ibid.; Alvarez to secretary of state, July 1, 1843, CD. The office of secretary of state was temporarily vacant at the time; Abel P. Upshur was sworn in on July 24, 1843.

74. Alvarez to Thompson, December 14, 1842, BR/Letter Book, pp. 41–42.

75. Alvarez to secretary of state, July 1, 1843, CD; Bent to Alvarez, February 28, 1843, BR, no. 62a.

76. Armijo, passport for Alvarez, April 3, 1843, BR, no. 129; Alvarez to secretary of state, July 1, 1843, CD.

77. Thomas Rowland to Alvarez, April 23, 1843, BR, no. 264.

78. Alvarez to secretary of state, July 1, 1843, CD.

79. Buchanan to Alvarez, March 19, 1846, quoted in John Bassett Moore, ed., *The Works of James Buchanan Comprising His Speeches, State Papers and Private Correspondence,* vol. 6 (New York: Antiquarian Press, 1960), pp. 423–24.

80. Waldo to Robert J. Walker, March 26, 1845, GSA.

81. Petition to the Department of Treasury, March 25, 1845; copies in ARPO and GSA.

82. Waldo to Honorable Leonard H. Sims, April 3, 1846, ARPO, microfilm 873, roll 8, frame 0577.

83. Alvarez to Buchanan, June 19, 1845, CD.

84. Ibid.

85. Buchanan to Alvarez, March 19, 1846, in Moore, *Works of James Buchanan,* pp. 423–24.

86. Alvarez to Buchanan, March 28, 1846, CD.

87. Alvarez to Buchanan, September 4, 1846, CD.

88. Buchanan to Alvarez, March 19, 1846, in Moore, *Works of James Buchanan,* pp. 423–24; seal in the MNM/HL. The official brass seal is about the circumference of a silver dollar and approximately an inch thick. It was cast at least as early as March, when Buchanan had the official papers drawn up, and reads: "Commercial Agency, Santa Fe, U.S.A."

Chapter 4

1. José M. Ponce de Leon, *Reseñas históricas del Estado de Chihuahua,* vol. 1 (Chihuahua, Mexico: Imprenta del Gobierno, 1910), p. 297. For Arista, see Thomas Falconer, *Letters and Notes on the Texan–Santa Fe Expedition, 1841–42,* ed. F. W. Hodge (1894; reprinted Chicago: Rio Grande Press, 1963), p. 36.

2. Ponce de Leon, "Manuel Armijo, el gobernador y comandante General de Departamento de Nuevo Méjico y sus habitantes," in *Reseñas históricas,* vol. 1, p. 302.

3. Lavender, *Bent's Fort,* p. 210; Josiah Gregg, *Commerce of the Prairies,* ed. Max L. Moorhead (1944; reprinted Norman: University of Oklahoma Press, 1954), p. 162. Moorhead agrees with David Lavender by including William Workman

and John Rowland as commissioners of Texas, p. 162, fn. 12.

4. Lavender, *Bent's Fort,* p. 205–206. Lavender's citation, p. 425, fn. 3, of the eventual outcome of the episode is wrong. The correct citation is Alvarez to secretary of state, July 1 (not December 18), 1842, CD. See also Memorial, p. 8; Alvarez to Guadalupe Miranda, March 12, 1841, WGR, no. 187. The last indicates that Alvarez had a little more success in pursuing the matter through less threatening channels, for Alvarez is thanking Armijo "for his goodness" in getting the assassins of Daley retried by the Supreme Court.

5. Lavender, *Bent's Fort,* p. 215.

6. Bent to Alvarez, January 16, 1841, BR, no. 44. Thomas Falconer, who claimed that Armijo knew as early as March 17, 1841, reasoned that the governor had received word from General Arista, who was a Mexican agent in Texas.

7. Lavender, *Bent's Fort,* p. 210.

8. Thomas Rowland to Alvarez, October 26, 1841, BR, no. 262.

9. Bent to Alvarez, February 19, 1841, BR, no. 47.

10. Bent to Alvarez, February 25, 1841, BR, no. 48; Bent to Alvarez, February 19, 1841, BR, no. 47.

11. Bent to Alvarez, February 25, 1841, BR, no. 48.

12. Bent to Alvarez, February 26, 1841, BR, no. 49; the titles are not given.

13. Bent to Alvarez, March 22, 1841, BR, no. 51. This whole affair is briefly described in Lavender, *Bent's Fort,* pp. 210–11.

14. BR, Manuel Alvarez, Diary, September 11 and 13, 1841 (hereafter cited as BR/Diary).

15. Memorial, pp. 20–21; BR/Diary, September 15, 1841, in which Alvarez suggests that one of the men was acquainted with Padre Martínez in Taos. For more on Brignoli and Carlos, see Falconer, *Letters and Notes,* pp. 38, 51; and George Wilkins Kendall, *Narrative of the Texan–Santa Fe Expedition* (London: David Bogue, 1845), p. 141.

16. Tyler, "Gringo Views," p. 29. There were some lighter moments, such as a letter Alvarez received from Bent in January 1841. Alvarez's friend related that Padre Martínez reported that the Texans were in California. Bent wondered how they got there and laconically recommended that Martínez should be made "Pope for his geographical knowledge." Bent to Alvarez, January 30, 1841, BR, no. 46.

17. BR/Diary, September 15, 17, and 19, 1841.

18. Memorial, p. 21; Alvarez to Miranda, September 14, 1841, MANM, reel 29, frame 1340; a copy attached to Memorial is numbered 26. The date appears to be incorrect. If, as the memorial implies, Alvarez met with Armijo after the arrival of the deserters, his letter would have been written on September 15, but as the letter indicates, he wrote a day later; it must actually have been written on September 16. The entry for September 25, 1841, BR/Diary, mentions that Armijo's government had resorted to mail censorship.

19. Alvarez to Miranda, September 14, 1841, MANM, reel 29, frame 1340.

20. Miranda to Alvarez, September 14, 1841, BR, no. 214; a copy attached to Memorial is lettered V.

21. Memorial, p. 21.

22. Alvarez to Miranda, September 15, 1841, MANM, reel 29, frames 1342–44.

23. BR/Diary, October 7, 1841.

24. Merchants to Webster, September 16, 1841, BR, no. 9a; a copy attached to Memorial is lettered Z.

25. Memorial, p. 23; see also BR/Diary, September 16, 1841.

26. Quoted from Gregg, *Commerce of the Prairies*, p. 163.

27. BR/Diary, September 16, 1841. The same Martín had demonstrated his volatile temper in December of the previous year when he broke into Vicar Juan Felipe Ortiz's house to confront the priest over a domestic matter; see Fray Angélico Chávez, *Très Macho, He Said: Padre Gallegos of Albuquerque, New Mexico's First Congressman* (Santa Fe, NM: William Gannon, 1985), p. 10.

28. There are minor variances in detail in the myriad accounts. A sampling includes Alvarez, Memorial, pp. 19–24; Josiah Gregg, *Commerce of the Prairies*, pp. 161–62; Kendall, *Narrative*, p. 246; and James Josiah Webb, *Adventures in the Santa Fe Trade, 1844–1847*, Southwest Historical Series, vol. 1, ed. Ralph P. Bieber (Glendale, CA: Arthur H. Clark, 1931), p. 263. Webb, who wrote a few years after the fact, demonstrates how rapidly the reputation was established. Recent histories have also helped to perpetuate the incident; for example, see Lavender, *Bent's Fort*, p. 216.

29. Memorial, p. 22.

30. Miranda to Alvarez, September 22, 1841, BR, no. 217.

31. Tyler, "Gringo Views," p. 31.

32. Miranda to Alvarez, September 23, 1841, BR, no. 218.

33. Hafen and Hafen, *Old Spanish Trail*, pp. 207–208.

34. John H. Lyman to Alvarez, August 8, 1841, BR, no. 175.

35. Ibid.

36. Falconer, *Letters and Notes*, pp. 16–17, 34.

37. Two years later Alvarez ventured the opinion that all the respectable people in New Mexico had determined not to resist the Texans. If Texas's Colonel William G. Cooke had fired but two guns he would have succeeded; see Philip St. George Cooke, "A Journal of the Santa Fe Trail," ed. William E. Connelley, *Mississippi Valley Historical Review* 12 (June 1925): 87. This is secondhand information and must be taken skeptically, especially since Alvarez left no other evidence of such an attitude.

38. Lavender, *Bent's Fort*, p. 217. Lavender claims that Kendall was the only American citizen, but Alvarez, Memorial, p. 28, intimated there were more.

39. Memorial, p. 28.

40. Miranda to Alvarez, October 1, 1841, BR, no. 221; and Gregg, *Commerce of the Prairies*, p. 163. Armijo had some justification for worrying about the arrival of more Texans because they seemed to keep coming in groups of varying sizes. Indeed, apparently because of their dire condition, the main force had broken into smaller groups. Santa Feans received reports of encounters with Texans when groups of the invaders were captured on three different dates in September. The reports came from the communities of Anton Chico, Las Vegas, and

Las Gallinas and are listed as follows: September 15, three prisoners; September 18, eighty-five prisoners; and September 30, twelve prisoners (see BR/Diary). News of the discovery of the Constitution of Texas in Las Vegas set off some immediate rejoicing among the people but could only raise suspicion in officials. The main force of 200 surrendered on October 7.

41. The attack and subsequent official delay shocked many people besides those directly involved; Joseph L. Eve, US chargé d'affaires to Texas, wrote a letter describing the "Mexican atrocity . . . recently having imprisoned the U.S. consul at Santa Fe." Eve to John Crittenden, April 3, 1842, in "A Letter Book of Joseph L. Eve, United States Chargé d'Affaires to Texas," ed. Joseph M. Nance, *Southwestern Historical Quarterly* 33 (1940): 370.

42. Miranda to Alvarez, September 28, 1841, BR, no. 219.

43. Miranda to Alvarez, October 1, 1841, BR, no. 221.

44. Armijo, passport for Alvarez and fifteen Americans, October 25, 1841, BR, no. 18.

45. Memorial, p. 30.

46. Ibid., pp. 30–32.

47. Ibid.

48. Gregg, *Commerce of the Prairies,* p. 163; Alvarez to Webster, March 2, 1842, CD; and James L. Collins to Governor William Carr Lane, December 10, 1852, quoted in its totality in *El Palacio* 19, no. 4 (November 1925): 206–11.

49. Alvarez to Webster, March 2, 1842, CD.

50. Alvarez to Webster, February 13, 1842, CD. Alvarez arrived in Washington at least by January 22, 1842. He stayed at Brown's Indian Queen Hotel on Pennsylvania Avenue, where he paid in advance for thirty-eight days; receipt from Brown's Hotel, January 22, 1842, AP/Business.

51. Alvarez to Webster, February 13, 1842, CD; Webster to Alvarez, February 16, 1842, BR, no. 307; and Alvarez to Webster, February 23, 1842, CD.

52. Memorial. (The original of this document, with copies of appended letters, is in CD.)

53. Alvarez to Webster, December 15, 1841, CD. Noel M. Loomis, *The Texan–Santa Fe Pioneers* (Norman: University of Oklahoma Press, 1958), p. 183, states that the first word of the Texans' capture came from Alvarez, which could be true. However, he dates the revelation to January 18, 1842, which probably is not true since Alvarez had crossed the plains and written to Webster at least as early as December 15. The *Daily Missouri Republican* (St. Louis) reported the story on December 24, 1841, and the *Niles National Register* (Washington, DC) reported it on January 8, 1842.

54. John Rowland to John White, speaker of the House, December 19, 1841, BR, no. 267; and William Boggs to General Leslie Z. Combs, December 28, 1841, BR, no. 94. In stark contrast to the usual fascination exerted by the Texan invasion is one letter, probably carried by Alvarez across the plains, in which the event is not mentioned. The writer merely related usual business; see James Magoffin to James Rowland, October 22, 1841; copy in MNM/HL.

55. Webster to Alvarez, February 16, 1842, BR, no. 307.

56. Alvarez to Webster, March 2, 1842, CD.

57. Webster to Alvarez, March 4, 1842, BR, no. 309.

58. See, for example, Jorge Ramírez to Alvarez, August 4, 1841, BR, no. 254.

59. Webster to Alvarez, February 16, 1842, BR, no. 307.

60. Official certificate attesting to Alvarez's naturalization, BR, no. 5.

61. Alvarez to Webster, May 4, 1842, CD.

62. See especially Kendall, *Narrative,* p. 246.

63. Alvarez to secretary of state, July 1, 1843, CD.

64. Cooke, "Journal," pp. 87–88.

65. Ibid., pp. 85, 88, 94, 227–31. Cooke's arrest of Snively and his men is well documented in many secondary sources. Also see John Tyler, Annual Message to Congress with Documents, December 3, 1844, Bound Serial Set [449], Senate Document 1, 28-2, pp. 36–40; this includes official correspondence relating to Cooke's disarming of Snively. Official Mexican reaction to Cooke's activities was satisfaction; see *Revista Oficial,* quoted in Ponce de Leon, *Reseñas históricas,* appendix 6, p. 308.

Chapter 5

1. Alvarez to secretary of state, July 1, 1843, CD; Dunham, "Manuel Alvarez," p. 195.

2. Alvarez to secretary of state, July 1, 1843, CD; see also Kelly (full name unknown) to Alvarez, February 3, 1842, AP/Business.

3. Charles Bent estimated that in specie alone, the Santa Fe trade sent up to a half-million dollars to Missouri, all without the benefit of the bill; Bent to Alvarez, April 29, 1843, CD; Alvarez to secretary of state, July 1, 1843, CD.

4. The itinerary is compiled from business receipts and hotel bills Alvarez saved; AP/Business and AP/Miscellaneous (see n. 15 below).

5. Memo of gold bullion dated August 25, 1843, AP/Business; Barry, *Beginning of the West,* p. 530; and receipt from Sanderson's Franklin House to Alvarez, August 30, 1843, AP/Business.

6. Barry, *Beginning of the West,* p. 449.

7. P. Harmony, Nephews and Company to Lamar, Campbell and Company; P. Harmony, Nephews and Company to Aguirre, Usugua, Fils and Uribanan, August 31, 1843 (copies): all in AP/Miscellaneous.

8. Aguirre, Solante and Murrieta to Alvarez, January 22 and 25, 1844, AP/Miscellaneous.

9. Letters of introduction by Marcial Antonio López, n.d., AP/Miscellaneous.

10. Autorisation particulière de visiter le palais de l'Elysée, November–December, 1843; permit to visit the Royal Chapel of Notre Dame, November 14, 1843; and permit to visit Fontainebleau, November 11, 1843, AP/Miscellaneous.

11. Alvarez to "Primo," January 18 and 27, 1844, AP/Ledger Book. These documents establish Alvarez's presence in London on the given dates and show his continuing concern for New Mexico and his family. The two drafts are the only known occasions on which he mentions his family outside of his will and a

family tree he drew. The *primo* (cousin) is Don José Luis Arias; Josefina, whom Alvarez mentions in both drafts, is Luis's sister.

12. Gregg to Alvarez, December 26, 1843, AP.

13. Various bills and receipts dated May 1 – October 1, 1843, AP/Business. Among the bolts of cloth, Alvarez had satin and French cashmere as well as cotton and wool.

14. Receipts dated May 1–11, 1843, AP/Business. The papers available today seem not to tell the whole story, for there are some gaps.

15. Definite dates surmised for his whole trip are as follows:
St. Louis, August 14, 1843; Chicago, August 15–16, 1843; Philadelphia, August 25, 1843; New York, August 31 – September 1, 1843; Europe, September 1843 – May 1844; New York, May 1–11, 1844; Philadelphia, May 13, 1844; Pittsburgh, May 20 and 27, 1844; St. Louis, June 1–10, July 9, 10, and 20; Independence, July 3–30, August 27. Note that these are dates established from the documents; any attempts to establish Alvarez's whereabouts otherwise are educated conjecture.

16. Receipt, Groton Hotel to Alvarez, September 1, 1843, AP/Business.

17. Jas. W. McKir to Alvarez, August 31, 1843, AP/Business (emphasis in the original).

18. Contract with Anthony Beelen, May 27, 1844, AP/Business.

19. A. Beelen to Alvarez, May 27, 1844, in "A Sidelight on the Santa Fe Trade, 1844," *New Mexico Historical Review* 46, no. 3 (July 1971): 264; original in AP/Business.

20. Passport, June 11, 1844, BR, no. 110.

21. Alvarez to Luis Arias; Alvarez to Peter Harmony, Nephews and Company; and Alvarez to Francisco Alfalla. All letters are dated April 3, 1844, and are found among his business papers. They are drafts written by Alvarez.

22. Contract, August 27, 1844, AP/Business.

23. Bent to Alvarez, August 14, 1844, AP/Miscellaneous.

24. Barry, *Beginning of the West,* p. 530.

25. Robledo to Alvarez, December 28, 1844, AP/Business.

26. Examples of inquiries made of the merchant are Juan Bernadet to Alvarez, December 28, 1844, and Padre Martínez to Alvarez, n.d.: both in AP/Business. The last citation solicited the consul's aid in building a road from Santa Fe to Taos.

27. Alvarez to Honorable Wilson Shannon, December 23, 1844, BR/Letter Book. Alvarez wrote the draft for this letter on December 14, 1844.

28. Alvarez to Buchanan, June 18, 1845, CD. The *Santa Fe New Mexican,* February 1, 1876, mentions in the obituary for ex–Chief Justice Joab Houghton that he was appointed US consul in 1844; the year is wrong, and officially he was never the US consul.

29. Alvarez to R. J. Walker, secretary of the treasury, June 18, 1845, BR/Letter Book, p. 49.

30. Lavender, *Bent's Fort,* p. 260; and Bent to Alvarez, February 4, 1846, BR, no. 70.

31. Cooke, "Journal," pp. 235–36 and fn. 53; Gregg, *Commerce of the Prairies,* pp. 337–38.

32. *Revista Oficial,* July 18, 1843, as quoted in Ponce de Leon, *Reseñas históricas,* appendix 6, p. 308.

33. Charles Bent to Alvarez, January 7, 1843, APUNM, reel 1, doc. 61. This document is not included with the original Alvarez Papers.

34. Bent to Alvarez, February 24, 1845, APUNM, reel 4.

35. Wethered to Alvarez, July 16, 1845, AP.

36. Theodore Wheaton to Alvarez, November 6, 1845, BR, no. 312.

37. Ibid.

38. Bent to Alvarez, n.d. [1846], AP.

39. Woods to Alvarez, September 14, 1846, AP.

40. Gregg to Alvarez, May 7, 1846, BR, no. 158 (emphasis in the original).

41. Gregg to Alvarez, September 14, 1846, AP; Gregg to Alvarez, September 14, 1846, BR, no. 159.

42. Bent to Alvarez, February 24, 1846, BR, no. 73. Ralph Emerson Twitchell, *The Military Occupation of New Mexico, 1846–1851* (Denver, CO: Smith-Brooks, 1909), pp. 63–64, points out the disparagement within the Hispanic population when Paredes took over Mexico.

43. Duffus, R. L. *The Santa Fe Trail* (New York: Longmans, Green, 1930),p. 184.

44. Charles Bent to Alvarez, March 2, 1846, BR, no. 75; Bent to Alvarez, March 4, 1846, BR, no. 76; and Bent to Alvarez, March 6, 1846, BR, no. 78.

45. Vigil y Alarid to Alvarez, April 24, 1846, BR, no. 302.

46. Bent to Alvarez, May 3, 1846, BR, no. 87; Alvarez to Vigil y Alarid, May 6, 1846, BR/Letter Book, p. 54.

47. Vigil y Alarid to Alvarez, May 5, 1846, AP.

48. Lavender, *Bent's Fort,* pp. 273–74.

49. W. G. Ritch, ed., *The Legislative Blue Book of the Territory of New Mexico* (Santa Fe, NM: Charles W. Greene, Public Printer, 1882), p. 133.

50. Rowland to Alvarez, February 28, 1846, BR, no. 265.

51. James Buchanan, secretary of state, to Alvarez, May 14, 1846, BR, no. 98.

Chapter 6

The chapter title is taken from Juan Bautista Vigil y Alarid's public address to Brigadier General Stephen Watts Kearny, translated and quoted in William A. Keleher, *Turmoil in New Mexico, 1846–1868* (Santa Fe, NM: Rydal Press, 1952), p. 16; original in Vigil Papers, NMSRC. Vigil y Alarid was then acting governor of New Mexico.

1. Webb, *Adventures,* pp. 185–86.

2. Alvarez to Buchanan, February 9, 1846, CD.

3. Alvarez to Francisco Baca y Torres, March 23, 1846, BR/Letter Book, p. 52; and Alvarez to Mrs. Robert Ferguson, March 28, 1846, BR/Letter Book, p. 52.

62. Lamar, *Far Southwest,* p. 71; Larson, *Quest for Statehood,* pp. 9, 10; and Ritch, *Bluebook,* p. 98.

63. J. V. Masten to "Father," December 17, 1847, MWF.

64. Sadlowski, "Manuel Alvarez," "Politico" chapter. Among the acts was a resolution calling for the translation of the Constitution into Spanish and another resolution relating to replevin.

65. *Santa Fe Republican,* December 11 and 18, 1847.

66. Ibid., January 22, 1848.

67. Ibid.; Lamar, *Far Southwest,* p. 71.

68. *Santa Fe Republican,* January 22, 29, and February 12, 1848.

69. Larson, *Quest for Statehood,* p. 11; *Santa Fe Republican,* February 12, 1848.

70. *Santa Fe Republican,* March 11, 1848.

71. Ibid., August 16, 1848.

72. Ibid.; see also Donald Chaput, *François X. Aubry: Trader, Trailmaker and Voyager in the Southwest, 1846–1854* (Glendale, CA: Arthur H. Clark, 1975), p. 61. Chaput cites the aforementioned *Republican* but mistakenly claims that a dozen or so merchants, plus Alvarez, Aubry, McKnight, and Wade Hampton, signed the petition.

73. *Santa Fe Republican,* August 15, 1848. The newspaper gives Wethered's name as Weatherhead in one place.

74. Larson, *Quest for Statehood,* pp. 13–14; Ritch, *Bluebook,* pp. 99–100.

75. Twitchell, *Military Occupation,* pp. 153–54.

76. Lamar, *Far Southwest,* p. 72; Sadlowski, "Manuel Alvarez," "Politico" chapter.

77. Larson, *Quest for Statehood,* p. 14, claims Alvarez did not attend; Sadlowski, "Manuel Alvarez," "Politico" chapter, offers the contrary view; and Ritch, *Bluebook,* pp. 99–100, does not mention him but also does not consider the walkout.

78. See Ritch, *Bluebook,* pp. 99–100, in which the memorial is given in full; originals of the "Petición del Pueblo de Nuevo Méjico . . . ," October 14, 1848, are found in TPUSS.

79. Larson, *Quest for Statehood,* pp. 15, 17–18.

Chapter 7

1. Keleher, *Turmoil,* p. 37.

2. Lamar, *Far Southwest,* p. 74.

3. Green, "Calhoun," pp. 331–32; George Archibald McCall, *New Mexico in 1850: A Military View,* ed. Robert W. Frazer (Norman: University of Oklahoma Press, 1968), pp. 65–66.

4. Hubert Howe Bancroft, *History of Arizona and New Mexico, 1530–1888* (San Francisco: History Company, 1889), pp. 447–48; Green, "Calhoun," p. 336.

5. Lamar, *Far Southwest,* p. 74.

4. Alvarez to Buchanan, February 9, 1846, CD.

5. Leo E. Oliva, *Soldiers on the Santa Fe Trail* (Norman: University of Oklahoma Press, 1967), p. 57.

6. Alvarez to Buchanan, September 4, 1846, CD.

7. George Rutledge Gibson, *Journal of a Soldier Under Kearny and Doniphan, 1846–1847,* Southwest Historical Series, vol. 3, ed. Ralph P. Bieber (Glendale, CA: Arthur H. Clark, 1935), p. 64; and Alvarez to Buchanan, September 4, 1846, CD.

8. Alvarez to Buchanan, September 4, 1846, CD. In this same letter, Alvarez described Armijo as perhaps "a good man in small matters . . . a small one in great affairs."

9. Ibid.; and Gibson, *Journal,* pp. 87–88.

10. Janet Lecompte, "Manuel Armijo and the Americanos," *Spanish and Mexican Land Grants in New Mexico and Colorado,* ed. John R. and Christine Van Ness (Manhattan, KS: Sunflower Press, 1980), pp. 59–60 (the same article is in *Journal of the West* 19 [July 1980]: 51–63).

11. Henry C. Connelly, September 29, 1848, and Major Philip St. George Cooke, February 21, 1849, both quoted in Keleher, *Turmoil,* pp. 31, 24, respectively; and Lecompte, "Manuel Armijo," p. 60.

12. See Keleher, *Turmoil,* p. 37, fn. 122; the report is meticulously itemized.

13. For a report of those efforts, see Alvarez to Buchanan, September 4, 1846, CD.

14. Bent to Senator Thomas Hart Benton, September 24, 1846, JWA. If James W. Goodrich is right, Kearny relied on Waldo's expertise when he made appointments in the new government; see Goodrich, "Earnest Pursuit," p. 169.

15. The other two were Ceran St. Vrain and David Waldo.

16. Memorandum of silver bullion, no. 47, and memorandum of gold bullion, no. 39, July 10, 1845: both in AP/Business.

17. Murrieta to Alvarez, August 4 and 18, 1845, account with Murrieta and Company, August 4, 1845, account with P. Harmony, Nephews and Company, July 25, 1845: all in AP/Business. Unlike Murrieta and Company, P. Harmony, Nephews and Company's name gives no hint of a reason for Alvarez's business; the only indication of why he chose them is that correspondence is in Spanish. A most telling document, however, is an announcement of the retirement of Don Manuel X. Harmony; the remaining associates were L. T. Juárez, Peter J. Francia, and Juan García. See Peter Harmony, Nephews and Company to Alvarez, January 1, 1845, AP/Business.

18. Contract with Bent, St. Vrain and Company, October 10, 1845, AP/Business.

19. Robledo to Alvarez, June 29, 1845, and Robledo to Alvarez, n.d. (1846): both in AP/Business.

20. P. Harmony, Nephews and Company to Alvarez, January 6, 1846, account with P. Harmony, Nephews and Company, December 31, 1846, and Harmony to Alvarez, June 24, 1846: all in AP/Business.

21. Duffus, *Santa Fe Trail,* p. 209.

22. S. Houck to Alvarez, October 20, 1846, AP.

23. Houck to Alvarez, November 30, 1846, AP.

24. Isaac Lightner to Alvarez, November 27, 1846, AP.

25. Martínez to Alvarez, April 12, 1847, BR, no. 182.

26. Marcy to James K. Polk, n.d., as quoted in US Congress, Senate, Insurrection Against the Military Government in New Mexico and California, 1847 and 1848, 56th Congress, 1st session, Senate Document 442 (hereafter Sen. Doc. 442); Secretary of War William L. Marcy to Colonel Sterling Price, June 26, 1847, in US Congress, House, California and New Mexico: Message from the President . . . Transmitting Information . . . on the Subject of California and New Mexico, 31st Congress, 1st session, 1850, Executive Document 17, 248 (hereafter Ex. Doc. 17).

27. Lewis Hector Garrard, a traveler who eventually published his journal, witnessed the trial and wrote of the paradox, probably after the fact: "Justice! Out upon the word, when its distorted meaning is the warrant for murdering those who defend to the last their country and their homes"; Garrard, *Wah-to-Yah and the Taos Trial* (1850; reprinted, Norman: University of Oklahoma Press, 1974), pp. 172–73.

28. Blair apparently inquired about the matter to the US Attorney General's Office; see Marcy to Price, June 26, 1847, Ex. Doc. 17.

29. Marcy to Price, June 11, 1847, Ex. Doc. 17.

30. Marcy to Price, June 26, 1847, Ex. Doc. 17.

31. Marcy to Price, June 26, 1847, Ex. Doc. 17.

32. Duffus, *Santa Fe Trail,* pp. 186–87. José María Pacheco, one of the survivors, overestimated the Texan force at 2,200 men. The ramifications of the ambush reached Chihuahua, where the governor, Mariano Martínez, wrote a rousing manifesto in which he hoped the Texans would now be overconfident, for they would be surprised at how Mexicans would defend their property, country, and dignity. Nine days later, Chihuahuan troops were dispatched to serve as auxiliaries in New Mexico under José Mariano Martínez. See "Manifesto of his Excellency the Governor . . . ," July 9, 1843, and *Revista Oficial,* July 18, 1843, in Ponce de Leon, *Reseñas históricas,* appendix 5, pp. 304–307.

33. Lavender, *Bent's Fort,* pp. 222, 239; and Duffus, *Santa Fe Trail,* pp. 186–87.

34. Sen. Doc. 442.

35. Bent to James Buchanan, October 22, 1846, JWA; original in the US National Archives, 9th Military Department Orders, vol. 5, p. 214.

36. *New York Tribune,* October 3, 1846.

37. Laws of the Territory of New Mexico (Santa Fe, 1846); copy in MNM/HL. This body of law is also referred to as the Kearny Code and Organic Law.

38. Marcy to Kearny, June 3, 1846, Ex. Doc. 17.

39. Marcy to Kearny, January 11, 1847, Ex. Doc. 17.

40. Robert W. Larson, *New Mexico's Quest for Statehood, 1846–1912* (Albuquerque: University of New Mexico Press, 1968), p. 7; Howard Roberts Lamar, *The Far Southwest, 1846–1912: A Territorial History* (New York: W. W. Norton, 1970), p. 70.

41. Calhoun to Orlando Brown, July 15, 1850, in James S. Calhoun, *The Official Correspondence of James S. Calhoun While Indian Agent at Santa Fe and*

Superintendent of Indian Affairs in New Mexico, ed. Annie Heloise Abel (Washington, DC: US Government Printing Office, 1915), p. 218.

42. John Greiner to G., October 1, 1851, in "Private Letters of a Government Official in the Southwest," ed. Tod B. Galloway, *Journal of American History* 3, no. 4 (1909): 546.

43. For some positive aspects of occupation, see The *Santa Fe Republican,* September 10, 1847. The importance of military expenditures is indirectly described by a contemporary when he explains that curtailment of such disbursements was drying up the availability of money; see Greiner to G., March 31, 1852, in Galloway, "Private Letters," p. 550.

44. Greiner to G., July 29 and October 1, 1851, in Galloway, "Private Letters," pp. 544–46.

45. Fletcher M. Green, "James S. Calhoun: Pioneer, Georgia Leader and First Governor of New Mexico," *Georgia Historical Quarterly* 39, no. 4 (1955): 331.

46. Calhoun to Brown, July 15, 1850, in Calhoun, *Official Correspondence,* p. 232.

47. Ygnacio Miera, Ronaldo Archiveque, et al., to Alvarez, June 10, 1847, AP. Padre Martínez also saw an advantage in Alvarez's multilingual talents; see Martínez to Alvarez, April 12, 1847, BR, no. 182.

48. Armijo to Alvarez, June 17, 1848, BR, no. 21, September 11, 1848, BR, no. 22, and June 21, 1850, BR, no. 25.

49. AP/Ledger Book, 1834, nos. 137–216. The year indicates Alvarez's long and early acquaintance with the concepts.

50. Ibid. The treatise is a handwritten, twenty-three page account of the Revolutionary War and American independence. Alvarez wrote his narrative fourteen to fifteen years before he would put his knowledge to practical use.

51. Collins to Alvarez, July 3, 1847, BR, no. 105, and July 4, 1847, BR, no. 106.

52. *Santa Fe Republican,* October 9, 1847; the report is dated September 29.

53. *Santa Fe Republican,* September 24, 1847.

54. Larson, *Quest for Statehood,* pp. 8–9; and Lamar, *Far Southwest,* p. 71.

55. Larson, *Quest for Statehood,* p. 9; and Sadlowski, "Manuel Alvarez" (third pa[rt] of the "Politico" chapter).

56. *Santa Fe Republican,* October 30, 1847; Sadlowski, "Manuel Alvarez," "Po[lit]ico" chapter.

57. *Missouri Republican* (St. Louis), August 29, 1856.

58. Lamar, *Far Southwest,* pp. 73–74.

59. Laws of the Territory of New Mexico, Section 10, p. 7. The code had [been] receiving favorable reviews from the local populace, who voiced fear [of] abolishment by the federal government. In light of easterners' reacti[on to] Kearny's action, it is no wonder the local populace was worried.

60. Ritch, *Bluebook,* p. 98.

61. Larson, *Quest for Statehood,* p. 9. Copies of all, or part, of Vigil's address [in] Ritch, *Bluebook,* pp. 98–99; Twitchell, *The Leading Facts of New M[exico] History* (Cedar Rapids, IA: Torch Press, 1912), vol. 2, pp. 264–66; and *S[anta Fe] Republican,* December 11, 1847.

6. Ibid., p. 73; and Larson, *Quest for Statehood,* p. 18. Deceit apparently played a role, for Alvarez received a report that the opposition party had run their man in Mora, St. Vrain, on the "Alvarez faction" platform; Juan Bernadet to Alvarez, September 20, 1849, AP/Business.

7. "Journal of the Convention of the Territory of New Mexico," Report of J. S. Calhoun, Indian agent at Santa Fe, New Mexico, Message from the president of the United States, 31st Congress, 1st session, Ex. Doc. 17 (hereafter "Journal of the Convention"); Larson, *Quest for Statehood,* p. 18.

8. McCall, *New Mexico in 1850,* p. 70, fn. 38. Weightman served as a paymaster with the rank of captain in a voluntary force of the Army of the West.

9. Larson, *Quest for Statehood,* p. 19; "Journal of the Convention," pp. 93–95.

10. "Journal of the Convention," pp. 96–97.

11. Larson, *Quest for Statehood,* p. 21; see also Keleher, *Turmoil,* p. 38.

12. *New Mexican* (Santa Fe), November 24, 1849.

13. Lamar, *Far Southwest,* p. 73; Victor Westphal, *The Public Domain in New Mexico, 1854–1891* (Albuquerque: University of New Mexico Press, 1965), pp. 3–4. Lamar points out that one of the motivations behind the 1849 convention was the confirmation of land grants, and Westphal, writing about events in 1853 when the first surveyor arrived in New Mexico, notes that the government's lack of action in land matters had become a source of agitation.

14. *New Mexican* (Santa Fe), December 8, 1849. The declaration was addressed "To The People of New Mexico."

15. James H. Simpson, *Navaho Expedition: Journal of a Military Reconnaissance from Santa Fe, New Mexico to the Navaho Country,* ed. Frank McNitt (Norman: University of Oklahoma Press, 1964), p. xiv; and Twitchell, *Military Occupation,* p. 162.

16. Larson, *Quest for Statehood,* p. 22. Although it has been generally accepted that Alvarez published the *Gazette,* there seems to be no tangible proof. Pearce S. Grove, Becky J. Barnett, and Sandra J. Hansen, eds., *New Mexico Newspapers: A Comprehensive Guide to Bibliographical Entries and Locations* (Albuquerque: University of New Mexico Press, 1975), p. 470, indicate that first editions of the *Santa Fe Gazette* came out in April 1851. Copies exist of 1851 editions; none from before that date.

17. Lamar, *Far Southwest,* p. 74.

18. Calhoun to Colonel W. Medill, commissioner of Indian affairs, October 29, 1849, Ex. Doc. 17. For more on this incident, see Chaput, *Aubry,* p. 84; and Marc Simmons, *The Little Lion of the Southwest: A Biography of Manuel Chaves* (Chicago: Sage Books, 1973), pp. 122, 142. Simmons's account is apparently about another White massacre that occurred in the southern part of the territory.

19. Weightman et al. to Houghton, July 24, 1849, WGR. Weightman cited no specifics outside of the public interest as reason for Houghton to resign. Among the names on the petition were statehood stalwarts Angney, Theodore Wheaton, and Palmer J. Pillans. No Spanish names appeared on the list.

20. Houghton, July 27, 1849, WGR.

21. For the duel, see Larson, *Quest for Statehood,* p. 70; William Keleher, "Texans

in Early Day New Mexico," *Panhandle-Plains Historical Review* 25 (1952): 17–18. Chaput, *Aubry,* pp. 158–59, has a good account of the barroom fight in which François Aubry died from knife wounds inflicted by Weightman.

22. *Santa Fe Weekly Gazette,* November 27, 1853.

23. Ibid., January 22 and November 27, 1853.

24. *Santa Fe Republican,* May 3, 1848.

25. Larson, *Quest for Statehood,* p. 22; Colonel McCall, as quoted in Sadlowski, "Manuel Alvarez," "Politico" chapter.

26. Quoted in Oliver LaFarge, *Santa Fe: The Autobiography of a Southwestern Town* (Norman: University of Oklahoma Press, 1959), pp. 7–8. Alvarez wrote the one-paragraph statement published with the list. The paper misread a couple of signatures and had Angney listed as "Auguay" and Juan F. Ortiz as "Juan F. Ortero (Vicar General)"; see draft, July 16, 1850, AP/Business, no. 29.

27. Weightman to Alvarez, July 19, 1850, AP.

28. Weightman to Alvarez, August 26, 1850, AP.

29. George W. Crawford, secretary of war, to Brevet Lieutenant George A. McCall, November 19, 1849, Ex. Doc. 17.

30. Larson, *Quest for Statehood,* p. 30; Lamar, *Far Southwest,* pp. 75–76; Sadlowski, "Manuel Alvarez," "Politico" chapter; and McCall, *New Mexico in 1850,* pp. 66–68.

31. Larson, *Quest for Statehood,* p. 31; Lamar, *Far Southwest,* p. 77; and Sadlowski, "Manuel Alvarez," "Politico" chapter.

32. Ritch, *Bluebook,* p. 100; Calhoun to Brown, July 15, 1850, in Calhoun, *Official Correspondence,* p. 218; Larson, *Quest for Statehood,* pp. 30–34, 36; Lamar, *Far Southwest,* p. 77; and Bancroft, *History,* pp. 447–48. New Mexican attitudes toward Texas stemmed not only from previous confrontations or racial bias. Missouri business houses in New Mexico had too much invested in the Santa Fe trade to allow Texas to divert its profits from Missouri's state coffers.

33. McCall, *New Mexico in 1850,* p. 109; Lamar, *Far Southwest,* pp. 78–79; Larson, *Quest for Statehood,* p. 37; Sister Mary Loyola, "The American Occupation of New Mexico, 1821–1852," *New Mexico Historical Review* 4, nos. 1–3 (July 1939): 242–43; and Loomis Morton Ganaway, *New Mexico and the Sectional Controversy, 1846–1861* (1944; reprinted Chicago: Porcupine Press, 1976), pp. 50–51.

34. Lamar, *Far Southwest,* p. 79.

35. Richard Weightman to the vice-president of the United States and president of the Senate, September 11, 1850, TPUSS.

36. Calhoun, *Official Correspondence,* p. 305. Connelly won by a big majority: 4,604 to 2,706.

37. Alvarez garnered 4,586 votes to St. Vrain's 3,456. Ritch, *Bluebook,* p. 100; Loyola, "American Occupation," pp. 242–43; McCall, *New Mexico in 1850,* p. 109, fn. 36; and Sadlowski, "Manuel Alvarez," "Politico" chapter.

38. Calhoun to Brown, July 15, 1850, in Calhoun, *Official Correspondence,* p. 217.

39. As quoted in Larson, *Quest for Statehood,* pp. 42–43.

40. "Communication of Manuel Alvarez," July 8, 1850, TPUSS; the address was given on July 4, 1850.

41. "Second Communication of Manuel Alvarez," July 8, 1850, TPUSS.

42. Bancroft, *History,* pp. 447–48; Loyola, "American Occupation," pp. 442–43; and McCall, *New Mexico in 1850,* p. 70.

43. McCall, *New Mexico in 1850,* p. 70. Within the context of the times, neither man's attitude was novel. Racial bigotry is one reason that New Mexico's statehood was delayed for more than sixty years after 1850.

44. Munroe to Alvarez, July 12, 1850, quoted in the *Congressional Globe,* 1852, 32d Congress, 1st Session, p. 328.

45. Alvarez to Munroe, July 13, 1850; Ibid., pp. 327–28.

46. Vigil to the county prefects, July 23, 1850, BR, no. 223.

47. Calhoun to Brown, July 15, 1850, in Calhoun, *Official Correspondence,* p. 218; see also Larson, *Quest for Statehood,* pp. 43–44; Lamar, *Far Southwest,* p. 80.

48. As quoted by Alvarez in Alvarez to Munroe, July 13, 1850, and cited in the *Congressional Globe,* 1852, 32d Congress, 1st Session, p. 327.

49. Loyola, "American Occupation," p. 243.

50. Larson, *Quest for Statehood,* p. 45.

51. Cabeza de Baca to Alvarez, August 4, 1850, BR, no. 32, and August 8, 1850, BR, no. 33.

52. Joint resolutions of the Senate and House of Representatives of the State of New Mexico, *Congressional Globe,* 1852, 32d Congress, 1st Session, p. 328; see also Twitchell, *Military Occupation,* pp. 191–92.

53. Weightman to vice-president of the United States, September 11, 1850, "Memorial of the Legislature . . . to Congress," and "Communication of Manuel Alvarez," July 8, 1850: all in TPUSS; Larson, *Quest for Statehood,* p. 57. Weightman also carried a certificate naming him senator of the United States, as proclaimed by "Manuel Alvarez, Acting Governor of the State of New Mexico," dated July 11, 1850, in TPUSS.

54. Weightman related how he had telegraphed the president but did not include the dispatches because of the prohibitive cost; Weightman to Alvarez, August 26, 1850, AP.

55. Taylor died just as Alvarez's and New Mexico's emissary reached the Missouri settlements. Fillmore sent the documents to Congress without comment; Lamar, *Far Southwest,* p. 81. For the whole story of Texas's claims to New Mexico, sectionalism, and the roles of Taylor and his successor Fillmore, see Holman Hamilton, *Prologue to Conflict: The Crisis and Compromise of 1850* (Lexington: University of Kentucky Press, 1964), pp. 47–48, 96–98, 103–109.

56. Weightman to Alvarez, September 14 and 18, 1850, AP.

57. As quoted in McCall, *New Mexico in 1850,* p. 71.

58. See Twitchell, *Military Occupation,* pp. 195–96; quotation from Weightman to Alvarez, September 14, 1850, AP (emphasis in the original).

59. Weightman to Alvarez, September 14, 1850, AP.

60. Special Order number 12, Colonel Munroe, March 2, 1851, FUA, microfilm, roll 1.

61. Conrad to Weightman, April 3, 1851, FUA, microfilm, roll 1.

62. Larson, *Quest for Statehood,* p. 78. Two good books on Webster's political ambitions and his handicaps are Robert F. Dalzell, Jr., *Daniel Webster and the Trial of American Nationalism, 1843–1852* (Boston: Houghton Mifflin, 1973) and Irving H. Bartlett, *Daniel Webster* (New York: W. W. Norton, 1978).

63. Weightman to Alvarez, September 18, 1850, AP.

64. Ibid.; Waldo to Webster, December 8, 1850, ARPO.

65. Archuleta to Alvarez, March 7, 1851, BR, no. 11. Archuleta had been Armijo's military commander and a reputed leader of the 1847 revolt. He took an active role in the local-rule faction and later served three terms as representative from Río Arriba to the House of the Territorial Legislative Assembly from 1853 through 1856; see Ritch, *Bluebook,* pp. 103–104.

66. Larson, *Quest for Statehood,* p. 60; unidentified correspondent to Webster, September 1, 1850, ARPO; and A. B. Babbit and John M. Bernksel to President Millard Fillmore, September 25, 1850, ARPO. Babbit and Bernksel had opposed Allen's appointment to the Utah post because of his "anti-Mormon" record.

67. Weightman to Alvarez, December 16, 1850, AP; *St. Louis Republican,* December 28, 1850, copy in ARPO. The *Louisville Courier's* article is mentioned in the *Republican.*

68. Weightman to Webster, December 26, 1850, ARPO, copy in AP; Waldo to Webster, December 8, 1850, ARPO, copy in AP.

69. Weightman to Fillmore, December 30, 1850, ARPO; copy "c" sent to Alvarez and is in AP; copy sent to Webster is in GSA. See also Twitchell, *Leading Facts,* p. 283. Twitchell may have used the gachupín labeling to conclude erroneously that Alvarez did not receive the appointment because he was not a US citizen. Larson, *Quest for Statehood,* p. 318, fn. 74, repeats the mistake.

70. Gallegos to Alvarez, January 20 and August 11, 1851, AP. Padre Gallegos was a priest educated in Durango and stationed in Albuquerque. During the late Mexican years, he had quietly echoed the anti-American, pro-Mexican attitude of his colleague, Padre Martínez. After occupation, Gallegos — like Martínez, who was also a political activist — ran afoul of Archbishop Jean Baptiste Lamy. Unlike Martínez, Gallegos sided with the local-rule faction totally, eventually being elected territorial delegate to the 33d Congress as well as serving as speaker of the House in New Mexico's Legislative Assembly on two occasions and as a member of the 1st Assembly Council from Bernalillo County; see Ritch, *Bluebook,* pp. 107–108, 119.

71. Weightman to Webster, January 18, 1851, ARPO; the copy in GSA has a notation that the letter was received and filed on February 4, 1851.

72. Weightman to Alvarez, January 15, 1851, AP.

73. Unidentified correspondent to Webster, September 1, 1850, ARPO.

74. Allen to Webster, March 21, 1851, ARPO.

75. Weightman to David G. Bissell, February 17, 1851, David G. Bissell Papers, Missouri Historical Society, St. Louis.

76. For an example of Armijo's activity, see Armijo to Alvarez, June 10, 1851, AP. The ex-governor even served a term from Bernalillo in the House of the Third Legislative Assembly; Ritch, *Bluebook,* p. 102.

Chapter 8

1. Weightman to Alvarez, May 6, 1852, AP. The change did not appear to startle Weightman, who implied that Messervy thought compromise better than Smith. Messervy even asked Weightman to join him!

2. Weightman to Alvarez, February 9, 1852, AP; Larson, *Quest for Statehood,* pp. 65–66. Among the Calhoun/Weightman antagonists in Washington, identified by Weightman, were Collins, Houghton, and Reynolds.

3. Petition of citizens of New Mexico preferring charges against Governor Calhoun, April 1851, and Collins and Houghton to Fillmore, December 24, 1850: both in ARPO, Fillmore M 873 R12. Eight people signed the declaration, including Messervy, Houghton, and Collins; they put in a good word for Hugh Smith, too, while praising Allen.

4. Sumner to Major General R. Jones, April 22, 1852; Calhoun to Sumner, April 18, 1852; Sumner to Calhoun, August 8, 1851; A. R. Woolley, E. H. Wingfield, and John Greiner to Luke Lea, commissioner of Indian affairs, n.d.: all in FUA.

5. H. Maxwell to Fillmore, August 28, 1851; Declaration of the Legislature, July 12, 1851; and Weightman to the president, April 14, 1852: all in ARPO, Fillmore M 873 R12.

6. William McKnight to Alvarez, June 17, 1852, AP/Business.

7. Weightman to Alvarez, May 6, 1852, AP.

8. Ibid.; Weightman to Fillmore, May 11, 1852, ARPO, Fillmore F 186 (copy in GSA).

9. Collins to Fillmore, April 16, 1852, ARPO, no. 183 (copy in GSA).

10. Messervy and Weightman to the secretary of state, December 16, 1852, ARPO, Fillmore F 194 (copy in GSA); both Messervy and Weightman denied the insinuation.

11. Messervy to Fillmore, June 2, 1852, ARPO, Fillmore M 873 R1.

12. Wingfield to Fillmore, June 9, 1852, ARPO, Fillmore F 189 (emphasis in the original; copy in GSA). Wingfield was Indian agent to the Southern Apaches in New Mexico; see Ritch, *Bluebook,* p. 124. For published correspondence between Munroe and Alvarez, see *Congressional Globe,* 32d Congress, 1st Session, House of Representatives, 1852, p. 327.

13. Certificate of appointment, August 20, 1851, BR, no. 99 (also in DSTP, T 17, R1); Lt. General Facundo Pino to Alvarez, October 3, 1851, AP.

14. Calhoun to Alvarez, March 26, 1852, BR, no. 100; Calhoun to Alvarez, March 30, 1852, BR, no. 101; Calhoun to "Whom it may concern," April 2, 1852, BR, no. 102. Calhoun apparently suffered from cancer; see Lawrence R. Murphy, "Antislavery in the Southwest: William G. Kephart's Mission to New Mexico, 1850–53," *Southwestern Studies* 54 (1978): 43.

15. Weightman to Alvarez, June 16, 1852, AP; Greiner did not receive the appointment.

16. Ibid.

17. David Whiting to Alvarez, July 1, 1852, BR, no. 313. Even Alvarez's non-Hispanic friends seemed to show their respect for him though they may have tried his patience — like many others, Whiting wrote to Alvarez in poor Spanish.

18. Wayne L. Mauzy, "Early Newspapers in New Mexico: *The Santa Fe Republican,* 1847–1849," *El Palacio* 2 (April 1960); *Santa Fe Republican,* March 18, 1848 (1st notice) and April 4, 1848 (2d notice). Alvarez sued a Jesús Acre for $150.

19. Bond for license to trade with Indians, June 3, 1850, WGR, no. 389.

20. Alvarez account with P. Harmony, Nephews and Company, May 20, 1846 – April 1847, April 20, 1847 – September 1, 1848, May 16, 1849, September 22, 1849, and May 29, 1849: all in AP/Business. Mention of Manuel Armijo's dealings is in Harmony, Nephews and Company to Alvarez, February 10, 1847, AP/Business.

21. Fauntain Hansford and Thomas W. Flounoy to Alvarez, July 4 and August 15; William W. McCoy to Alvarez, December 25, 1847; Solomon Houck to Alvarez, September 16, 1848; J. R. Palmer to Alvarez, October 30, 1849; William Clark to Alvarez, November 7, 1849: all in AP/Business.

22. Contract with Concordland Hall, August 30, 1848; contract with Waldo and Waldo, October 4, 1848; contract with William S. McKnight and J. H. McCutchan, August 25, 1848: all in AP/Business.

23. Houck to Alvarez, June 18, 1847; Trinidad Gabaldón to Alvarez, October 16, 1847; Pedro Olivares to Alvarez, May 20, 1848: all in AP/Business.

24. McCoy to Alvarez, April 22, 1847, AP/Business.

25. François Lafarez to Alvarez, January 1849, AP.

26. For the first instance, S. Carel to Alvarez, July 30, 1849; for the second, Peter David to Alvarez, no date, 1853: both in AP/Business.

27. H. Gosselin to Alvarez, March 10, 1853, AP.

28. McCoy to Alvarez (account included), October 1, 1852, AP/Business. Alvarez and the Waldos had known each other too long to be formal in their business arrangements; implicit throughout this letter is a casual and mutual trust.

29. Receipt of payments, September 30, 1852, AP.

30. Note on E. T. Davies, June 6, 1850, AP/Business; an acknowledgment of payment is written on the note.

31. Gonzales to Alvarez, September 24, 1849, AP/Business.

32. Tenorio to Manuel Chaves, October 13, 1849, AP/Business.

33. McCoy to Alvarez, April 22, 1847; receipt from John Simms, August 18, 1850; and receipt from Alvarez, October 2, 1850: all in AP/Business.

34. McCoy to Alvarez, November 1, 1848, AP/Business.

35. John Lewis to Alvarez, October 26, 1848, AP/Business.

36. C. H. Merritt, sheriff of Santa Fe County, to Alvarez, April 3, 1849, AP/Business.

37. Hereford to Alvarez, April 13, 1849 (two letters): both in AP/Business; Hereford to Solomon Sublette, March 9, 1850, Sublette Papers, Missouri Historical Society, St. Louis, MO. Hereford was on his way to Chihuahua and mentioned

that prices there did not justify paying duties for goods on their way to that city.

38. Ibid. (first letter).

39. Capoulade to Alvarez, January 8, 1848, AP/Business (Capoulade's first name is not given).

40. Smyth and Shelly to Alvarez, October 10, 1849, AP/Business.

41. Houck to Alvarez, November 1, 1848, AP/Business.

42. Memorandum of gold bullion, April 2, 1849, AP/Business.

43. Olivas to Alvarez, March 29, 1849, AP/Business.

44. Wethered to Alvarez, May 20, 1850; Beaubien to Alvarez, January 7, 1850: both in AP/Business.

45. See, for example, Juan Bernadet to Alvarez, June 22 and October 16, 1849; Capoulade to Alvarez, January 8, 1848: all in AP/Business.

46. Hereford to Solomon Sublette, March 9, 1850, Sublette Papers, Missouri Historical Society, St. Louis, MO.

47. Angney to Alvarez, December 10, 1850, AP/Business; see also McCall, *New Mexico in 1850,* p. 53.

48. Angney to Alvarez, February 1, 1851, AP/Business.

49. Angney to Alvarez, April 1, 1851, AP/Business.

50. Angney to Alvarez, December 10, 1851, AP/Business.

51. Sunseri, "Sheep Ricos," p. 6.

52. Angney to Alvarez, January 28, 1852, AP/Business.

53. Angney to Alvarez, January 30, 1852, AP/Business.

54. Ibid.; Fournier to Alvarez, August 7, 1852: both in AP/Business.

55. Fournier to Alvarez, August 7, 1852; Angney to Alvarez, September 1, 1852: both in AP/Business. Fournier also gave credit to a three-week rain.

56. Angney to Alvarez, January 30, 1852, March 13 and April 15, 1854; Fournier to Alvarez, June 9, 1852, February 15, August 23, and September 12, 1853: all in AP/Business. Although much older, Fournier seems to have come from the same mold as Angney. The two partners deserved each other, and Alvarez, who must have been amused, tolerated them.

57. Fournier to Alvarez, April 15 and September 12, 1853: both in AP/Business.

58. Michael Cearrole to Alvarez, November 5, 1852, AP/Business. Angney apparently mistook Alvarez's herd for another shipment on his behalf.

59. Dryden to Alvarez, September 12, 1852, AP/Business.

60. Ibid.

61. Angney to Alvarez, October 26, 1852, AP/Business.

62. Angney to Alvarez, November 3, 1852, AP/Business.

63. Angney to Alvarez, January 31, 1853, AP/Business. If Fournier ever met Alvarez in New Mexico, this may have been the occasion. No letters survive from Angney's last mailing in October 1852 to this letter, but Angney writes that Fournier, "of this date," gives the information. That seems to indicate a letter, and indeed one survives for that date; see Fournier to Alvarez, January

31, 1852, AP/Business.

64. Fournier to Alvarez, January 31 and April 15, 1853: both in AP/Business. By this time Alvarez had started handling Fournier's New Mexico business.

65. Aubry to Alvarez, March 3, 1853, AP/Business; Sunseri, "Sheep Ricos," p. 6.

66. Aubry to Alvarez, March 15, 1853; Angney to Alvarez, March 15, 1853: both in AP/Business.

67. Aubry to Alvarez, March 15, May 4 and 22, 1853: all in AP/Business. Another agent was sent to San Diego after Rowland's refusal.

68. Aubry to Alvarez, May 4 and 22, 1853; Angney to Alvarez, July 31, 1854: all in AP/Business. Alvarez went so far as to inquire from friends in Missouri about the respective worth of Spanish and French merino sheep. Solomon Houck replied that Spanish merinos were worth $5 to $30 and the French variety from $30 to $300; Houck to Alvarez, April 28 and May 26, 1853: both in AP/Business.

69. Sunseri, "Sheep Ricos," p. 5; and Philip St. George Cooke, William H. C. Whiting, and François X. Aubry, *Exploring Southwestern Trails, 1846–1854*, Southwest Historical Series, vol. 3 (Glendale, CA: Arthur H. Clark, 1938), p. 56.

70. Chris Emmett, *Fort Union and the Winning of the Southwest* (Norman: University of Oklahoma Press, 1965), pp. 109–10; John Greiner to G., May 12, 1851, in Galloway, "Private Letters," p. 542.

71. *Las Vegas Daily Optic* (Las Vegas, NM), July 17, 1891, as related by H. H. Green; Emmett, *Fort Union*, pp. 9–10.

72. *Santa Fe Weekly Gazette*, February 26, 1853. The letter was published in its entirety at this relatively late date, and in Spanish as well as English in subsequent editions.

73. Weightman to Alvarez, May 6 and September 10, 1852, AP. For a nice history of the US adjudication of lands, as well as the problems that procrastination caused, see Westphal, *Public Domain*.

74. Albert James Diaz, *A Guide to the Microfilm of Papers Relating to New Mexico Land Grants* (Albuquerque: University of New Mexico Press, 1960), pp. 19, 62, 67; and Sadlowski, "Manuel Alvarez," last page of text.

75. Brevet Major J. H. Carlton to Mr. Robbins Sumner, superintendent of the farm, Ocaté River, December 15, 1852, FUA; Cooke to M. R. Sumner, November 29, 1853, JWA.

76. Colonel J.F.K. Mansfield, "Inspection Report of Mansfield," FUA, Records of the War Department, Office of the Adjutant General, Miscellaneous File, with map; *Las Vegas Daily Optic* (Las Vegas, NM), July 17, 1891. One reason for Ocaté's value is that it was right on the mountain branch of the Santa Fe Trail; see "Inspection Report" map.

77. Robert W. Frazer, "Army Agriculture in New Mexico, 1852–1853," *New Mexico Historical Review* 50, no. 4 (October 1975): 317–18. There was debate about the program. Some believed the farms would fail; see Lt. Colonel Philip St. George Cooke to Mr. M. R. Sumner, November 16, 1853, JWA.

78. Samuel B. Watrous to Alvarez, April 12, 1856, AP. Watrous later had a community outside of Las Vegas and by Fort Union named after himself; see T. M. Pearce, ed., *New Mexico Placenames: A Geographical Dictionary* (Albuquerque:

University of New Mexico Press, 1965), p. 178. Watrous was harvesting grass at the Ocaté, which indicates that Alvarez did not limit activity to the army.

79. Frazer, "Army Agriculture," pp. 317–18. For examples of attempted rentals and purchases, see John W. Duran to Alvarez, March 23, 1856; B. Machowich to Alvarez, February 11, 1856: both in AP. The latter is also quoted in Frazer.

80. All of the contracts and receipts of rent payment are in AP/Business, 1850–1856.

81. For the López property, see contract with Debous and Beiner, April 1, 1853, and contract with Charles Lerouge, March 9, 1854: both in AP/Business. For the Weaverly House, see contract with John Stein, June 17, 1852, AP/Business. For the Ortiz residence, see contract with Harry J. Jones, September 10, 1850, AP/Business.

82. See, for example, contract with Harry J. Jones, September 10, 1850; contract with John Stein, June 17, 1852: both in AP/Business.

83. Contracts with Louie P. Mullen, August 9, 1850, J. B. Wood, September 6, 1850, Stein, June 17, 1852, which locate the Weaverly House on the north side of the plaza, John M. Yaeger, September 1, 1852, Doctor E. Yuba, March 1, 1853, and Charles Lerouge, October 20, 1855: all in AP/Business. The last contract mentions the López property on the north side of the main street, and the accounts of the September 1841 assassination attempt on Alvarez locate his store and residence on the plaza. See also Reconnaissance of Santa Fe and Its Environs Made by the Order of Brigadier General Kearny, August 19, 1846, Lt. W. R. Emory and Lt. J. F. Olner, MNM/HL. The tentative location of Alvarez's buildings is the present location of the Catron building.

84. Rio Arriba County Deed Book No. 2 (copy), pp. 61–22, Conver Collection, Folder 5, Box 255. Alvarez's purchase took place on October 20, 1849, although Elias Clark, the county recorder, did not list the transaction until January 4, 1854. A subsequent listing notes that Charles Blumner purchased a house "bounded on the south by the main plaza" and "on the west" by "Manuel Alvarez, deceased"; Deed Book No. 2, p. 243.

85. Oath and certification of the Office of Public Building Commissioner, January 17, 1853, and Commission of Public Buildings to Governor David Merriwether, September 15, 1853, WGR, no. 555; commission of office, January 15, 1853, BR, no. 166.

86. See Merriwether to Alvarez, January 13, 1854, AP.

87. William Messervy, acting governor, to Houghton, DSTP; Houghton to the commission, May 28, 1853, WGR, no. 584.

88. Commissioners to Merriwether, September 15, 1853, WGR, no. 602, and September 29, 1853, WGR, no. 604. Merriwether's request coincided with a report the commission had been compiling for the comptroller of the US Treasury Department, which Congress used as a base for their allocations for public building.

89. Commissioners to Merriwether, September 15, 1853, WGR, no. 602.

90. Houghton to Lane, February 26, 1853, WGR, no. 565; Commissioners to Merriwether, September 29, 1853, WGR, no. 604.

91. Elisha Whittlesey, comptroller, to commissioners, December 29, 1853, WGR, no. 619.

92. Merriwether to Alvarez, January 13, 1854, AP.

93. Lamar, *Far Southwest,* pp. 90–91. Lamar is the main reporter of Houghton's illegal activities, yet he misses the significant reports the commission passed to Governor Merriwether — the commission accounted for the overruns.

94. Collins to Alvarez, April 17, 1854, BR, no. 107.

95. See Collins to Alvarez, June 17, 1854, BR, no. 108; Collins to Alvarez, July 26, 1854, BR, no. 109; and Lamar, *Far Southwest,* p. 91.

96. Fournier to Alvarez, October 19 and December 16, 1854, October 12, 1855: all in AP/Business.

97. McKnight to Alvarez, February 16, 1856, AP; Lane to Alvarez, December 20, 1853, BR, no. 168; Martínez to Alvarez, August 26, 1853, BR, no. 189, and September 13, 1853, BR, no. 190; and Houck to Alvarez, November 24, 1853, AP/Business.

98. Mother Superior Maria Magdalena to Alvarez, May 10, 1856; Waldo Hall and Company to Alvarez, November 5, 1852: both in AP; and J. M. de Uria Nafarrondo to Alvarez, July 9, 1850, BR, no. 224.

99. Taladrid to Alvarez, February 27, 1855, WGR, no. 282, January 9, 1856, WGR, no. 283, and May 8, 1856, WGR, no. 284; Taladrid to Most Reverend Jean Baptiste Lamy, July 14 and 23, 1856, AASF, no. 29.

100. Fournier to Alvarez, July 25, 1853; Vicente Armijo to Alvarez, December 29, 1850; Pillans to Alvarez, September 1850; bill of exchange to Weightman, April 25, 1853; bill of exchange to Alvarez, May 24, 1853; Waldo and Company to Alvarez, March 1, 1854; and McKnight to Alvarez, February 16, 1856: all in AP/Business.

101. Houck to Alvarez, October 26, November 24, and December 27, 1853: all in AP/Business.

102. Houck to Alvarez, January 25, 1854, AP/Business. The Carr-Gallegos election pitted two of Alvarez's confidants in opposition, and, although he was not physically involved, the barroom fight between Weightman and Aubry that resulted in the latter's death also involved two of Alvarez's close friends.

Epilog

1. Fournier to Alvarez, November 23, 1853, December 16, 1854, and February 16, 1855: all in AP/Business.

2. Fournier to Alvarez, September 18 and October 19, 1854: both in AP/Business.

3. Fournier to Alvarez, October 19, 1854, AP/Business.

4. Fournier to Alvarez, September 12, 1854, February 16 and March 25, 1855: all in AP/Business.

5. W.W.H. Davis to Charles McKiblin, February 28, 1855, BR, no. 120; Taladrid to Alvarez, February 27, 1855, WGR, no. 282.

6. Fournier to Alvarez, March 25 and May 10, 1855: both in AP/Business.

7. Fournier to Alvarez, May 4 and 10, 1855: both in AP/Business.

8. Fournier to Alvarez, May 10, 1855, AP/Business.

9. Fournier to Alvarez, May 10, August 10, and September 15, 1855: all in AP/Business. In Italy, Alvarez boarded seventeen days (August 8–24) in the Hotel de Francia y San Luis; receipt, Hotel de Francia, August 1855, AP.

10. While in Paris, Alvarez received an invitation from a Carlos [A.?] asking him to participate with him in his first mass; Carlos [A.?] to Alvarez, "Sunday morning," AP. The initial is unclear, but if it is an A, it might stand for Arias; if so, Alvarez probably participated in mass for a newly ordained relative. A contrary opinion is supported by the fact that the letter is written in French rather than Spanish.

11. McKnight to Alvarez, November 22, 1855, AP.

12. Two certificates of appointment, both dated February 26, 1856, AP.

13. Fournier to Alvarez, May 10, 1855, AP/Business.

14. *Missouri Republican* (St. Louis), August 29, 1856.

15. Benjamin Franklin to a Minister of the Gospel, June 6, 1765, in AP/Ledger Book, 1834.

16. Perea, "Santa Fe," pp. 182–83.

17. Weightman to Alvarez, November 16, 1852, AP. The shipment included *Historia de la conquista de México* and a history of the United States in Spanish.

18. Waldo to Honorable Robert J. Walker, March 26, 1845, ARPO. Like other petitions cited in this book, this one is a register of everyone of any importance in the trade.

19. Perea, "Santa Fe," pp. 182–83.

20. AP/Ledger Book, 1834, no. 287.

21. Ibid., no. 285. The Battle of San Pascual north of San Diego in which Kearny escaped death and defeat when rescued by the navy is described in many secondary sources.

22. Ibid., nos. 349 and 354.

23. Ibid., no. 788.

24. AP/Ledger Book, 1834.

25. *Missouri Republican* (St. Louis), August 29, 1856. Apparently, this is the only contemporary notice of Alvarez's death.

26. Ibid.; Burial, Santa Fe, 1856, AASF, microfilm, reel 88, frame 34. Reverend Etienne Avel records that Manuel Alvarez died at home. Two witnesses (to his Catholic burial) were Carlos Sumter and José Mereuere (the name is not clearly legible). There is no mention of the burial site, and my conclusion that Alvarez was buried at the Parroquia is drawn from negative evidence: A burial site is at a particular church, which is named for anyone buried anywhere but at the Parroquia. Interestingly, subsequent excavations at Saint Francis Cathedral hint that Alvarez was most likely buried outside the Parroquia's north wall in an area that is now in the interior of the larger cathedral, which was built around the old Parroquia; see Bruce T. Ellis, *Bishop Lamy's Santa Fe Cathedral with Records of the Old Spanish Church* . . . (Albuquerque: Historical Society of New Mexico — University of New Mexico Press, 1985), pp. 39, 80, 170, 180, and passim.

Selected Bibliography

Archival Sources

Manuel Alvarez Papers. New Mexico State Records Center and Archives, Santa Fe. Also on microfilm and organized differently, in the Coronado Room, University of New Mexico, Albuquerque.

Applications and Recommendations for Public Office During the Administrations of Polk, Taylor, and Fillmore, 1845–1853. Microfilm 873, roll 1. United States, Department of State, Washington, DC.

Archivol General de la Nación. Guerra y Marina, 1841–1842. Mexico City.

Archivol General de la Nación. Justicia y Negocios Eclesiásticos. Mexico City.

Archives of the Archdiocese of Santa Fe. Special Collections. Albuquerque, New Mexico.

James W. Arrott Collection. Thomas C. Donnelly Library, New Mexico Highlands University, Las Vegas.

David G. Bissell Papers. Missouri Historical Society, St. Louis.

Pierre Chouteau-Maffitt Collection. Missouri Historical Society, St. Louis.

William Clark Papers. US Office of Indian Affairs, St. Louis Superintendency, Kansas State Historical Society, Topeka.

Consular Dispatches, Santa Fe, Manuel Alvarez. Record Group 199, vol. 1. US National Archives, Washington, DC.

Conver Collection. Rio Arriba County Deed Book 2. History Library, Palace of the Governors, Museum of New Mexico, Santa Fe.

Department of State Territorial Papers. New Mexico, Calhoun Records, 1851–1872. Microfilm T17, roll 1. US National Archives, Washington, DC.

Dispatches from US Ministers to Mexico, 1823–1906. Powhatan Ellis, March 15, 1823 – December 11, 1906. US Department of State, Record Group 59, microfilm 97, roll 1. US National Archives, Washington, D.C.

Andrew Drips Papers. Missouri Historical Society, St. Louis.

Fort Union Archives. Special Collections, microfilm roll 1. Thomas C. Donnelly Library, New Mexico Highlands University, Las Vegas.

Everett D. Graft Collection. The Newberry Library, Chicago.

Inventory of all goods, chattels, and credits of Manuel Alvarez, deceased. History Library, Palace of the Governors, Museum of New Mexico, Santa Fe.

Land Grant File. New Mexico State Records Center and Archives, Santa Fe.

Last will and testament of Manuel Alvarez. Copy. History Library, Palace of the Governors, Museum of New Mexico, Santa Fe.

Abiel Leonard Collection, 1786–1909. State Historical Society of Missouri, Columbia.

Abiel Leonard Papers, 1769–1928. Western Historical Manuscripts Collection, University of Missouri, Columbia, MO.

Charles Lucas Collection. Missouri Historical Society, St. Louis.

Mexican Archives of New Mexico. New Mexico State Records Center and Archives, Santa Fe.

Mexican War File. Missouri Historical Society, St. Louis.

Papers of the US General Services Administration, Diplomatic Branch. US National Archives and Records Service, Washington, DC.

LeBaron Bradford Prince Papers. New Mexico State Records Center and Archives, Santa Fe.

Benjamin Read Collection. New Mexico State Records Center and Archives, Santa Fe.

William G. Ritch Papers. Henry F. Huntington Library, Art Gallery and Botanical Gardens, San Marino, CA.

St. Louis General Records, Deed Books. St. Louis City Hall, St. Louis, MO.

Santa Fe Trade Papers. Missouri Historical Society, St. Louis.

Solomon Sublette Papers. Missouri Historical Society, St. Louis.

Territorial Papers of the US Senate, 1789–1873. New Mexico, Record Group 46. US National Archives, Washington, DC.

Donaciano Vigil Papers. New Mexico State Records Center and Archives, Santa Fe.

David Waldo Papers. Missouri Historical Society, St. Louis.

Benjamin Davies Wilson Collection. Western and Spanish Section, Henry F. Huntington Library, Art Gallery and Botanical Gardens, San Marino, CA.

Books and Articles

Anderson, J. O. "Taos Uprising Legends." *El Palacio,* no. 12 (1948): 331–37.

Bancroft, Hubert Howe. *The History of Arizona and New Mexico, 1530–1888.* San Francisco: History Company, 1889.

Barreiro, Antonio. *Ojeada sobre Nuevo México.* Puebla, Mexico: 1832. Trans. and ed. Carrol H. Bailey and J. Villasana Haggard in *Three New Mexico Chronicles: The Exposición of Don Pedro Bautista Pino, 1812; The Ojeada of Lic. Antonio Barreiro, 1832; and The additions by Don José Agustín de Escudero, 1849.* Albuquerque, NM: Quivira Society Publications, 1942.

Barry, Louise. *The Beginning of the West: Annals of the Kansas Gateway to the American West, 1540–1854.* Topeka: Kansas State Historical Society, 1972.

Bartlett, Richard A. *Nature's Yellowstone: The Story of an American Wilderness That Became Yellowstone National Park in 1872.* Albuquerque: University of New Mexico Press, 1974.

Beachum, Larry M. *William Becknell: Father of the Santa Fe Trade.* Southwestern Studies 68. El Paso: Texas Western Press, 1982.

Bender, Averam B. *The March of Empire: Frontier Defense in the Southwest, 1848–1860.* Lawrence: University of Kansas Press, 1952.

Binkley, W. C. "New Mexico and the Last Stage of the Texan-Santa Fe Expedition." *Southwestern Historical Quarterly,* no. 3 (1919): 260–71.

Binkley, William C. "Reports from a Texas Agent in New Mexico, 1849." In *New Spain and the Anglo-American West: Historical Contributions, Presented to Herbert Eugene Bolton,* vol. 2. Los Angeles: n.p., 1932.

Bloom, Lansing. "Editorial Notes, Our First Press." *New Mexico Historical Review,* no. 1 (1937): 107–10.

———. "Ledgers of a Santa Fe Trader." *El Palacio* 14, no. 9 (May 1923): 133–36.

———. "New Mexico Under Mexican Administration." *Old Santa Fe* 2 (October 1914): 119–69.

Calhoun, James S. *The Official Correspondence of James S. Calhoun While Indian Agent at Santa Fe and Superintendent of Indian Affairs in New Mexico.* Ed. Annie Heloise Abel. Washington, DC: US Government Printing Office, 1915.

Calvin, Ross, ed. *Lieutenant Emory Reports.* Albuquerque: University of New Mexico Press, 1968.

Chaput, Donald. *François X. Aubry: Trader, Trailmaker and Voyager in the Southwest, 1846–1854.* Glendale, CA: Arthur H. Clark, 1975.

Chávez, Fray Angélico. *Archives of the Archdiocese of Santa Fe: 1678–1900.* Washington, DC: Academy of American Franciscan History, 1957.

———. *Très Macho, He Said: Padre Gallegos of Albuquerque, New Mexico's First Congressman.* Santa Fe, NM: William Gannon, 1985.

Cleland, Robert Glass. *This Reckless Breed of Men: The Trappers and Fur Traders of the Southwest.* New York: Alfred A. Knopf, 1950.

Connelly, W. E., ed. "A Journal of the Santa Fe Trail." *Mississippi Valley Historical Review,* no. 1 (1925): 72–98.

Congressional Globe. 32d Congress, 1st Session, 1852.

Convention, 1849: Journal of New Mexico Convention of Delegates to Recommend a Plan of Civil Government, September 1849. Santa Fe: New Mexican Printing Company, 1907.

Cooke, Philip St. George. "A Journal of the Santa Fe Trail." Ed. William E. Connelley. *Mississippi Valley Historical Review* 12 (June 1925).

Cooke, Philip St. George, William H.C. Whiting, and François X. Aubrey, *Exploring Southwestern Trails, 1846–1854.* Southwest Historical Series, vol. 2. Ed. Ralph Bieber. Glendale, CA: Arthur H. Clark, 1938.

Coombs, Franklin. "Coomb's Narrative of the Santa Fe Expedition in 1841." Ed. F.W. Hodge. *New Mexico Historical Review,* no. 3 (1930): 305–14.

Copeland, Fayatte. *Kendall of the Picayune.* Norman: University of Oklahoma Press, 1943.

Cox, Michael. "Through the Governor's Window, 1821–1846." *El Palacio* 80, no. 3 (1974): 22–28.

Davis, W.W.H. *El Gringo or New Mexico and Her People.* Santa Fe, NM: Rydal Press, 1938.

Diaz, Albert James. *A Guide to the Microfilm of Papers Relating to New Mexico Land Grants.* Albuquerque: University of New Mexico Press, 1960.

Duffus, R. L. *The Santa Fe Trail.* New York: Longmans, Green, 1930.

Dunham, Harold H. "Manuel Alvarez." In *The Mountain Men and the Fur Trade of the Far West,* vol. 1. Ed. LeRoy Hafen. Glendale, CA: Arthur H. Clark, 1965.

———, ed. "Sidelights on Santa Fe Traders: 1839–1846." In *1950 Brand Book,* vol. 6. Denver, CO: Westerners–University of Denver Press, 1950.

Dye, Job Francis. *Recollections of a Pioneer, 1830–1852.* Los Angeles: Glen Dawson, n.d.

Ellis, Bruce T. *Bishop Lamy's Santa Fe Cathedral with Records of the Old Spanish Church* . . . Albuquerque: Historical Society of New Mexico–University of New Mexico Press, 1985.

Emmett, Chris. *Fort Union and the Winning of the Southwest.* Norman: University of Oklahoma, 1965.

Eve, Joseph L. "A Letter Book of Joseph L. Eve, United States Chargé d'Affaires to Texas." Ed. Joseph M. Nance. *Southwestern Historical Quarterly,* no. 3 (1940): 96–116.

Falconer, Thomas. *Letters and Notes on the Texan–Santa Fe Expedition, 1841–1842.* Ed. F. W. Hodge. 1894; reprinted Chicago: Rio Grande Press, 1963.

Feirman, Floyd S. "The Spiegelbergs of New Mexico, Merchants and Bankers, 1844–1893." *Southwestern Studies,* no. 4 (1964): 3–48.

Ferris, Warren A. *Life in the Rocky Mountains.* Ed. P. C. Phillips. Denver, CO: Old West Publishing, 1940.

Forrest, Earle R. *Missions and Pueblos of the Old Southwest.* Glorieta, NM: Rio Grande Press, 1979 (originally Cleveland: The Arthur H. Clark Co., 1929).

Frazer, Robert W. "Army Agriculture in New Mexico, 1852–1853." *New Mexico Historical Review* 50, no. 4 (October 1975): 313–34.

Galloway, Tod B., ed. "Private Letters of a Government Official in the Southwest." *Journal of American History,* no. 4 (1909): 541–54.

Ganaway, Loomis Morton. *New Mexico and the Sectional Controversy, 1846–1861.* 1944; reprinted Chicago: Porcupine Press, 1976.

Garrard, Lewis Hector. *Wah-to-Yah and the Taos Trail.* 1850; reprinted Norman: University of Oklahoma Press, 1974.

Gibson, George Rutledge. *Journal of a Soldier Under Kearny and Doniphan, 1846–1847.* Southwest Historical Series, vol. 3. Ed. Ralph Bieber. Glendale, CA: Arthur H. Clark, 1935.

Goodrich, James W. "In the Earnest Pursuit of Wealth: David Waldo in Missouri and Southwest, 1820–1878." *Missouri Historical Review* 46, no. 2 (1972): 155–84.

Green, Fletcher, M. "James S. Calhoun: Pioneer, Georgia Leader and First Governor of New Mexico." *Georgia Historical Quarterly* 39, no. 4 (1955): 309–47.

Gregg, Josiah. *Commerce of the Prairies.* Ed. Max L. Moorhead. 1944; reprinted Norman: University of Oklahoma Press, 1954.

Grove, Pearce S., Becky J. Barnett, and Sandra J. Hansen, eds. *New Mexico Newspapers: A Comprehensive Guide to Bibliographical Entries and Locations.* Albuquerque: University of New Mexico Press, 1975.

Hafen, Leroy R. *The Mountain Men and the Fur Trade of the Far West.* Glendale, CA: Arthur H. Clark, 1965.

Hafen, Leroy R., and Ann W. Hafen. *The Old Spanish Trail: Santa Fe to Los Angeles.* Far West and the Rockies Historical Series, 1820–1875. Glendale, CA: Arthur H. Clark, 1954.

Hamilton, Holman. *Prologue to Conflict: The Crisis and Compromise of 1850.* Lexington: University of Kentucky Press, 1964.

Hammond, George P., ed. *The Thomas O. Larkin Papers,* vol. 1. 1951; reprinted Berkeley: University of California Press, 1953.

Hodge, F. W., ed. "Letter Dated Santa Fe, July 29, 1841, Reproduced from *Niles National Register.*" *New Mexico Historical Review* 5, no. 3 (July 1930): 209–304.

Horgan, Paul. *Lamy of Santa Fe: His Life and Times.* New York: Farrar, Straus & Giroux, 1975.

Houck, Louis. *A History of Missouri,* vol. 2. Chicago: R. R. Donnelley & Sons, 1908.

———. *The Spanish Regime in Missouri: A Collection of Papers . . . ,* vol. 2. Chicago: R. R. Donnelley & Sons, 1909.

Hyde, George E. *Life of George Bent: Written From His Letters.* Norman: University of Oklahoma Press, 1968.

Insurrection Against the Military Government in New Mexico and California, 1847 and 1848, 56th Congress, 1st Session, Senate Document 442, pp. 4–5.

Irving, Washington. *The Adventures of Captain Bonneville U.S.A. in the Rocky Mountains and the Far West.* New York: G. P. Putnam's Sons, 1898.

James, Thomas. *Three Years Among the Mexicans and the Indians.* Chicago: Keystone Books, 1962.

James L. Collins to Governor William Carr Lane, December 10, 1852. In "Perils of the Santa Fe Trail in Its Early Days (1822–1852)," ed. Benjamin Reed. *El Palacio* 19, no. 4 (November 1925): 206–11.

Johnston, Abraham R., Marcellos B. Edward, and Philip G. Ferguson. *Marching with the Army of the West, 1846–1848.* Southwest Historical Series, vol. 4. Ed. Ralph P. Bieber. Glendale, CA: Arthur H. Clark, 1935.

Keleher, William A. "Texas in Early Day New Mexico." *Panhandle-Plains Historical Review* 25 (1952): 13–28.

———. *Turmoil in New Mexico, 1846–1868.* Santa Fe, NM: Rydal Press, 1952.

Kendall, George Wilkins. *Narrative of the Texan–Santa Fe Expedition.* London: David Bogue, 1845; New York: Harper & Brothers, 1844.

Kenner, Charles L. *A History of New Mexican–Plains Indian Relations.* Norman: University of Oklahoma Press, 1969.

LaFarge, Oliver. *Santa Fe: The Autobiography of a Southwestern Town.* Norman: University of Oklahoma Press, 1959.

Lamar, Howard Roberts. *The Far Southwest, 1846–1912: A Territorial History.* New York: W. W. Norton, 1970.

Lane, William Carr. "The Letters of William Carr Lane." Ed. Ralph P. Bieber. *New Mexico Historical Review,* no. 2 (1928): 179–203.

———. "William Carr Lane Diary." Ed. William G. B. Carson. *New Mexico Historical Review* (1964): 274–332.

Larson, Robert W. *New Mexico's Quest for Statehood, 1846–1912.* Albuquerque: University of New Mexico Press, 1968.

Lavender, David. *Bent's Fort.* Garden City, NY: Doubleday, 1954; reprinted Lincoln: University of Nebraska Press, 1972.

Laws of the Territory of New Mexico. Ed. S. W. Kearny. Santa Fe, NM: n.p., October 7, 1846.

Lecompte, Janet. "Manuel Armijo and the Americanos." In *Spanish and Mexican Land Grants in New Mexico and Colorado.* Ed. John R. and Christine Van Ness. Manhattan, KS: Sunflower Press, 1980.

———. *Pueblo, Hardscrabble, Greenhorn: The Upper Arkansas, 1832–1856.* Norman: University of Oklahoma Press, 1978.

———. *Rebellion in Rio Arriba: 1837.* Albuquerque: Historical Society of New Mexico–University of New Mexico Press, 1985.

Loomis, Noel M. *The Texan–Santa Fe Pioneers.* Norman: University of Oklahoma Press, 1958.

Loyola, Sister Mary. "The American Occupation of New Mexico, 1821–1852." *New Mexico Historical Review* 4, nos. 1–3 (July 1939).

Lucas, James A. "Letters to the Editor of the Mesilla Valle-Democrat." *New Mexico Historical Review,* no. 1 (1964): 16–31.

McCall, George Archibald. *New Mexico in 1850: A Military View.* Ed. Robert W. Frazer. Norman: University of Oklahoma Press, 1968.

McClure, Charles. "The Texan–Santa Fe Expedition of 1841." *New Mexico Historical Review,* no. 1 (1973): 45–56.

McMurtie, Douglas C. "The History of Early Printing in New Mexico." *New Mexico Historical Review* 4 (1929): 372–410.

Manning, William R. "Diplomacy Concerning the Santa Fe Trail." *Mississippi Valley Historical Review,* no. 4 (1915): 516–31.

Mattes, Merrill J. "Behind the Legend of Colters Hell: The Early Exploration of Yellowstone National Park." *Mississippi Valley Historical Review* 36, no. 2 (September 1949): 251–82.

———. "Exploding Fur Trade Fairy Tales." In *Probing the American West.* Ed. K. Ross Toole et al. Santa Fe: Museum of New Mexico Press, 1962.

Mauzy, Wayne L. "Early Newspapers in New Mexico: *The Santa Fe Republican,* 1847–1849." *El Palacio* 2 (April 1960): 39–52.

Moore, John Bassett, ed. *The Works of James Buchanan Comprising His Speeches, State Papers and Private Correspondence,* vol. 6. New York: Antiquarian Press, 1960.

Morgan, Dale L. *Jedediah Smith and the Opening of the West.* Lincoln: University of Nebraska Press, 1953.

Murphy, Lawrence R. "Antislavery in the Southwest: William G. Kephart's Mission to New Mexico, 1850–53." *Southwestern Studies* 54 (1978): 31–43.

———. "The Beaubien and Miranda Land Grant." *New Mexico Historical Review,* no. 1 (1967): 27–48.

Oliva, Leo E. *Soldiers on the Santa Fe Trail.* Norman: University of Oklahoma Press, 1967.

Parker, David W. *Calendar of Papers in Washington Archives Relating to the Territories of the United States (to 1873).* Washington DC: Carnegie Institute of Washington, 1911.

Parkman, Francis. *The Oregon Trail*. 1849; reprinted Clinton, MA: Airmont, 1964.

Parrish, William J. "The German Jew and the Commercial Revolution in Territorial New Mexico, 1850–1900." *New Mexico Historical Review* 45, no. 1 (1960): 1–29.

Perea, Francisco. "Santa Fe As It Appeared During the Winter of 1837 and 1838." Ed. W.H.H. Allison. *Old Santa Fe* 2 (October 1914): 170–83.

Pletcher, David M. *The Diplomacy of Annexation: Texas, Oregon and the Mexican War*. Columbia: University of Missouri Press, 1973.

Ponce de Leon, José M. *Reseñas históricas del Estado de Chihuahua*, vol. 1. Chihuahua, Mexico: Imprenta del Gobierno, 1910.

Prince, LeBaron Bradford. *Historical Sketches of New Mexico*. Kansas City, MO: Ramsey, Millet & Hudson, 1883.

Reno, Philip. "Rebellion in New Mexico — 1837." *New Mexico Historical Review* 40, no. 3 (1965): 197–214.

Ritch, William Gillet. *Illustrated New Mexico*. Santa Fe Bureau of Immigration, 1885.

————, ed. *The Legislative Blue Book of the Territory of New Mexico*. Santa Fe, NM: Charles W. Greene, Public Printer, 1882. Reprinted as *New Mexico Blue Book, 1881*. Albuquerque: University of New Mexico Press, 1968.

Rittenhouse, Jack D. *The Santa Fe Trail: A Historical Bibliography*. Albuquerque: University of New Mexico Press, 1971.

Robidoux, Orral Messmore. *Memorial to the Robidoux Brothers: A History of the Robidouxs in America*. Kansas City, MO: Smith-Grieves, 1924.

Robinson, D., ed. "Records of Fort Tecumseh." *South Dakota Historical Collections*, vol. 9 (1918): 93–167.

Sadlowski, Walter D., Jr. "Manuel Alvarez: Merchant and Trader, Consul and Commercial Agent Politico." Unpublished manuscript. History Library, Palace of the Governors, Museum of New Mexico, Santa Fe.

Sánchez, Pedro. *Memories of Antonio José Martínez*. Trans. Guadalupe Baca-Vaughn. Santa Fe, NM: Rydal Press, 1978.

Sibley, George Champlin. *The Road to Santa Fe: The Journal and Diaries of George Champlin Sibley*. Ed. Kate L. Gregg. Albuquerque: University of New Mexico Press, 1952.

"A Sidelight on the Santa Fe Trade, 1844," *New Mexico Historical Review* 46, no. 3 (July 1971): 261–65.

Simmons, Marc. *The Little Lion of the Southwest: A Biography of Manuel Chaves*. Chicago: Sage Books, 1973.

Simpson, James H. *Navaho Expedition: Journal of a Military Reconnaissance from Santa Fe, New Mexico to the Navaho Country*. Ed. Frank McNitt. Norman: University of Oklahoma Press, 1964.

Smith, Ralph A. "The King of New Mexico and the Doniphan Expedition." *New Mexico Historical Review,* no. 1 (1963): 29–55.

Stanley, F. *Cuidad Santa Fe: Mexican Rule, 1821–1846.* Pep, TX: n.p., 1962.

Sunder, John E., ed. *Matt Field on the Santa Fe Trail.* Norman: University of Oklahoma Press, 1960.

Sunseri, Alvin. *Seeds of Discord: New Mexico in the Aftermath of the American Conquest, 1846–1861.* Chicago: Norton-Hall, 1979.

———. "Sheep Ricos, Sheep Fortunes in the Aftermath of the American Conquest, 1846–1861." *El Palacio* 83, no. 1 (1977): 3–8.

Townley, John M. "El Placer: A New Mexico Mining Boom Before 1846." *Journal of the West* 10, no. 1 (January 1971): 102–15.

Tyler, Daniel. "Governor Armijo and the Tejanos." *Journal of the West,* no. 4 (1973): 589–99.

———. "Governor Armijo's Moment of Truth." *Journal of the West* 11, no. 2 (April 1972): 307–16.

———. "Gringo Views of Governor Manuel Armijo." *New Mexico Historical Review* 45, no. 1 (January 1970): 23–46.

———. *Sources of New Mexican History, 1821–1848.* Santa Fe: Museum of New Mexico Press, 1984.

Twitchell, Ralph Emerson. *The Leading Facts of New Mexican History.* 5 vols. Cedar Rapids, IA: Torch Press, 1912.

———. *Old Santa Fe: The Story of New Mexico's Ancient Capital.* Santa Fe, NM: Santa Fe New Mexican Publishing, 1925.

———. *The Military Occupation of New Mexico, 1846–1851.* Denver, CO: Smith-Brooks, 1909.

———. *The Spanish Archives of New Mexico.* 2 vols. Cedar Rapids, IA: Torch Press, 1914.

United States Congress, House, *California and New Mexico: Message from the President . . . Transmitting Information . . . on the Subject of California and New Mexico.* 31st Congress, 1st Session, 1850, Executive Document 7.

Walker, Henry Pickering. *The Wagonmasters: High Plains Freighting from the Earliest Days of the Santa Fe Trail to 1880.* Norman: University of Oklahoma Press, 1966.

Walter, Paul A. F., ed. "Historical Society Meeting." *El Palacio,* no. 25 (1927): 637.

Webb, James Josiah. *Adventures in the Santa Fe Trade, 1844–1847.* Southwest Historical Series, vol. 1. Ed. Ralph P. Bieber. Glendale, CA: Arthur H. Clark, 1931.

Weber, David J. *The Extranjeros: Selected Documents from the Mexican Side of the Santa Fe Trail, 1825–1828.* Santa Fe, NM: Stage Coach Press, 1967.

———. *The Mexican Frontier, 1821–1846: The American Southwest Under Mexico.* Albuquerque: University of New Mexico Press, 1982.

———. *The Taos Trappers: The Fur Trade in the Far Southwest, 1540–1846.* Norman: University of Oklahoma Press, 1971.

———, ed. *Foreigners in Their Native Land: Historical Roots of the Mexican Americans.* Albuquerque: University of New Mexico Press, 1973.

Westphal, Victor. *The Public Domain in New Mexico, 1854–1891.* Albuquerque: University of New Mexico Press, 1965.

"Wethered, Samuel, Jr., to Manuel Alvarez, March 27, 1844." In "A Sidelight on the Santa Fe Trade, 1844." *New Mexico Historical Review* 46, no. 3 (July 1971): 261–64.

White, John Barber. "The Missouri Merchant One Hundred Years Ago." *The Missouri Historical Review* 13, no. 2 (1919): 91–111.

Windham, Margaret Leonard. *New Mexico 1850 Territorial Census,* vol. 4. Albuquerque: New Mexico Genealogical Society, 1976.

Young, Otis E., ed. "Mexican Edict of Expulsion." In *The First Military Escort on the Santa Fe Trail, 1929.* Glendale, CA: Arthur H. Clark, 1952.

Index